RE-INVENTING MARRIAGE

RE-INVENTING MARRIAGE

A Re-view and Re-vision

Christopher L. Webber

MOREHOUSE PUBLISHING
Harrisburg, PA

Morehouse Publishing
P.O. Box 1321
Harrisburg, PA 17105

Library of Congress Cataloging-in-Publication Data
Webber, Christopher.
    Re-inventing marriage / Christopher L. Webber.
        p.   cm.
    Includes bibliographical references and Index.
    ISBN 0-8192-1616-X (paper)
    1. Marriage—Religious aspects—Christianity.   2. Sex role—Religious aspects—
Christianity.   I. Title.   II. Title: Reinventing marriage.
BV835.W42   1994   94-10246
234'.165'09—dc20   CIP

Printed in the United States

iv

Acknowledgments

No writer is an island, as John Donne might have said, and this book could not have been written without much help from many people. The Wardens, Vestry, and members of Christ Church, Bronxville, gave me the gift of time in the form of a six-month sabbatical; the Council of the Diocese of New York, with the advice and support of Comptroller Michael MacPherson and the Rt. Rev. Richard Grein, gave me a study grant; the Rev. Karen Henry gave me the gift of confidence that all would be well in the parish in my absence. The Rev. William Doubleday invited me to teach the course in Canon Law at the General Theological Seminary that got me thinking about questions of marriage in the first place. The Library Staff at St. Vladimir's Seminary were generous in allowing me easy access to their resources. St. Deiniol's Library in Wales provided the quiet and supportive place where I could bring the project to a conclusion.

I am grateful also to those who have advised me along the way: Dr. Peter Whitely, who helped get me started in the area of sociology, the Rev. R. J. O'Connell, S.J., and the Rev. Joseph Leinhard, S.J., who helped me think about St. Augustine and enabled me to make use of the Fordham University Library; the Rev. Richard Norris, who guided me in my thinking about the patristic period; Dr. Alice Stone Ilchman, who provided resources at Sarah Lawrence College; Rabbi James Perman and Rabbi Susan Grossman, who helped me find resources on Judaism; the Rev. Roger White, who was generous in loaning me books from his library; and Margaret Arnold, who researched the story of Captain David Hand.

I am also much indebted to those who have read various drafts, given me much valuable advice, and saved me from countless errors: the Rt. Rev. Walter Dennis, the Rev. Richard Corney, Dr. Warren Ilchman, and Dr. Elisabeth Gruner. Naturally, they are not responsible for whatever opinions I insisted on in spite of their advice.

Invaluable also were the friendship, support, and counsel of the staff and residents of St. Deiniol's College: Sub-Warden Richard Legg, Carolyn Legg, Ann Welsh, the Very Rev. Jack Greenhalgh, the Rev. Ronald Harris and Gwenneth Harris, the Rev. William Black, the Rev. Peter Brain, and Sarah McNamer.

Unlike St. Paul, St. Augustine, and St. Thomas Aquinas (among others), I have not had the disadvantage of writing about marriage without first-hand experience. Whatever else I may know or think about marriage, my wife and I have had thirty-five years to learn about it together and I begin, I must admit, with a hopeless prejudice toward marriage on the basis of those years and that experience of love. Peg has been patient in my absence, careful in proofreading, and insightful in criticism and suggestion; but above all she has given me the evidence that marriage can be what the Bible says it can be: a way to know the depth and richness of the love of the eternal God.

Contents

The spirit and the body were understood mostly as parallel aspects of being a person; the process of their integration was hardly imagined.   — Peter Brown

I am married with the Etenga.   — quoted by Joseph Thiel

Go, take for yourself a wife of whoredom and have children of whoredom, for the land commits great whoredom by forsaking the LORD.   — Hosea 1:2

Let us rejoice and exult and give him the glory, for the marriage of the Lamb has come, and his bride has made herself ready.   — Revelation 19:7

A wedding is not a pageant or a theatrical performance.
                                    — John Chrysostom

. . . how much . . . better for me . . . to be called mistress than wife — so that affection alone . . . and no force of a nuptial chain (should) constrain me.   — Heloise to Abelard

INTRODUCTION

Reinventing Marriage

"Reinventing marriage" may sound like that proverbially useless exercise called reinventing the wheel. At some level, marriage needs no reinvention; people will still get married no matter what shape our church and society may give it. But few stone-age or even medieval people would recognize the materials out of which today's wheels are built or have any understanding of the cars, trains, and planes, to which they are attached or the destinations toward which we turn them. Chariot wheels still turn as well as ever, but they would hardly begin to meet our modern needs. And why should we make life hard for people? Marriage, as old an invention as the human race, has accumulated tons of unnecessary baggage over the years and has not always put its best face forward. To sort out the baggage, to discard whatever may have outlived its usefulness, to put the essential elements together in a way appropriate to the world we now live in: this is what I mean by reinvention.

Of course, every marriage is to some degree an invention. Madeleine L'Engle's title for the story of her marriage, *Two-Part Invention,* sums up what most married people know: that they are always improvising because they are always faced with unprecedented situations and have to face them with someone with whom they are still getting acquainted.

But in a more general sense as well, the Christian Church has spent nearly two thousand years inventing marriage and those two millennia are based on another two millennia of Judaism which in turn is built on all the millennia of human existence before Abraham and Sarah. Along the way the church has also absorbed elements of marriage traditions from Greek and Roman civilization and the Germanic folkways of Northern Europe. One purpose of this book is to retell that story and, in doing so and seeing how much our understanding of marriage has changed in that time, to help prepare the way for the reinventions needed as we begin the next millennium.

Another purpose of this book is to suggest some immediate and practical steps that Christians might take today to help those setting out to invent a life together. Each such couple writes on a blank slate but the handwriting they use has been learned from others and may not really fit their own individual needs. There was a time when life changed slowly and the expectations of those beginning a marriage were almost entirely shaped by those around them. Traditions were clear and no one moved very far from the traditional path. That is no longer true. We have enormous freedom to improvise but all too little guidance how best to use that freedom.

Three images occur to me as ways of understanding what this book is all about. The first is the rather mechanical word "reinvention" which I have already discussed. The word suggests not the building of something new and unprecedented but rather taking apart a piece of machinery that doesn't operate very well and putting it back together somewhat differently in the hope that it may run better. Of course, marriage is not a machine, not mechanical at all; but perhaps the image is helpful nonetheless.

The second image comes from a guide book to Kyoto that I read many years ago. It was called "a contemplative guide." The first and largest part of the book was a history of the city of Kyoto emphasizing those periods which produced the great shrines and temples for which Kyoto is famous. Part 2 described the major shrines. And Part 3, a very small part of the book, told the reader how to get to each shrine, what bus to take and where to get on and off. This book before you is something like that. It begins with a long (too long?) history of the city of marriage and the people who have lived in it; then it describes the major aspects of marriage, the buildings we have erected: sacramental, theological, procreational, and human-relational; this leads to suggestions for redesigning these buildings to make them more accessible and usable; finally, there are some practical suggestions: how to get there.

The third image for understanding this book is drawn from mountain climbing. Whether in the Adirondacks or the Himalayas, mountain climbing often involves a long hike through dense forest before the climber can obtain any views. Perhaps this book is a little like that in that it involves a long hike through sometimes dense forest before we come out into the open and gain some perspective on the world through which we were climbing. It would, I suppose, be possible to drop down on a mountaintop by parachute or helicopter, and perhaps the view would be the same. I am not sure, however, that it is possible actually to understand the scenery if you haven't walked through it first.

This book, then, involves first a long walk through the history of Christian marriage. Sometimes the woods are so dense as to be almost impenetrable; at other times the woods are sparse and we can move along rapidly. The objective does at last come into view, and we can try to understand not only how we have gotten where we are, but also how we might go forward more intelligently.

As the bibliography at the end will indicate, there is a vast literature being produced these days on the subject of marriage, ranging from "how-to" manuals to massive theological studies. That the institution of marriage — indeed, the relationships between men and women — are already shifting and changing is widely recognized. This book is intended to be a voice in the middle of that conversation, saying first, "Wait a minute; let's look at how we got here in the first place," and second, "Now that we've got that clear, how about re-building this way?"

A good conversation involves several voices, hearing, considering, responding. I hope this book will be seen as an invitation to take part in an ongoing conversation through which we can learn more about the full potential that human marriage holds.

CHAPTER ONE

Dueling With Dualism:
How It All Began

*T*he early church found it hard to deal with marriage in a
positive way. Theologicans were concerned for reason and
control, but these values were drawn largely from pagan sources,
not Jewish or Christian faith.

FROM THIS DAY BACKWARD

Captain David Hand sailed a ship in the whaling trade and died in 1840 at the age of eighty-one. They buried him in a cemetery in Sag Harbor, New York, and set a marble slab over his grave. Not far away, another marble slab commemorates Hannah, his wife, who died in 1835, five years before her husband, at the age of sixty-nine. Between those two stones are four smaller stones that fill out the story of Captain Hand's life. The first commemorates Susannah, wife of Captain David Hand, who died in 1791 in the twenty-seventh year of her life. A short poem reminds the reader that life is short and uncertain. The next stone marks the grave of Mary, wife of Captain David Hand, who died in the thirty-second year of her life. A short poem tells us, "The Almighty spoke and she was gone..." Beside her lies Hannah, wife of Captain David Hand, who died in the thirtieth year of her life. The poem on her stone, legible when my family moved to Sag Harbor in 1949 but now worn beyond reading, summed up the situation neatly: "Behold! ye curious mortals passing by, how thick the partners of one husband lie..." Nor was that the end of the story. A fourth stone in the row marks the resting place of Charlotte, also wife to Captain David Hand. She died at the age of thirty in 1800. Hannah — *the second Hannah* — was Captain Hand's fifth wife and the only one to survive the childbearing years.

Two centuries have passed since Captain David Hand began to marry the young women of Sag Harbor. In that time, our expectation of marriage has changed more radically than in all the centuries of human life before it. Presumably Captain Hand's first four wives died in child-birth or soon after. We can picture his ship returning from the year-long and two-year-long explorations of the world's oceans that brought whale oil to the lamps of nineteenth century Americans and wealth to the pockets of those few whaling captains who survived and imagine the captain coming down the gangplank to learn that his wife had died in labor or shortly afterwards. Then, while the ship was being outfitted for the next voyage, the captain would marry again only to repeat the cycle. Those who pledged themselves to each other "till death us do part" before this century were not often making a long commitment. Frequent though divorce may be in the late twentieth century, the average marriage lasts longer now than it did then. In fact, the frequency of divorce today is caused, at least in part, by the fact that we have so much longer in which to live with the consequences of our commitments.

Look in the bookstores or study the list of best selling books and you will find volumes on sex, love, and marriage prominently featured. "Marriage is in trouble," we are told and, no doubt, it is. We yearn for stable relationships for ourselves and secure homes for our children. Lacking historical perspective, we look at the marital chaos of our time and ask, "What are we doing wrong?" But we are facing the full implications of a lifelong commitment for the first time in the history of the human race. We have no precedent for an average life-span of eighty years and more and no experience in guiding couples through all the changes that such a span of years can bring.

Nor is our increased life-span the only change of circumstances that faces marriage as an institution in our time. Marriage once was an economic partnership with clearly understood roles. Marriage once had the continuity of the tribe and the production of legitimate heirs as primary concerns. Marriage once was carefully regulated by church and state and reinforced by economic and social pressure. Marriage once was prepared for by careful family negotiations and transitional rituals through which a young man and woman were incorporated into a role with clearly under-stood responsibilities. The radically changed economic circumstances of our day have sheared away almost all the built-in support, eliminated the delineation of roles, and undermined our best efforts to find peace and security in our domestic relations. When we turn to the church for guidance, we find the church still attempting to work from outworn models shaped by the philosophers of pre-Christian Greece, the social conditions of the Roman empire, and medieval Europe.

That a faith centered on the proposition that "God is love" should deal so ineptly with marriage is one of the great ironies of Christian history. The fact is, however, that the church, all unwittingly, has generally taken its teaching and practice from the world around it rather than from its own revelation. Surely the time has come, surely the needs of married people compel us, to reexamine our history, to see how we came to be where we are, and to ask the radical questions that will enable us to discover, perhaps for the first time, patterns for Christian marriage drawn from our own faith and appropriate to the world in which we live.

We will suggest that it is time to separate Christian marriage from state licensing, to reconsider the relationship between marriage and childbearing, to redefine the nature of marriage as a sacrament, and to reinvent the ancient practice of betrothal under church sponsorship. We believe a reinvention of marriage can help couples build more truly Christian marriages, better marriages, better prepared to endure and thrive in a society like ours. But to understand the logic of these proposals, we need to understand much more clearly how we have come to be where we are. The story of marriage in the early Christian church is critical for that understanding.

In the earliest days of the church, many believed that it was better not to marry at all, that continence was preferable to marriage. If church members could not attain to that standard, then they might be allowed to marry, but still they would be advised to avoid any sexual relations, if possible. Finally, however, the theologians conceded that sexual relations were permissible but only with the clear and sober purpose of procreation and never, never, for the sake of pleasure.

Clement of Alexandria, for example, suggested that if sexual relationships were necessary, they should be confined to the night. Origen believed that the Holy Spirit was always present with married Christians except during sexual intercourse, a time when it would not be appropriate for the Spirit to be on hand.[1] St. Augustine taught that marriage "is the least imperfect form of copulation. The sexual act is a sin, but while it is mortal in fornication it becomes venial in marriage and can be redeemed."[2] Even more strikingly he wrote, "A man who is too ardent a lover of his wife is an adulterer, if the pleasure he finds in her is sought for its own sake." [3]

These are not opinions commonly heard from today's pulpits.

Where did this attitude come from? The first Christians were Jews, and Judaism has always had a very positive view of marriage. Judaism insisted, for example, that rabbis should be married; indeed, contrary to Clement, the Talmud taught that it is a particular mitzvah (good deed) for scholars to have intercourse on Friday night, thus joining the holiness of the Sabbath with the holiness of marital sex.[4] But Christians have honored continence, and the Roman Catholic church has insisted on a celibate priesthood. Why the change? Is there something in the teaching of Christ that would seem to promote such an attitude?

This is not a very positive way to begin our study of marriage, but "first the bad news" seems to me a useful way to begin. Strong and persistent voices have questioned the value of marriage throughout the church's history and inevitably left their impact on us, however subconsciously. To redesign the building, we need to know what foundation blocks it rests on, who put them there, and why. If we intend to replace them, we need to be sure the building can stand without them. So we begin not exactly at the beginning but with the first great leaders and teachers after the age of the New Testament. What did they say and why did they say it? What can we learn from them? It's not always an easy story to follow, but once through it we can turn to the Bible itself and begin our own exploration of God's purpose.

Four themes are central to this exploration: dualism, reason and control, continence (or virginity),* and procreation.

DUALISM

The life of the early church was dominated by a struggle with dualism. Sex is a very physical thing, but marriage is something more. No couple should get married until they have become aware that their love has an element that is more than bodily attraction, more even than the light in her eyes and the radiance of his smile: something indefinable and yet very real, something "bigger than both of us."

But what is that something? What is love itself? To ask such a question, to believe such a question can be asked and answered, is to move beyond the realm of science. We find ourselves using words like "spiritual," by which we mean something we experience but cannot actually grasp, like friendship, courage, and sympathy. We know these things exist, but scientific tests can find no trace of them at all, let alone analyze their ingredients. So we call them "spiritual," and then we need to explain what we mean by that. The relationship between the physical and the spiritual is at the heart of the problem that Christians, and all thoughtful people, have pondered over the years. Are they two aspects of reality? Is one bad and the other good? How can we live in a physical world and give spiritual reality its proper place?

Virginity in the Patristic era as today, could be a gender-neutral term, but most often it referred to women. We will use the term *virginity* when our sources use it, but otherwise we will speak of continence unless we are referring specifically to women.

The world in which the first Christians lived had already asked itself these questions and worked out various answers. Some of the commonly accepted answers divided existence into two separate realms and rejected the material realm as unimportant at best and evil at the worst. Many of the first Christian theologians had grown up outside the church and had studied in schools where some such form of dualism was taught. Inevitably dualism influenced and sometimes divided Christianity but neither theologians nor philosophers had adequate tools with which to combat dualism effectively. "The spirit and the body," a modern theologian writes, "were understood mostly as parallel aspects of being a person; the process of their integration was hardly imagined."[5]

In the end, however, the Christian faith always rejected dualism. Two people in love will also reject it. They know, as the church knows, that the body is real and love is real, that both are good, that the body is fulfilled by love, and that love needs a body for its expression. God's love for the world was expressed in the human body of Jesus Christ; a woman's love for a man and a man's love for a woman are expressed through physical actions. We know about "Platonic love," but it isn't very satisfying; a man and a woman can sit for a while at opposite ends of the couch and admire each other, but eventually they move toward the center and let their love find expression. In the early days of the church, however, there were many who preferred to stay at opposite ends of the couch, or half way toward the center, and some of them called themselves Christians. Sometimes, in fact, the battle between Christianity and the various kinds of dualism was fought not only inside the church but even inside individual faithful Christians struggling for answers that made sense both for themselves and their friends and even their enemies. That struggle, internal and external, left a deep mark on the church's understanding of marriage.

The fundamental Christian assertion was clear, however, and Augustine, who had belonged to a group of dualists called Manicheans earlier in his life, knew it as well as anyone:

> So I saw plainly and clearly that you have made all things good, nor are there any substances at all which you have not made, and because you did not make all things equal, therefore they each and all have their existence; because they are good individually, and at the same time they are altogether very good, because our God made all things very good.[6]

It was because Augustine saw this clearly that he finally became a Christian, but sometimes teachers we have left behind long ago still have their influence. Sometimes when we really want to fit in to a new neighborhood or a new group of friends, we are completely unaware of an accent or mannerism that still makes us different. And sometimes when we get into an argument with former colleagues, we concede many points in the hope of winning them over. Some think that Augustine, for example, never got over being a Manichean, and some think he conceded too much to them in order to persuade them. Either way, the tension between flesh and spirit in Augustine is strong, and most modern Christians would feel that Augustine remains far too suspicious of the flesh and its power.

It isn't easy *not* to be a dualist. The great religions of the world, centered as they are on the things of the spirit, have always found it difficult to value highly the things of this world; renunciation is a common theme. Christianity, though Archbishop William Temple once called it "the most avowedly materialist of all the great religions,"[7] has not escaped that tendency either. Any discussion of soul and body or flesh and spirit or this world and the next or especially of good and evil can easily take us in the direction of dualism, and Christians have not always been careful to maintain a clear distinction between a material world which may be very corrupt but which remains fundamentally good and redeemable and, on the other hand, a world at war with God which cannot be redeemed and can only be renounced. It is hard to keep that difference clear. But whenever the issue was clearly forced upon them, it was dualism that the Christians rejected.

They rejected it when they spotted it, but they did not always spot it. How could they help but pick up some of their neighbors' accents and never notice? So we find in the writings of the early centuries a constant concern for the conflict between the body and the spirit. Ambrose of Milan, who taught Augustine the Christian faith, wrote that "it is not possible to be at one with God and with the flesh at the same time" and that the body, while a "superb work of art," is, nevertheless, "the enemy of the soul."[8] If that isn't dualism, what is it?

REASON AND CONTROL

Faced with that direct question, Ambrose and Augustine, Origen and Clement might have responded this way: "Ah, but you have missed the point. The issue is not one between good and evil as the Manicheans say, but rather between order and disorder. The world and the flesh are not inherently evil, but they have become disordered and uncontrolled. We hope, with God's help, to restore a right order in God's world so that, as the apostle Paul has written, 'All things (may) work together for good for those who love God.' We know that the physical body is a part of God's good creation, not simply a prison for the spirit, but the body is subject to evil influence and we have to be very careful not to let it get out of control. It's the spirit's lack of proper control over the body that makes us captives of the flesh when our will is to belong to God."

We might be tempted to say something very much like that ourselves. Don't we find ourselves torn between the goals we set ourselves and the constant distractions of daily living? We want to exemplify the ideal, deeply devoted couple, but he forgot to pick up a loaf of bread on the way home and she forgot to pay the electric bill. Petty things drag us down from our noble goals. And if our goals are truly noble — love of God, the deep unity of our spirit with the divine — we will, inevitably, find the world around us to be very often a distraction and obstacle, sometimes God's enemy and ours.

Life for the first generations of Christians was, by any standard, an overwhelming challenge. Survival in a time when most human beings lived with the constant threat of crop failure and consequent starvation, and all human beings lived with the specter of uncontrollable disease and death, wasn't easy to begin with. Add to that the hostility of the Roman government and the consequent peril of persecution, and it would seem that no additional challenges were needed. But whether life seems dominated by the need to find enough flour to make a loaf of bread or the need to get the trash sorted before the next collection day, the pressure of material concerns remains, and with it the constant sense — for those who care — that the soul is being neglected.

So it was that St. Paul, after his conversion, went into the desert to be free to consider God's call. And so it was that almost from the beginnings of the church there were schools of thought questioning the goodness of the physical body and the material world. Before long there were Christians withdrawing from society to free themselves as completely as possible from its pressures and distractions and to seek God in solitude.

To live in an ordinary human community, even in the smallest unit, a family, is to live daily with the feeling that life is not fully under control. No one likes that feeling. To denounce the material things that constantly complicate our lives is one response; to attempt to rid ourselves of them is another. In view of the fact that first-century Judaism had produced a monastic community of sorts on the shores of the Dead Sea and that the Gospels begin with the call of John the Baptist to the desert, it is hardly surprising that a few devout Christians almost from the first had been drawn to the desert. There, in isolation from material things, they could hope to find that sense of control and unity that is so elusive in a house where there are bills to pay and dishes to wash and a telephone that rings.

The monastic movement in those early centuries was one response to this perceived lack of control. By going out to the desert, Christians could find a simpler environment within which the body could be more readily disciplined and brought into subjection. But the body was not simply rejected; on the contrary, Anthony of Egypt and his followers in the early fourth century learned that the soul could be refined by bodily discipline. "In the desert tradition, the body was allowed to become the discreet mentor of the proud soul."[9]

Most Christians, of course, could not just move to the desert. But the need for control mattered to them nonetheless. Late in the fourth century, Ambrose of Milan faced the same issue of control in his very different circumstances. Milan in his day was, in effect, a frontier settlement. The slow decline of the Roman Empire, the shift of the center of gravity to Constantinople from Rome, and the increasing pressure of barbarian tribes to the north had left cities like Milan feeling like insecure outposts of empire, and every failure of discipline was a threat to the security of society itself. In these unsettled circumstances, what was valued at every level and in every relationship was discipline and order. Ambrose, we are told, refused to ordain a friend of his whose gestures seemed uncontrolled. He found himself unsettled by the awkward stride of another.[10] These things mattered. The body must be under control, society must be under control; there must be unity and integrity.

Yet as these early Christian theologians contemplated human nature in its fallen condition, they saw that the flesh is not subordinate to the human spirit and will. Most specifically, they saw that the sexual organs were moved by passion rather than reason. Imagine that! But it upset them to observe this division within the body. They called it lust, and it troubled them and they wished it might be controlled. They were sure that any sensible person would want it to be controlled. If, as they believed, reason is what makes us human, then reason should have control of our lives. St. Augustine felt that strongly:

> What friend of wisdom and holy joys, being married...would not prefer, if this were possible, to beget children without this lust, so that in this function of begetting offspring the members created for this purpose should not be stimulated by the heat of lust, but should be actuated by his volition, in the same way as his other members serve him for their respective ends?... but sometimes this lust importunes them in spite of themselves, and sometimes fails them when they desire to feel it...[11]

Augustine had noticed that some people could wiggle their ears either one at a time or both together and that others could move the hair on their head backward or forward at will or sweat or break wind or weep with perfect control. Who then could deny the possibility, he inquires, that God might have given us equal control of our sexual organs, and no doubt did in the Garden of Eden? But when those first human beings failed to obey God, God, as punishment, arranged that our members would not obey us.[12] Augustine had a wonderful vision — what better illustrates the difference between his world and ours — of a time in the Garden of Eden when sexual relations were always calm and reasonable:

> The man, then, would have sown the seed, and the woman received it, as need required, the generative organs being moved by the will, not excited by lust...[13]

We may find it hard to imagine that as wonderful, but Augustine couldn't imagine anyone not wishing for such a world. Indeed, he thought it self-evident that anyone who could control their sexual desire to the point of eliminating it would obviously be delighted:

> For what Christian men of our time being free from the mar-riage bond, having power to contain from all sexual inter-course...would not choose rather to keep virginal or widowed continence, than (now that there is no obligation from duty to human society) to endure tribulation of the flesh, without which marriages cannot be...[14]

But the point is not so much rejection as control of the body and its passions. The issue is control, and while the result may be a concern similar to that of the dualist groups for the subordination of the flesh, it may be more accurate to see it as based not so much on dualism as on the philosophers' desire for a controlled and rational universe. Indeed, underlying the struggle of these early Christians was an unexamined assumption that the mind *should* control the body, that human life should be entirely rational and logical and unmoved by emotion or sensuality. The Bible does not say, "Be reasonable," but they seemed to think it did. Our own assumptions tend to an equally unexamined con-trary position, that the sensual is an important, even central aspect of human life and should be recognized, enjoyed, and honored. The cur-rent Episcopal Book of Common Prayer, for example, tells us that the marriage of a man and a woman was ordained by God "for their mutual joy," but that assumption is not in the Bible either. Our age, like that of the early Christians makes assumptions that may have more to do with what our neighbors believe than what the Bible teaches, but the tra-ditions of marriage that we have inherited were based on the beliefs of those who lived in the first Christian centuries and they, in turn, were deeply influenced by their neighbors.

The desire for control over the sensual aspects of life must, inevitably, focus at last on human sexuality. That is not, of course, the whole story. It is not only in relation to sex that our desires lack perfect discipline; food, possession, and position can lead to disordered desires also. Augustine himself noted that while he had been able to conquer his sexual desires with a single once-for-all act of renunciation, the desire to eat too much or too well was new again at every meal.[15] He began his essay "On Continence" with a discussion of the need to control the mouth — in this case, what goes out, not what comes in![16] Augustine even confessed himself to be unsure whether the church should use music in its services since music was capable of inciting the senses with a "dangerous pleasure."[17] For the pagan philosopher Porphyry, it was food, not sex, which was the crux of the problem; blood and meat were the primary symbols of the uncontrolled human desire.[18] For still others the desire for public office was evidence of disorder in human life. It may well be, in fact, that we, with our obsession with various kinds of diet, including vegetarianism, and our suspicion of politicians, will find more in common with the ancient world when we ponder these non-sexual expressions of greed and lust.

Of course, not all Christians in that day focused their attention on sex. For at least one anonymous Christian of the late fourth century, it was Adam's lust for land which had cost him Eden. But for most, whether pagan or Christian, it was evident that sexual desires were the acid test of rational control and the most pressing problem to be solved. Pagans, however, were satisfied with a regulated and limited sex life;[19] Christians held up a higher ideal: no sex at all.

Some, in fact, have argued that, as the age of the martyrs passed, Christians felt a need to find some new symbol of self-sacrifice, some way to offer themselves as the martyrs had done. To sacrifice one's life is the acid test of faith, but, if that option is not available, the sacrifice of one's sexual life may be almost as convincing a proof of the fervency of belief. And perhaps Christians also felt a need to mark themselves off from the rest of the world in some clear and obvious way. Jews had circumcision and kosher laws. Christians had abandoned those boundary lines, but sexual renunciation could provide evidence of faithfulness and act as a boundary between those dedicated to this world and those dedicated to the next.[20]

Concern for control was not the concern of Christians only. Christians may have believed that they were simply working out the implications of the Gospel; in fact a desire for more perfect control seems to have been the response of pagan philosophers and heretics as well to the chaotic insecurity of their common life. Valentinus, a Gnostic philosopher of the second century, praised Jesus for being, above all, self-controlled:

. . . he ate and drank in a unique manner, without evacuating his food. He had such power of self-control that the food within him did not undergo corruption, since he himself did not have to undergo corruption.[21]

What Christians had to say about control needs to be seen in this larger context. Of course they worried about control of the bodies' functions; everyone did. The wonder is that they, unlike Valentinus and certain others, managed to keep their worries from escalating out of all proportion.

CONTINENCE

For Western Christians at the end of the second millennium, perhaps the most puzzling aspect of the patristic teaching is the ranking of marriage as second best to continence. Quite apart from the fact that our culture does not value chastity or virginity at all, there is, in Scripture, God's command to the man and the woman to replenish the earth. How can a church full of virgins and celibates accomplish that goal?

But clearly Christians of the first centuries took for granted the desirability of continence. So Augustine, having written thirty-five chapters in *defense* of marriage, then immediately wrote fifty-seven chapters in *praise* of virginity. And note that he had to write a defense of marriage but needed only to praise virginity. He was concerned that virginity "not only . . . be set forth, that it may be loved, but also . . . admonished, that it be not puffed up."[22] In other words, virginity was so obviously good that no defense was needed, only a caution against undue pride. And virginity was so good that the reward would be eternal: virginity, being better than marriage, says Augustine, will have a greater reward.[23]

Augustine himself cited scripture as the reason for honoring continence. The scriptural command to replenish the earth seemed to him to be directed only to humanity before the time of Christ. Augustine found in the Hebrew Scriptures not only a command to replenish the earth but a chronicle of men and women who took quite extraordinary measures to fulfill it. Abraham, for example, made use of his servant Hagar to acquire an heir when Sarah could not conceive. Jacob took two wives. Solomon in his wisdom encumbered himself with wives and concubines almost beyond number. But Augustine saw this as quite reasonable, since the earth needed to be populated if God's plan for human redemption was to be carried out. Now, however, God's plan was complete and the need for populating the earth was past.

In particular, Augustine cited St. Paul, and especially the first letter to Corinth,** to support his view. Looking back from our vantage point in the twentieth century, we might not only challenge the scriptural interpretation of our illustrious predecessors of ours but also ask whether his belief that time was short might not have made its impact. Today we might interpret the second letter to Corinth rather differently. We would be likely to discount stands taken in view of an imminent end of time and emphasize rather Paul's warnings of the dangers of an unconsidered continence and of married partners unilaterally declaring an end to their sexual relationship. But do we really understand the letter better than Augustine did, or does our society simply predispose us toward a different viewpoint than that toward which his society predisposed him? In their own view, at least, the theologians of the early church could find much support in scripture for their advocacy of virginity and celibacy. From our perspective, looking backward, we might wonder whether their belief that time was short and the prevailing mores of their culture might not have been the determining factors shaping their ideas.

The belief that Christ's return was imminent and that practical living arrangements could be decided on that basis was, of course, a formative influence on the scriptures they cited. Why make career plans, if your career may be interrupted at any moment by the silver sound of angelic trumpets? Why commit yourself to a marriage if the short time remaining might better be spent in prayer? Even Clement and Origen in the second and third centuries must have understood that the countdown might not be in days or weeks or even months, but their authority was St. Paul and Paul had written with no such understanding. When Augustine and Ambrose were writing, nearly four hundred years of Christian experience indicated that the last judgment was not necessarily around the next corner, but their thinking was shaped by Origen, Cyprian, and others whose thinking was shaped by St. Paul's sense of an impending end of history. Furthermore, they also lived under such a sense of impending doom due to the mounting pressure on the empire that past experience no longer seemed a sure guide. Nearly three centuries in which the threat of martyrdom never entirely disappeared had been followed by a time of mounting crisis as the Roman Empire began to crumble. These were not years in which to construct a theology of long-term relationships.

On the contrary, the shortness and uncertainty of human life combined with the gospel hope of a new age to come (indeed, already beginning to manifest itself) were the primary influence on the first Christian

---

**See the full discussion in chapter five.

thinkers. They were living, it seemed to them, in "the last hour of a long night that would vanish with the dawn." And in that light, the ordinary human concerns for food and the other bodily needs were radically transformed.

> The body was poised on the edge of a transformation so enormous as to make all present notions of identity tied to sexual differences, and all social roles based upon marriage, procreation, and childbirth, seem as fragile as dust dancing in a sunbeam.[24]

So scripture and the tradition formed by scripture supported the priority given to continence and for women, at least, the culture itself provided grounding also. Almost every human society has, in fact, acknowledged continence until marriage as a value for women. Why? Whatever value we may still ascribe to premarital virginity is almost certainly rooted in fidelity and honor. For non-Christian or pre-Christian cultures, as well as for Christians for many centuries, the issues at stake were those of property and heredity. Marriage, as we shall see, had much to do with the orderly transmission of property. A family needs an heir to whom property and tradition can be transmitted. But if a woman is not a virgin, who can be sure of the legitimacy of children? How can the security of the inheritance be assured?[25] So premarital virginity was an almost universal value. But Christians who believed that time was short and who saw the church as the virgin bride of Christ[26] discovered a reason to commend virginity as a permanent commitment. Some groups, indeed, would have taken the process one step further and urged perpetual virginity on all. Clement of Alexandria in the second century and Augustine in the fourth found themselves therefore fighting a battle on two fronts: against their society in defense of virginity and against heretical groups in defense of marriage. Thus, whatever sources we find in the general culture for the commitment to virginity, they were not such as to justify Christian practice. That Christian men should be celibate and Christian women be given to lifelong virginity annoyed such disciplined pagans as Porphyry.[27] Sexual abstinence in that culture remained a dissonance and mark of distinction, but less so than it is in ours.

The honor given virginity in the early church and the preference for it over marriage, may also reflect the way in which marriage was lived out in that very different world. For centuries we have been content to understand that world through its leaders and literature. Today we are beginning to look at society as a whole, at life as it was known to "those who have left no memorial."[28] Peter Brown cautions us to beware of the assumption that Anthony of Egypt and others like him were in any way typical of their time.[29] Most Christians in Egypt never lived in the desert, and the fact that there are millions of Christians in Egypt today would indicate that there were many who continued to marry and be given in marriage. But those marriages (as we shall see) were not necessarily like ours, and that, too, may help to explain why virginity was praised.

Cranmer's familiar opening exhortation for a wedding service does, eventually, mention the "help and comfort" the one spouse may give to the other, and it asks the bride and groom for a commitment "to love and to cherish" each other. Later we will ask what that may have meant to a late medieval couple. In the early centuries of the church it would normally have been quite secondary to other considerations. To begin with, marriage was normally arranged by the families with an eye first of all to economics. Girls quite often were betrothed at a very early age, six to eight years old being not uncommon. Such early betrothals ensured the necessary mate for a boy and girl and the virginity of the woman. Perhaps also, as in China and India in more recent times, an early marriage was more economical for both families.[30] A man needed a woman to keep house and produce children. A wife needed a husband to provide food and shelter. In a time when "plague, pestilence, and famine . . . battle and murder and . . . sudden death" were all too familiar, it was important that arrangements be made so that life could be carried on.

The partners in an arranged marriage might, of course, become affectionate or even fall in love, such things are not impossible, but the hard, daily work of maintaining life would have left little time for the sort of companionship we seek today. It is also not impossible that parents might choose more wisely for their children than those under the early influence of post-pubertal hormones could do. But the combination of early arranged marriages and harsh living conditions seems unlikely to produce a marriage of affectionate and loving companionship. Anthropologist Jack Goody points out that "early familiarity may involve a reduced role for sex. Accommodation and acceptance are not the same as affection, love and desire, although these latter may develop with time."[31] It is also apparent in societies where girls are betrothed and married without consent that such arrangements are a major cause of suicide.[32]

How could love and a sense of companionship develop and flourish under such circumstances? Girls were not educated with that in mind. They were, after all, a charge on the estate. A simple method of limiting family size was the exposure of unwanted infants, and those unwanted were most likely to be girls. They were betrothed early, in part to save the cost of feeding them further, and before that they were often fed less well than their brothers. Once the church had begun singing the praise of virginity, Christian parents found a more humane way to reduce their costs: daughters could be given to the church as virgins. Exposure was regarded as sinful, but a virgin needed no dowry.[33] Whether destined for marriage or the church, education for women was, of course, not equal.

Once married, only the poorest women, those who had to work outside the house to help maintain the family, were often seen outside their homes. The invisibility of women in Greek society was such that lawyers had to go to some lengths to prove that women who had married and borne children had actually existed.[34] Even today, we are told, a Greek man will omit mention of daughters when enumerating his children.

Such societies are caught in a classic version of the vicious cycle: a woman whose role is to keep house and raise children will be raised with that and not love and companionship in mind. Therefore women would be less capable of providing love and intimate companionship. Augustine seems, in fact, to have been puzzled by God's decision to create a woman after realizing that it was not good for the man to be alone. "If man perchance were weary of being alone," he wrote, "how much more suited for common life and good conversation would have been two male friends living together than a man and a woman?"[35] There were, however, exceptions. Women with a sense of adventure, who managed to free themselves from the constraints of the normal family, could acquire a knowledge of the world and a familiarity with the marketplace. Such women would not be wives, but they might become mistresses and concubines. Demosthenes, in one of his orations, provided the classic analysis: "Mistresses we keep for the sake of pleasure, concubines for the daily care of our persons, but wives to bear us legitimate children and to be faithful guardians of our households." [36] Interestingly, Augustine, who lived with a concubine for thirteen years and, pending an arranged marriage which never took place, took a mistress after that,[37] wrote essays on marriage and virginity but not on concubinage. Perhaps he found women less satisfactory for companionship than men because he had never really been able to see them as more than sexual instruments. All the years that he lived with a concubine apparently provided no material for an essay to go with those on virginity and marriage.

The subordination of wife to husband was assumed both outside the church and within it. Augustine declared that St. Paul "has made known to us certain three unions, Christ and the church, husband and wife, spirit and flesh,"[38] or, to summarize it differently, Christ, husband, and spirit constitute one side of a balance while church, wife, and flesh make up the other. Further, he says that "the former consult for the good of the latter, the latter wait upon the former."[39] Clement of Alexandria had expressed it in a more practical form when he wrote of the value of marriage:

Physical illnesses also reveal how necessary marriage is. The loving care of a wife and the depth of her faithfulness exceed the endurance of all other relatives and friends, just as she surpasses them in sympathy. Above all, she prefers to be always at his side and truly she is, as Scripture says, *a necessary help.*[40]

Perhaps Clement, having never married, was unaware that wives also can become ill. But Clement inherited his attitude honestly from both his Greek and Jewish teachers. The last chapter of the Book of Proverbs, for example, having criticized nagging and contentious wives in earlier chapters, praises the wife who rises early and works to provide for her household so that her husband can be "known in the city gates, taking his seat among the elders of the land."[41]

For a woman, the demands and trials of marriage could involve not only an economic battle but a physical battle as well. The Jewish wife who termed her husband *baal* used the word used in other Semitic cultures to speak of a high god;[42] it meant "lord" and "master." An equivalent term was used for the husband in the Greek family: he was the *kyrios* or "lord."[43] The Roman husband was the *pater familias* and, while the experts may argue about how frequently his power of life and death was used over his immediate family, it seems unquestionable that it was used sometimes. The disobedient child could be put to death and was, at least occasionally. The wife was under the same control, and, this obviously did produce a society in which women were commonly beaten.

Augustine remarks on the relationship between his mother, Monica, and the husband to whom she was "given" and "whom she served as her lord." She learned to deal with his violence, Augustine tells us, by patience and reason, with the result that

> while many matrons, whose husbands were more gentle, carried the marks of blows on their dishonoured faces, and would in private conversation blame the lives of their husbands, she would blame their tongues, admonishing them gravely, as if in jest: "That from the hour they heard what are called the matrimonial tablets read to them, they should think of them as instruments whereby they were made servants . . ." And when they, knowing what a furious husband she endured, marvelled that it had never been reported, nor appeared by any indication, that Patricius had beaten his wife, or that there had been any domestic strife between them, even for a day, and asked her in confidence the reason of this, she taught them her rule, which I have mentioned above . . .[44]

Seldom are we given so clear an insight into the reality of human lives in another era. And as Monica obviously took it for granted that marriage was like that and had to be wisely and patiently accepted, so Augustine also never questioned this aspect of marriage. John Chrysostom, half a century earlier, had been eloquent in urging husbands to be gentle with their wives:

> [S]he who is your life's partner, the mother of your children, the very reason for your happiness . . . must not be restrained by fear and threats, but by love and a gentle disposition. What sort of union is it, when the wife trembles before the husband? What sort of pleasure will the husband himself enjoy, if he lives with a wife who is more a slave than a free woman?[45]

This concern is lacking in Augustine who, in all his writing and preaching about marriage, never suggests that Christians might seek to set a better example in this respect. Unlike many others in his own day (and others), he maintains clearly that men and women are equals in nature and mind and intelligence, but the female is to be subject to the male.[46] He cannot, apparently, imagine a world in which that subjection might be imposed without force or in which subjection itself might give way to a relationship of true equality.

Generalizations about the way other people and societies viewed marriage can lead to oversimplification and distortion. The picture of Rebekah being brought back willingly to Isaac as a wife sight unseen and with a ring in her nose is difficult for us to look at with appreciation, but we are told that Rebecca went willingly and that Isaac loved her.[47] We are likely to find more congenial the story of how Jacob served his future father-in-law, Laban, seven years to win Rachel's hand "and they seemed to him but a few days because of the love he had for her."[48] Love between husband and wife was clearly not unknown in former times, but it was not a priority and the soil it had to grow in was very stony and dry.

Even the birth and nurture of children, which we imagine will draw a couple together, was more likely in earlier times to be seen simply as a matter of economic necessity, or as another burden. For the wife, in fact, childbirth was a mortal danger. The incidence of death in childbirth was high and so was the rate of infant mortality.

Ephraim of Edessa understood the hardship of childbirth well enough to make freedom from it one of the joys of paradise:

> There find their sweet repose
> Wives with bodies broken
> Through pregnancy's dire curse,

Through birth's hard labors,
There do they see their babes,
That they buried with sighs,
Feed like the new born lambs,
Deep in the green of the Garden.[49]

In an economy of scarcity, additional mouths to feed were not easily satisfied either. The exposure of infants reflected that harsh reality. Children were sought as helpers and heirs, but they were also a danger to the wife and a burden to the husband. They were part of the economic equation of marriage in a world where the economic aspects of marriage dominated.

Under these circumstances, it is not surprising that the early church praised continence as a source of freedom. There is a profound theological sense in which discipline produces freedom. The disciplined athlete whose body is most completely under control is able to run the best race, skate the most perfect figures, and strike out the fewest times. And the disciplined follower (the "disciple") of Christ can, as St. Paul pointed out more than once, experience most fully "the perfect liberty of the children of God."[50] For those who pondered deeply Paul's meaning, the liberty he spoke of was most directly gained by sexual abstinence. To be free of the constraints of marriage was to belong, not to one other human being or a small family unit, but above all to that invisible society of human and angelic beings bound together in the body of Christ and the communion of saints. Peter Brown writes eloquently of the freedom such a belonging offered:

> Bonds based on physical paternity, on physical love, and on social roles derived from the physical person seemed peculiarly evanescent when compared with the resonant unity of a universe that strained toward the embrace of Christ . . . the humble, physical bonds of human marriage, based as they were on a momentary adjustment of the spirit to the heavy climate of earth, appeared peculiarly insubstantial. A time would come when all relations based upon physical kinship would vanish.[51]

For St. Augustine in particular, sexual activity was a slavery, a bondage, an addiction. His own upbringing and psychological development produced this reaction, one that may seem exaggerated, if not pathological, to people of our very different time. But in our time or his, there are surely some people who are addicted to sex and who can find their salvation, as addicts must, only in abstinence.[52] Fortunately, Augustine knew well that what was slavery for him might be freedom for others and that marriage was not to be condemned simply because he himself was not able to find his own freedom within it. The difficulty is that the power of Augustine's prose was such that his own self-analysis tended to become normative for Christians after him. Something in it also seemed to resonate with a deep fear of sex in the Western psyche. Thus Augustine's need to be free of sexual activity became a standard for Western Christians for more than a thousand years thereafter.

> He opened the sluice-gates of Latin Christian literature, quite as drastically as had Jerome, to let in the hard male puritanism that Romans relished in their ancestors and in their favorite authors. An ancient Roman's harsh distrust of sensual delight and a fear that the body's pleasures might weaken the resolve of the public man added a peculiarly rigid note to Augustine's evocation of human beings forever exposed to a merciless concupiscence. He created a darkened humanism that linked the pre-Christian past to the Christian present in a common distrust of sexual pleasure. It was a heavy legacy to bequeath to later ages.[53]

The most persuasive aspect of that legacy was that it was based on some hard rock truths: discipline *is* the door to freedom and marriage in those centuries was a burden in ways that we can barely begin to understand.

We can recognize that virginity did in fact open doors of freedom and opportunity for women in particular. Whatever assumptions about the role of women the church might have acquired from its culture, the gospel and the writings of St. Paul offered another possibility, however latent and unfulfilled. (It remains unfulfilled in our own day also however much credit we may wish to claim for "progress" in the area.) Paul had written that there is "neither male nor female for all are one in Christ Jesus."[54] We will examine this claim in more detail later, but surely something of that spirit does seem to have made a difference in the life of the Christian church from the very beginning. Women like Phoebe and Priscilla were prominent in the leadership of the first Gentile churches.

The discipline of the church led indirectly to a growing supply of women available for leadership roles. Widowhood was all too common in a day of low life expectancy; widows in their twenties were not unusual, but remarriage was frowned on. If people needed to be married, once was thought to be more than enough. Remarriage outside the church was especially discouraged, and women of wealth and position would have found few opportunities for marriage within the little Christian communities. The church in Antioch included three thousand widows and virgins by the end of the fourth century. Since these were women who had no life outside the church, their leadership skills almost inevitably would have been put to use.

Women were also prominent among the martyrs; the public witness to their faith made by women like Blandina and Perpetua[55] would have helped earn other women the right to roles of leadership. But Perpetua may already have been a leader in a house church. That was a role played by women from the beginning if they had a house large enough to be used for Christian gatherings. Perpetua was married and worried in prison about her infant. The stark necessity of survival made it difficult for many women in her position to play leadership roles, but widows and virgins, those who by fate or decision had been set free from the need to toil for the survival of a family, could and did find an opportunity within the church to develop such leadership gifts. The decision for virginity might, as we have said, have been made by the family, but since it would have provided an opportunity to be educated and set free from the burdens of childbirth, domesticity, and a husband chosen by others, such a decision might often have been very welcome. For a woman in those circumstances, freedom from sexual exploitation was freedom indeed.

PROCREATION

For most Christians, freedom from the demands of sex would not have been possible. Like most other human beings, they would have followed the normal path of marrying and giving in marriage. Ambitious parents, like Augustine's, might have sent a young man off to school and deliberately prevented him from marrying until a socially advantageous match could have been arranged. Most parents, however, would have arranged a marriage early and the young man or woman would have had very little say in the matter. And oddly, the same Christian church that so exalted celibacy and virginity would have told them that procreation was now their solemn obligation. That the two messages, continence and procreation, were not altogether consistent appears evident in the shifting stance taken by theologians as the church grew.

That the message changed may well have been due to its origins in cultures in which the church was located as well as in the church's own gospel. Procreation was clearly mandated in Judaism and the Greco-Roman world as well. The fragility of every family and society in the face of disease and conflict necessitated the constant generation of new human beings. It was important, then, that male and female begin to reproduce as soon as possible: a Jewish male could marry at thirteen and a girl at puberty, which was assumed to be twelve years and six months.

Marriage among both Jews and Greeks was considered obligatory, and marriages that were unfruitful were not allowed to continue. A Jewish male who was still unmarried at eighteen could be compelled to marry and if, after ten years, the marriage had produced no children, it could be legally dissolved. Apparently, the ten year limit was based on the story of Abraham who took a second wife only after Sarah had remained barren for ten years after they came into Canaan,[56] but it is interesting to note that Plato's *Republic* also prescribes that couples without children after ten years are to be divorced.[57] Perhaps, then, the allusion to Abraham and Sarah provides a rationalization for a requirement common to both cultures.

In some circumstances, the need for fruitfulness outweighed even the need for marriage. In Sparta, a marriage was not made public until the wife was pregnant[58] in order to ensure that the woman would be able to contribute to the population of the community. In time of war, the need for more men to replenish the community would have become even more urgent. It is said that in Sparta soldiers were sent home during a war to make sure that the women, being impregnated, were able to contribute to the war effort.[59] During the Peloponnesian War, even the less martial Athenians temporarily put aside the rules requiring formal marriage between men and women. Citizens were allowed to produce legitimate children from other wives than their own in order that the supply of citizen-soldiers might be maintained.[60]

However negative the views of some philosophical schools toward marriage, the need to replenish the community could not be set aside. Even a Stoic philosopher like Musonius held that sexual intercourse "is justified only when it occurs in marriage and is indulged in for the purpose of begetting children."[61] The rabbis, like the philosophers, saw the need of procreation as urgent for the life of the community. In the *Talmud* they wrote, "He who does not engage in procreation of the race is as though he sheds human blood."[62]

Christians were capable of taking a radically different attitude toward this aspect of procreation because their faith was founded on resurrection. Whereas the pagan world could find hope of immortality only in personal fame or in one's descendants (and fame, then as now, was harder to come by) Christians were by definition people who had accepted the gift of eternal life in their baptism. From that perspective, there was no overwhelming need to produce heirs to carry on one's name. Along with the belief that the world's remaining time was short, the belief in resurrection contributed powerfully to the Christian stance on continence.

Nevertheless, there is always a strong incentive to win the approval of society at large, and it is therefore not surprising to find documents from the second century demonstrating that Christianity was a faith consistent with the ideals of contemporary society and drawing a picture of the monogamous Christian couple devoting themselves to the responsible duty of procreation.[63]

On the subject of procreation, Clement of Alexandria echoed the pagan philosophers:

> By all means, then, we must marry, both for the sake of our country and for the succession of children and for the completion of the world . . . For if people do not marry and produce children, they contribute to the scarcity of human beings and destroy both the cities and the world that is composed of them.

To those who argued that there was no need to populate the earth since they lived already in the power of resurrection, Clement responded that they might logically abstain also from eating and drinking since these activities, too, will not be important in the age to come.[64] Methodius, appealing a generation later to Christians living through the final period of persecution, turned the traditional argument specifically to the benefit of the church. Chastity may receive greater honor, he wrote, but marriage is not to be despised since it is a source of new Christians and even of martyrs.[65]

But when the age of persecution had ended, the subject of procreation began to appear in another light. As the half-converted masses began to press into the church in the wake of Constantine's conversion, the need to produce more such semi-Christians seemed far less pressing. John Chrysostom said that marriage had once had two purposes,

> to make us chaste, and to make us parents. Of these two, the reason of chastity takes precedence . . . especially now when the whole world is filled with our kind . . . Now that resurrection is at our gates . . . the desire for posterity is superfluous. . . . So there remains only one reason for marriage, to avoid fornication.[66]

Augustine, looking back over the span of history, thought that there was "a mysterious difference in times." In the age of the patriarchs, procreation had been a good and necessary task since God's purpose could not be carried out without enough actors on the stage. Now, however, the cast of characters was sufficiently large and holiness could take precedence over fruitfulness.

For in these [people today] the very desire of sons is carnal, but in those [of the Old Covenant] it was spiritual in that it was suited to the sacrament of that time. Forsooth now no one who is made perfect in piety seeks to have sons, save after a spiritual sense; but then it was the work of piety itself to beget sons even after a carnal sense; in that the begetting of that people was fraught with tidings of things to come, and pertained unto the prophetic dispensation.[67]

Augustine could break free of the secular insistence on the need for procreation but still the philosopher's need for control remained. Plato had urged that the bride and groom should remain sober so they would be in control of themselves as they embarked on the adventure of marriage. And they should give careful attention to the begetting of children, since that which is good and excellent can only be produced when people pay attention to what they are doing.[68] Thus, no pleasure could be taken in the work of procreation.

The Christian married couple must "descend with a certain sadness" to that particular task: for in the act of married intercourse itself, their very bodies spoke to them of Adam's fall . . . Only in a city at the end of time . . . would the ache of discord, so faithfully mirrored in the flesh by sexuality, give way to . . . a fullness of peace.[69]

In the meantime, however disordered the human desires might be and however earnestly the church might hold up virginity and continence as a better way, the church would also maintain the biblical insistence on the goodness of creation and the goodness of marriage. In the tension between these viewpoints, the Christian understanding of sexuality and marriage has continued to be developed.

Because these first centuries set the pattern for later Christian thinking about marriage, a brief summary may be useful.

We begin with the first centuries of the church's life because it was in those years that a Christian doctrine of marriage was first elaborated. However strange the viewpoint may be to us, it is this understanding of sexuality and marriage which has remained normative through most of the church's history. Only in recent times has a significantly different outlook developed. But how can we move ahead without a clear sense of where we come from and without attempting to distinguish the sources of the various strands in our tradition?

What has been evident as we have surveyed the teachers of the first Christian centuries is how much of their thought was shaped by the culture that surrounded them and how much, in turn, that culture was shaped by the sheer necessity of economic survival. We cannot simply dismiss this as irrelevant. This is, after all, God's world, and if that world forces certain behavior patterns on us, it may be that God has a purpose in that also. Each strand in the tradition must be weighed and valued and we, in assessing it, must try to be conscious of our own cultural biases and the economic realities that shape our own instincts and assumptions. It is not an easy task!

Perhaps the strongest cultural influence on the early church was the dualism that shaped so much of the philosophy and religion from which the first Christians came. Even though they might have consciously rejected much of it, there was inevitably a continuing influence, however subconscious. Men like Clement and Augustine were conscious also of the need to make Christianity appear reasonable and commendable to those outside the church. Insofar as they could maintain that the Christian church exemplified the highest standards of pagan morality and culture, they would do so. We do the same, and in displaying those aspects of our life that the culture approves of and playing down those that are in conflict with the culture, our effort to influence the culture results as well in the culture influencing us.

Dualism was a powerful force in the early Christian centuries, and a pervasive influence in every human society aware of a conflict between its highest ideals and the contrariness of life as experienced. At a conscious level, the early Christian theologians rejected dualism, but many modern scholars accuse them of dualism nonetheless. They themselves, I believe, would have spoken of the need for control and for enabling the rational will to impose its vision on the disobedient flesh. Of course, that also was the language of pagan philosophers, but Christians then, lacking our perspective, accepted it as something obvious to everyone.

The stress on virginity, in a different way, set the church apart even from a society that valued virginity highly. For that late classical society, virginity was of economic and political importance and played a role in some aspects of pagan religion, but it was not seen as a higher way nor, in most cases, as a lifelong commitment. Among Christians, the lingering sense of an imminent end of time, reinforced by persecution and the decay of the Roman Empire, combined with the stress on control of the unruly body to create a cult of continence and virginity. The monks in the Egyptian desert exemplified the control that was possible and the potential use of the body to discipline the spirit and win a certain spiritual freedom. The women who dedicated themselves to virginity, however, often found it a way to be free of the burden of marriage and childbearing and to gain recognition and leadership within the Christian community.

For some Christian women at least, the men's need to control sexuality which placed women under restraint in so many cultures, created a new freedom and opportunity. It may be possible to argue that the very downplaying of marriage as second best enabled Christians to look again at the relationship between men and women. It may be possible to argue that the women who renounced marriage in that era (or for whom it was renounced) helped to enable the women of a later era to reshape marriage into a more truly human partnership.

Peter Brown reminds us that our knowledge of that time comes in large part from individuals who were by no means typical of their time. It has been estimated that two-thirds of the population of the Roman Empire in the time of the apostles held the status of slaves. They made up the larger part of the Christian church as well, but they were not the bishops and theologians whose ideas have come down to us. "The day-to-day life of Christians is a darkened landscape, intermittently lit up for us by the flashes of polemical fireworks that crackled far overhead."[70]

There are, undoubtedly, questions we would like to ask that can no longer be answered. But those occasional flashes do reveal something, and a later age, having only that record, may be more influenced by them than was their own. That Augustine, in particular, left his mark on the church for ages to come can hardly be denied. Our task is to understand as well as we can what forces shaped the thought that shaped the church we have inherited, to look at the developing institution of marriage in context and, by doing so to prepare the ground for a reexamination and reshaping of marriage for our own world.

CHAPTER TWO

All Sorts and Conditions:
Marriage in Other Cultures

*W*hat have other societies done about marriage? In most of
them, economic considerations have shaped the institution
of marriage. Families have made financial arrangements for the
security of their daughters and to ensure the future of the social
unit. Love, freely chosen, is a recent development.

In the high plains and mountains of Tibet, the basic resources by
which life is sustained have always been in short supply. Sufficient
resources are available so long as everyone is careful and so long as there
are not too many mouths to feed. In such a world, polyandry makes
perfect sense. It has been the custom, therefore, for the eldest son to
marry first, and for one or two of his brothers to share the same wife. If
there are other sons in the family, they will go into a monastery. Thus
one family remains one family generation after generation and the
population is stable.[1]

The Nayar people of the Malabar coast of India, on the other hand,
developed a pattern of life that needed no marriages at all. The men
were a warrior caste who spent their reproductive years in barracks or
at war; sexual relationships for them were informal and occasional.
Since the men were seldom present for long, the women were allowed
to take as many as ten "temporary husbands" but, for a more stable
arrangement, they considered it a privilege to be engaged as servants in
Brahmin households where the Brahmin men often took them as
concubines. Thus the tribe was conveniently reproduced without the
need of marriage.[2]

A Portuguese traveller in the sixteenth century reported that the kings
of the Malayalam Brahmin were allowed to have a mistress and children
but not to marry nor to have their sons succeed them to the throne. Instead, it was the custom that their brothers succeed them first, and
then their sisters' sons.[3]

Sociologists and anthropologists can provide us with a wide variety of interesting tales of patterns of sexual behavior in other times and places. We should not assume that marriage has always been a simple story of boy meets girl and lives happily ever after. But there do seem to be broad general patterns of human sexual behavior which form an immediate background for the development of marriage customs within the Christian church. Of most importance for our understanding of this development is an awareness of the political and economic factors that have governed and shaped the institution of marriage in most societies through most of human history. Marriage as romantic love, the free choice of a young man and young woman to marry each other for love alone, is a late development in the story of the human race and for most people has become the rule rather than the exception only in the latter part of the twentieth century.

For other ages and other societies, marriage was a matter of political and economic security. Solomon had seven hundred wives not, presumably, because he loved them* or because he needed that many outlets for his sexual drives, but because they represented the system of alliances on which his throne rested. His first wife was the daughter of the Pharaoh and we are told specifically that he took her in "a marriage alliance with Pharaoh king of Egypt."[4] His wives were the daughters of the leading men of Israel and the kings and great men of surrounding nations. The multitude of wives was a sign of his political, not his romantic, accomplishments.

Two and a half millennia later, Henry VII of England arranged for his son, Arthur, to be married to Catherine of Aragon because an alliance with Spain would enable him to dominate France, the ancient enemy. When Arthur died before his father, it seemed only logical to pass Catherine on to Arthur's younger brother. The fact that church law forbade a woman to marry her deceased husband's brother seemed far less important to the English king, the Spanish emperor, and the Roman pope than the political advantages to be gained.** And no one seems to have asked Henry or Catherine. Marriage was not and seldom had been a matter of individual affections but one of alliances between clans and families and nations.

In traditional societies, marriage can be defined as "an association between two persons for mutual support and the procreation and rearing

---

*The Bible does say he "loved many" foreign women (1 Kings 11.1), but "love" has many levels, and we may be safe in suggesting that quantity reduces quality.

**The fact that a chain of events set in motion to unite nations wound up dividing churches is extremely interesting but not directly relevant to our theme.

of children" and one that "usually has all the aspects of alliance between groups of kin."[5] The sense of belonging to a clan or lineage group takes precedence over any personal preference to such a degree that individuals will speak of themselves as married to a tribe ("I am married with the Etenga") rather than to an individual.[6] Since such marriages are primarily a matter of tribal concern, it is unusual to question the choice of a life partner made by the elders of the group. Love of parents and love of children will ordinarily outrank love of marriage partner. More important than the particular marriage partner chosen is the opportunity to take a full part as a man or woman in the life of the group, and, since that depends on marriage, what matters is to accept the partner selected and move on to the adult role opened up by marriage.[7] Those who refuse to play their appointed role could expect to be ridiculed and, ultimately, driven out of the common life — which means death.[8] Such patterns are common today in parts of Africa and Asia, for example, and were customary also among the noble families of Europe until rather recently.

Even when the concerns of family began to take precedence over tribe or clan (in medieval Europe, for example), the chief objective was still to carry on a lineage and, if possible, to "marry up": To find a partner for one's son or daughter through whom the family would be connected with another family of higher status or greater wealth. A marriage formed on such a basis might not preclude love or even affection, but where such qualities were absent in a relationship it was sometimes possible to buy one's way out. In nineteenth-century China, Cantonese women working in the silk factories could free themselves of unhappy ties by using their savings to buy secondary brides for their husbands.[9]

Because the cementing of a marriage bond could bring specific benefits to the family, a daughter had measurable economic and political value. Her departure from a family left them the poorer unless her value was replaced in some way. Many societies, therefore, developed a system of dowry or bride-price and negotiated contracts in which the obligations of both families were clearly specified. But whether the provision for the bride was seen as a dowry or bride-price, whether it was given by the bride's family or the groom's, the primary purpose of these customs was to ensure the future security of the daughter; the money or other gifts usually were set aside in some way for that purpose.[10] In Taiwan in the 1930s, for example, wealthy families would provide dowries for their daughters that included not only land and a supply of essential commodities sufficient for a lifetime but even money for her funeral.[11] The underlying assumption was that a woman could not earn her own living and needed to be secure against the possibility of divorce or of her husband's death. In this respect, the situation of daughters paralleled that of sons: the sons would inherit land or other wealth at their father's death while the daughters were, in effect, given their share of the inheritance when they departed in marriage.

The use of the term *bride-price* can give the impression of a simple economic exchange between men: the father, in effect, selling his daughter to the future husband for an agreed amount of money. The daughter, in this perspective, has a certain value and the father must be compensated for her loss. In Jewish tradition, for example, the Mishnah provides that

> A daughter is . . . perceived as the property of her father; he collects bride-price from the man who marries her or from one who seduces or rapes her (Exodus 22.15-16; Deut. 22.28-29) whether or not the violator marries the girl. The bride-price compensates for loss of the daughter's virginity treated as the father's economic asset.[12]

But the bride-price can also be the bride's economic asset. If she is of full age, she can negotiate the marriage settlement herself, and if she is divorced or her husband dies, the settlement is a lien on her husband's estate and must be paid to her by her husband's heirs.[13] The value of the marriage settlement, moreover, can be raised or lowered if the husband or wife should neglect their marital duty. If the husband is neglectful, he must increase the settlement by a fixed amount per week; if the wife is neglectful of her husband, the settlement is diminished and she will have less to take away in the event of divorce.[14]

The marriage contract in some societies specified the terms under which the dowry would be used and controlled. If the wife controlled it, she might still use it to buy her husband additional land or to support his business. The economic advantage to the husband was such that Plautus could say, "Most of you have dames for wives who bought you with their dowries."[15] How could the husband divorce a wife whose wealth was critical to his own success? Even if the husband controlled the dowry during the marriage, it would come back to the wife on his death or in the event of divorce. Marcus Aurelius became emperor by marrying the emperor's daughter, and so, when it was suggested to him that he divorce her, he retorted, "What, and return her dowry?" The dowry would have been the empire itself![16]

While a dowry of that size was obviously not usual, dowries could leave a widow in comfortable circumstances. In the life of the early Christian church the fact that the remarriage of widows was discouraged created a significant pool of women whose resources were available to the church and who themselves therefore were able to take an influential place in the church's life.

More important to our understanding of the development of a theology of marriage within the church, however, is the apparently universal pattern of negotiation and contract. Whatever the understanding was of the economic and personal issues involved, marriage in most societies had to do with a contractual relationship. The church simply accepted that understanding and built a theology upon it.

To think of marriage in terms of a formal contract negotiated by the families of the bridal pair is so unnatural to us that we may greatly misunderstand some of the implications. What it did not mean in most cases was that two strangers were suddenly thrust upon each other and told to "sink or swim" unlike Henry VIII and Ann of Cleves, who had not laid eyes on each other until she arrived in London for the marriage. The ordinary couple were more likely to have grown up in the same community, and negotiations would have consumed a significant period of time during which acquaintance might be deepened.

In most societies also there was a period of betrothal during which the couple might become very well acquainted. In some societies, that developing acquaintance included full sexual rights, and children born in that time were considered legitimate.[17] It seems, in fact, that in some societies the betrothal might be terminated if pregnancy did not occur. There was often no single moment or event that could be said to make the marriage complete and final.[18]

The betrothal period was also a time for families to draw closer together. In many societies, the payment of the bride-price was spread over a period of years and accompanied with certain ceremonies and festivities that served to unite the families more closely.

It must also be emphasized that marriage was not necessarily a "religious" event. We can observe a range of behavior, but for those who think in terms of American history and Supreme Court rulings to label it "religious" or "secular" may be to impose the wrong categories on the event. We would see a clear difference between the marriage in Hindu India, which sociologists describe as a "sacrament," a ceremony involving a nuptial fire and the reading of sacred texts,[19] and the customs of ancient Greece, which required only the drawing up of a betrothal agreement and the public registering of the relationship.[20] Greek custom was directed largely at ensuring the legitimacy of children for purposes of inheritance but, essentially, when a man and a woman lived together, that created the marriage. Nonetheless, Hindu and Greek alike were simply observing the customs of their society, and both would have understood that society to be an integral whole without boundaries marking secular or sacred realms.

A clearer case can be made for describing the traditional Jewish marriage as "secular" simply because it existed in such striking contrast and conflict with the customs of the surrounding peoples. Again and again in the Old Testament we find the prophets denouncing those who adopted the cultic practices of the Canaanites and others. Canaanite religion had to do with the fertility of the soil and the marriages. The coupling of male and female in marriage imitated the coupling of male and female deities. Temple prostitutes were available for the same purpose. However shocking this may have been to prophetic sensibilities, it must have been an enormous temptation for the Jewish people, with their nomadic, desert background, to learn from their Canaanite neighbors the proper way to encourage the crops to grow. The Book of Exodus describes the result:

> . . . when they prostitute themselves to their gods and sacrifice to their gods, someone among them will invite you, and you will eat of the sacrifice. And you will take wives from among their daughters for your sons, and their daughters who prostitute themselves to their gods will make your sons also prostitute themselves to their gods.[21]

If we describe a marriage which imitates the marriage of the gods as a religious marriage, then a marriage which rejects any such imitation might properly be described as secular. But the God of the prophets was not a God to be influenced by fertility rites; their God had chosen to act in human history out of a covenant love for the people of Israel. There was no divine prototype of marriage to imitate, it required no priests and no religious ceremony. So marriage for them could be described as "secular" or "worldly," but it was understood that that world was shaped and governed by God's loving purpose.

Marriage in ancient Israel, in many ways, had more of the character of a commercial transaction than a religious event. According to Mishnaic law, "A wife may be acquired in three ways . . . by money, by deed, or by intercourse." Notice that a wife is acquired in the same way as any other property: "by money, by deed, or by usucaption (long possession)." In the case of a wife, of course, intercourse constitutes usucaption.[22] The understanding of the woman as an object acquired is reinforced by the fact that in the marriage ceremony it is the man who speaks, not the woman.

Yet it is not the woman as a person who is treated like a piece of property, but the woman in her sexual function. In other respects, the personhood of the woman is strictly protected; even in her sexual function, it is her rights which are defined, not the husband's. She has a right, for example, to intercourse on a regular basis, depending only on the man's occupation. If he is a sailor, she has a right to his attentions only once in six months; if a camel driver once a month; if a laborer, once every other day; but daily if he is unemployed.[23]

All of this, however, has to do with the regulating of society in what we would now call its "secular" aspect. Yet to judge ancient marriages according to our standards of "sacred" and "secular" risks anachronism. That was not the way the people of those societies thought.

Roman marriage customs display a more obvious distinction between sacred and secular. In ancient Rome, marriage was clearly a religious event. Roman religion was centered on the household gods and each husband and wife served as priests of the household shrine. Through marriage a woman was inducted into her husband's religion; he carried her over the threshold in a simulated capture and then shared with her a piece of a special cake, so establishing communion with her and with the household gods.[24] Though a contemporary caterer might be surprised to hear it, the experts tell us that this form of marriage died out by the middle of the first century of the modern era.[25] What had developed in its place was a form of marriage as secular in its own way as that of the Jews, and an understanding of marriage that has continued to influence Western societies more deeply even than the custom of the wedding cake.

From ancient times, Roman citizens, including women, had had a remarkable freedom in terms of marriage. In the fifth century before the time of Christ, the Law of the Twelve Tables provided free marriage as an option available to women. A girl could chose at the age of twelve, which was the acknowledged age of marriageability, to declare herself a free woman and, although she then usually chose a guardian to administer her estate, she was free to betroth herself and to marry whomever she might choose; no one had the relationship to her of *pater familias.* True, custom required fidelity of her while allowing her husband easy access to concubines, prostitutes, and female slaves, but nonetheless her status was unique in the world of that day. She was regarded as her husband's equal in social status and was equally entitled to dissolve the marriage if she chose.[26]

By the time of the empire and the birth of the Christian church, this freedom had replaced the ancient religious ceremonies with a free marriage that was a transaction with no stated form at all. No exchange of gifts was needed and no contract was required unless great wealth and estates were involved. It sufficed that both parties to the marriage be citizens, that they have the desire and will to be married to each other, and that their mutual consent be verified.[27] The Emperors Theodosius in the fifth century and Justinian in the sixth century both affirmed this "mutual consent" form of marriage.[28]

We will see, as we trace the story further, how it developed that Christian marriage draws its inspiration from the uniquely secular background of Roman and Jewish tradition. But first we must look directly at what the Bible tells us about marriage.

CHAPTER THREE

From Eve to Bathsheba: The Hebrew Scriptures

*T**he story of Adam and Eve, seen through the lens of patriarchal societies, has been used to re-enforce values which that story may not, in fact, contain. We tend to use the term covenant to express our current values — and they may not be there either. The Song of Songs reminds us that the sublimity of love is grounded in fleshly reality — and that, at least, has not changed.*

The biblical story, we are often told, begins in a garden and ends in a city. The Judaeo-Christian tradition is centered in the history of God's dealing with a chosen people; it worships a God revealed in history. The Jews invented that linear sense of time that we now take for granted. Surrounded though they were by people who thought of time in terms of recurring cycles, the Jews had come to think of time as a succession of events through which God was working out a purpose yet to be fulfilled. Time had a beginning, a continuation, and an end.

We who are born into a society with that sense of history will inevitably find it difficult to recognize that there could be any other way of thinking. What else could time be but linear? The Jews had learned to think that way before they came into the promised land but there they encountered a settled, agricultural people, the Canaanites, for whom life was not linear at all. For them, life was a succession of seedtime and harvest, a recurring cycle of events in which one year might be better or worse than another but in which there was no development from one time period to the next.

We sometimes speak of a time as a flowing river, but a river is a better analogy for the cyclical sense of time than the linear for the beginning and middle and end are always present; the water flows past but the river does not change. Even though there may be times of flooding and times of drought, the river is always there from beginning to end and the water within it, constantly flowing past, only creates an illusion of movement and change. In a society that understands time in that way, there will be recurring festivals marking the annual return of spring floods and summer drought. These festivals enable human beings to participate in the cycle as their ancestors have done and as their descendants would do. Every year, people take part in the same event. Jews and Christians, too, have their annual cycle of events and the celebration of those events has some roots in ancient festivals of planting and harvest. But the Jew and the Christian, with their linear sense of history, risk thinking of the events being celebrated simply as past, so diminishing their sense of participation. A modern writer speaks of "the pastness of God's presence" and how "the Jewish tradition has devoted much of its energy to the re-creation of contemporaneity . . . most obviously in that theater of the recovery of experience that is known as the Passover Seder."[1] The book of Deuteronomy speaks eloquently of how God's actions in the past are truly present now and for all time:

> The LORD our God made a covenant with us at Horeb. Not with our ancestors did the LORD make this covenant, but with us, who are all of us here alive today.[2]

Having adopted a linear sense of history, however, the problem is how to make the seminal events of that history real for those who were not there. Even the eucharist, in which Christians celebrate Christ's promise to be present, becomes all too easily a celebration of memory, of real absence rather than real presence because we are prisoners of a linear understanding of history: if we are here, how can we be there? Marriage, too, is transformed by that sense of history. Newly married couples may imagine themselves as setting out on a journey rather than being incorporated into a way of life. They may see themselves as travellers setting out on a long and lonely journey rather than as new members of the community of the married.

All of this should be kept in mind when we come to suggesting other ways to celebrate marriage today. For the moment it serves primarily to set into context certain biblical passages that bear on the subject of marriage. We need to see them not so much as source material from the past but as visions not yet fulfilled. If it has taken the world several thousand years to catch up with the Jewish concept of linear time, it may take us a few more years still to modify that understanding again in view of Albert Einstein's theory that time is relative. Time, the scientists tell us now, is not linear after all; it bends and flows in eddies; the star I see today is, or was, at a distance measured by time across space that is curved. Perhaps the light the Bible throws on the subject of marriage might be imagined, then, as flowing not only from the past but also from the future. The light we see now flows from novas that erupted long ago. Stars that provide only dim light to us may already have erupted into novas that will be bright beacons for future generations. In the biblical vision, events take place which have been long foreseen, and present events are shaped both by a prophesied future and by a remembered past.

If, then, we begin our analysis of the biblical view of marriage with the story of Adam and Eve, it is not out of any concern to begin at the beginning. In fact, the Jewish people had been entering into marital relationships long before the story of Adam and Eve was written down, and Semitic peoples had undoubtedly been marrying each other even before the story was first told. The institution of marriage as they knew it would have shaped that story as they told it and wrote it.

If our intention were simply to look at the development of the institution of marriage in the Bible, we might most logically begin with the marriages recorded in the book of Genesis. But a book that records the ten generations from Adam to Noah without mentioning a single woman's name is not a very good source book for the study of marriage as an institution. That men and women came together in marriage seemed so obvious that it is taken for granted and seldom mentioned. We are told of husbands and wives but not of their getting married. Surprisingly, the marriage of Isaac and Rebekah is the first mentioned and Genesis mentions only two others: the marriage of Abraham to Keturah and the marriage of Er and Tamar. Did you remember that Abraham married Keturah? Does it matter? Abraham's marriage to Sarah takes place "off stage" and is never discussed but that, clearly — and the relationship with Hagar — is what matters. The marriage of Er and Tamar, is significant only because Er "was wicked, and the Lord slew him," and because Onan, his brother, refused to do his duty by the widow. Those, for better or worse (to borrow an appropriate phase), are the marriages recorded in Genesis. And the rest of the Hebrew Scriptures adds very little of importance. The marriages of David and Solomon are, in their own way, interesting studies but there is, to be honest about it, not a lot to learn from them about marriage as an institution.

We can, however, learn a great deal if we can break loose from a narrow searching of the historical record and ask the Bible a different kind of question. We will do better if we set out not so much to ask what marriages took place and what they were like as to seek to understand the vision of what marriage might be and ought to be, to look forward more than back. And that study does begin with the story of Adam and Eve.

FIRST WITNESS: ADAM AND EVE

Let me begin with a caution: we hear what we want to hear. Any husband or wife can tell you that — about his or her spouse! We come to the story of Adam and Eve with a particular set of expectations shaped, not by the Bible, but by the world around us. Even the best and most original minds, therefore, may still come away having seen very much what they expected to see, with a vision limited or even contradicted by assumptions they are unable to question. So Augustine, although he lived in a society that assumed the inequality of male and female, was able to see in the creation story evidence of equality in nature, mind, and intelligence. Augustine could see what the Bible was saying but still could not transcend the views of his society enough to question the subordination of the female to the male.[3] Similarly, *The Interpreter's Bible,* in discussing the story of the creation in chapter one of Genesis, says nothing about the implications for male and female relationships of the statement, "male and female he created them; in the image of God created he them." Concerning God's judgment on the man and the woman in chapter two, it does say that the subordination of the woman to the man ordained in that passage is "a consequence of the disorder which has infected the relationship of man to man."[4] When that was written, just after the middle of the twentieth century, nothing more needed to be said because no further questions were likely to be asked. As for the relationship between Adam and Eve being discussed in terms of "man to man" — well, we can understand that that was the way they used language in those days, but such a use of language can't help but influence ways of thinking, can it?

There are, however, several other questions to ask, and the first might be: what exactly is implied by the two creation stories in Genesis about male and female relationships? We are given two answers. The first answer is simple and straightforward: God created humankind in his image, in the image of God he created them; male and female he created them (Gen. 1.27).

Both male and female are made in the image of God; there is no indication of difference in status between them.

But chapter two is much more complex. It sets out a two-stage process of creation in which God first formed a man and then formed a woman from the man's rib. That has traditionally been read as evidence of man's superiority. Even the New Testament, in the first letter to Timothy, declares:

> I permit no woman to teach or to have authority over a man; she is to keep silent. For Adam was formed first, then Eve . . .[5]

Phyllis Trible has argued that such an interpretation of Genesis is un-justified by a closer reading of the Hebrew. She maintains that the first reference to "Adam" is generic and better translated "earth creature"; that only after Eve's appearance does Adam become a proper name and the original "earth creature" become differentiated into male and female. Indeed, when the second chapter of Genesis speaks of the time when there was still no one to till the ground, the Hebrew says there was no *adam* (2.5) but it is not, at this point, a proper name.[6] The older trans-lations, in the usage of their day, properly translated it as "man," and the New Revised Standard Version says "there was *no one* to till the ground." So, when God creates one to till the ground, it can be argued that this is simply "an adam," a human being with no specific gender. Thus male and female come to be when the human being is made to sleep and God divides the one into male and female beings with proper names.

Even if we find this analysis unpersuasive,[7] need we accept Augustine's assumption that first is better? What is the logic of that? In chapter one of Genesis, every creeping thing that creeps on the earth was made before humankind, but it is the human beings who are given "dominion . . . over every living thing."[8] In chapter two all the other life forms were formed after the man and before the woman. So, by Augustine's logic, if we consider only chapter two, the woman would be sub-servient to every other living thing.

But clearly we are taking our own society's way of thinking and in-terpreting these ancient stories accordingly. A feminist society might just as easily conclude that because the woman was formed last, it was her natural function to rule. Not only was the woman made last, but the man was made of mere dust of the earth while the woman was made of human flesh and bone. Clearly, then, the woman should have preeminence.

We would do better, however, to recognize that these are questions that the document was not necessarily designed to answer. What we can discover — and it is a remarkable discovery — is that neither story provides an ordering of domination in human relationships. Rather, domination results from the disordering of creation in which the man and the woman have failed to follow the instructions they were given and are required to live with the result.

Required for how long? The man, we should remember, is con-demned to toil with the ground but no one has ever suggested that no man therefore can try another occupation. Cain, the story goes, did till the soil, but his brother Abel kept sheep — and won approval. Does that indicate that men and women must continue forever to live out the initial consequences of disorder? If, with God's help, human beings are able to overcome some of the consequences of the Fall, is there anything to prohibit it? If, at long last, men and women can return to the equality in which they were created, would that not be a sign of the kingdom? Jesus apparently thought so; it has often been noted that he treated women with a respect not otherwise evident to us in his day.

But ask another question: what does it mean that "for the man there was not found a helper as his partner"?[9] The King James Version (1611) translated the phrase as "helpmate," the Revised Standard Version (1971 edition) says "a helper fit for him," and the New Revised Standard Version (1989) "a helper as his partner." Even our translations reflect our social ideals. However we phrase it the word "help" or "helper" seems to imply an assistant — unless we have learned that the same word is used elsewhere to describe God's own role in relationship to God's people. It is for God's "help" that the psalmist cries out, and it is "God our helper" who responds again and again to that cry:

> Our soul waits for the LORD; he is our help and shield.
> (Ps. 33.20)
> . . . you are my help and my deliverer; do not delay, O my God.
> (Ps. 40.17)
>
> . . . my help and my God . . . (Ps. 42.11 and 43.5)
> You are my help and my deliverer; O LORD, do not delay!
> (Ps. 70.5)

So the woman is created to fill the role in relation to the man that God plays in relation to God's people. Is that a role of subordination?

In short, if we ask these stories to answer the questions that concern us today, we begin to see that the answers that others have found in them are not necessarily the only ones. We begin to see that a relationship of equality between men and women may do equal or better justice to the scriptural text.

But if those are appropriate answers, why has it taken us so long to hear them? The evident answer in all the material we have examined so far is that human society evolves slowly and human beings are not likely to hear answers to questions they have not yet asked, nor answers that require a radical rethinking of inherited patterns. These passages seem to function as a kind of "timed release" medication, slowly assimilated and slowly opening human society to a message that even the original author may not have fully imagined. Yet they must have had some idea of the impact of their words because they do not simply reflect the society that produced them. Compare, for example, the passage we have looked at with these words of Confucius:

> The woman's duty is to prostrate herself submissively before her husband in such a way as to have no will of her own, but to demonstrate a perfect form of obedience.[10]

That kind of answer to our questions about human relationships is not found in the book of Genesis. Rather, we find there instead something more like a vision of human relationships both as they might have been and as they might become, a vision given in the thought forms of a society very different from ours but providing a mirror image neither of that society nor our own. Time, as we are beginning to learn, is relative: past and future both provide us with goals to shape the present.

SECOND WITNESS: THE COVENANT

Five books make up the Pentateuch or Torah, the foundation document of Judaism and of the Christian Bible. Most people have probably set out at one time or another to read the Bible. They start out with a sense of adventure, hoping to learn the story of their faith and find guidance for their lives. Most of those who set out on that journey of discovery probably do well enough through Genesis and into Exodus. There are slow spots and some confusion, but the stories of Adam and Eve, Cain and Abel, Noah and the Flood, and the long tale of Joseph in Egypt keep them going. Exodus starts off well too with the plagues and the crossing of the Red Sea and the handing down of the Ten Commandments. But as the chapters go by, the impediments seem to pile up. The final chapters of Exodus read like an Altar Guild inventory in a high church parish:

> They made on the breastpiece chains of pure gold, twisted like cords; and they made two settings of gold filigree and two gold rings, and put the two rings on the two edges of the breastpiece; and they put the two cords of gold in the two rings at the edges of the breastpiece.[11]

And then Leviticus begins with chapter after chapter describing the cutting up of animals and the throwing about of their blood until the squeamish will be glad to get back to the more controlled violence of their television sets. The long genealogies, the "begats," can easily stifle enthusiasm also. No wonder the family Bible often accumulates dust.

But almost at the center of the Pentateuch, just past the midpoint of the book of Leviticus, is a passage which, if you can dig your way through to it, shines out like buried gold. The nineteenth chapter of Leviticus, part of what is known as "The Holiness Code," begins with words that summon humanity to an unimagined potential: You shall be holy, for I the LORD your God am holy (Leviticus 19.2).

The man and woman, tempted by the serpent, were told, "You will be like God, knowing good and evil," but, in the event, they knew only that they were naked. Now, after the violence of their escape to the desert they are offered as a gift what they attempted to seize on an otherwise peaceful day in the garden: as God is holy, so shall God's people be.

Yet even this high calling comes in a jumble of marvelous idealism and irrelevant taboos. In one verse we are told to love our neighbor as ourself and in the very next verse we are warned to refrain from sowing two kinds of seed in one field or using two kinds of stuff in one garment. We are told to care for the poor and the sojourner and to pay wages on time, yet only a few verses later, we learn that slaves are not to receive the same justice as others.

There are passages in the book of Leviticus which must have been studied carefully and must have guided the daily lives of farmers and merchants. They are down-to-earth, practical passages that have nothing to say to us. On the other hand, there is the summons to a year of jubilee when slaves are to be set free and debts forgiven and unity restored. "Proclaim liberty throughout the land to all its inhabitants," it commands, and the words are engraved on the Liberty Bell and echo in the long story of the struggle for human freedom. Yes, but was the jubilee year ever observed? No one knows. Some scholars suspect that some of the laws of Leviticus are only a vision of what life ought to be like and were never carried out. But they are the words that continue to form and challenge human society toward a better future.

Here again, as in the creation story, we are offered a strange and wonderful mixture of past, present, and future. Many scholars spend their lives trying to disentangle the various strands of the Pentateuch or the book of Leviticus or even the Holiness Code. It seems to contain laws from, indeed, the time of Moses, some fourteen centuries before the time of Christ, but it also contains elements that seem to come from the post-exilic period of Israel's history some eight or more centuries later. The final editing of the Pentateuch may date from a thousand years after the time of Moses, perhaps four hundred years before the birth of Jesus. Yet it is presented as a single document describing historical events in linear sequence.

The point of all this is that we are looking here at some of the core material of the covenant between God and God's people. We are approaching the subject of covenant, the key word in modern discussions of the meaning of marriage. The use of that word in that context is based, at least in theory, on its use in the Bible.

"Covenant" is, after all, a word — like all words — with various shades of meaning. We shall examine these in the context of the contemporary discussion of marriage; for now, the task is to see what the word means in the Bible.

That search should be easy. What word could be more fundamental to our faith than the word that provides a title for the two main divisions of the Bible? But Christopher Brooke provides a useful warning:

> Nothing is so ill recorded as what everyone knows and takes for granted; it is the fundamental customs which are most difficult to trace.[12]

"Covenant" fits that description; a word that occurs over three hundred times in the Bible but is never defined. Three times in the first two books of the Bible God makes a covenant, once each with Noah, Abraham, and Moses.[13] Three times human beings make a covenant with each other: Abraham with Ahimilech, Isaac with Ahimilech, and Jacob with Laban.[14] But what is a covenant? Obviously you are supposed to know. And if you don't, then you have to guess from the context and whatever other clues can be found. A word used without definition invites the reader to create a definition and the great danger is that we will read into the word what we want to make it say because of who we are and where we live and the way we would like it to be. What we most want the word to say, in a world that values freedom and detests inflexible commitment, is something about freedom, a commitment on God's part but not ours. A word like that will be very popular and widely used, especially in relation to the area of life in which we make the deepest commitments and in which our exercise of freedom is most deeply challenged.

Theodore Mackin, for example, defines covenant by contrasting it with the narrow legalism of contract:

> Parties to a contract negotiate its terms; each leads from a position of relative strength, even if the qualities of the two strengths be unequal. . . . But in the Yahweh-Israel covenant there was no negotiating, no setting of terms by Israel, no claiming in justice by either. The relationship began with an

act of self-giving, rescuing love on the part of Yahweh. He took an entirely gracious initiative and did so in complete freedom. He invited Israel into a love-relationship. This invitation she was free to accept or reject. And even after both had entered the covenant, both remained free. In the historical scenario of the metaphor Israel was free to prove faithless, and she had the power to void the covenant. The only effect she could not work was to destroy Yahweh's love. He chose freely to pursue her despite her unfaithfulness. The permanence of their relationship came from his unfailing will to have her as his spouse.[15]

This is an appealing picture, surely, but is there, in fact, such a clear contrast in the Bible between contract and covenant and so clear a definition of covenant?

In the first place, as we have already noted, covenants existed not only between God and Israel but also between human beings. Whatever the covenants with God may consist of, those between human beings have to do with an exchange of sheep for water rights, a military agreement, and the settling of a family squabble.[16] There was no gracious self-giving initiative, but rather there was negotiating and setting of terms as there would be in a contract. Sometimes, in fact, the Hebrew word *berith* is translated as "treaty" and "compact." Ben-hadad, king of Syria, for example, having been defeated in battle and fearing for his life, offered back to King Ahab of Israel the cities his father had captured from Ahab's father and the right to establish bazaars in Damascus.[17] Modern versions of the Bible call the arrangement a "treaty"[18] but the Hebrew word is *berith* and elsewhere that word is normally translated "covenant."

But are the covenants between God and Israel so gracious, self-giving, and permanent? Noah is promised that there will be no more floods, no universal destruction, and that is, in a way, gracious and self-initiated, but most of the human race has been drowned as a prelude. The covenant with Abraham that promised one without an apparent heir an heir-apparent and descendants innumerable must have seemed an act of overwhelming generosity to one without such hope, but the price was circumcision, an indelible mark of estrangement between Abraham's descendants and the rest of the human race. The gift of the Ten Commandments has been the boast and pride of the Jewish people from the time of Moses onward. "What other great nation," Moses asked them, "has statutes and ordinances as just as this entire law that I am setting before you today?"[19] "I will delight in your statutes," sings the psalmist, "I will not forget your word."[20] But how free is that gift? "If you spurn my statutes . . . and break my covenant," God tells them:

I in turn will do this to you: I will bring terror on you; con-
sumption and fever that waste the eyes and cause life to pine
away. You shall sow your seed in vain, for your enemies shall
eat it. I will set my face against you, and you shall be struck
down by your enemies; your foes shall rule over you, and you
shall flee though no one pursues you. . . . You shall eat the
flesh of your sons, and you shall eat the flesh of your daughters. I will destroy your high places and cut down your incense altars; I will heap your carcasses on the carcasses of
your idols. I will abhor you. I will lay your cities waste, will
make your sanctuaries desolate, and I will not smell your
pleasing odors. I will devastate the land, so that your enemies
who come to settle in it shall be appalled at it.[21]

Some gift! It is appropriately the letter to the Hebrews, the New
Testament book which has most to say about the covenant, which also
tells us, "It is a fearful thing to fall into the hands of the living God."[22]

There are, of course, better things to be said of the biblical idea of
covenant. Fraught with peril though our relationship with God may be,
it is, nonetheless, the source of our life; it is our strength and hope and
joy. Above all, it is a personal relationship; the God of Abraham, Isaac,
and Jacob is one with whom a deeply personal relationship is possible.
Just as the human relationships most important to us are often nurtured
around the dining table, so covenant, in the Bible, is often created by
the sharing of food: when Isaac and Ahimilech had made an agreement,
Isaac "made them a feast, and they ate and drank."[23] And, of course, the
New Covenant was given at supper among friends.

Having said this much, we need to say one thing more. A word that
speaks of human relationships and has a special relationship with feasting may begin to sound like a word that can be used to discuss marriage.
The usage that occurred to the prophets, however, was framed the
other way around. It began with Hosea, a man who lived in the eighth
century before Christ. He tells what appears in the Bible as a very short
and simple story in two parts:

The LORD said to Hosea, "Go, take for yourself a wife of
whoredom and have children of whoredom, for the land
commits great whoredom by forsaking the LORD." So he went
and took Gomer daughter of Diblaim, and she conceived and
bore him a son.[24]

The LORD said to me again, "Go, love a woman who has a
lover and is an adulteress, just as the LORD loves the people

of Israel, though they turn to other gods and love raisin cakes."
So I bought her for fifteen shekels of silver and a homer of
barley and a measure of wine. And I said to her, "You must
remain as mine for many days; you shall not play the whore,
you shall not have intercourse with a man, nor I with you."[25]

The whole fourteen chapters of the book of Hosea are centered around
these two brief passages but, even in these five verses, the message is
already plain. Hosea understands that the relationship between God
and Israel has been like that between himself and Gomer. God has
loved an unfaithful people; God has paid a price for a people who have
committed adultery with other gods. Hosea does not use the relationship between God and Israel to point a lesson about marriage; he uses a
basic human instinct about the need for faithfulness in marriage to
point a lesson about Israel's faithlessness to God.[26]

The humanity of Hosea's prophecy is striking and profoundly moving. It plays on very basic and personal human feelings: the love between
husband and wife, between parent and child, and the deep sense of
hurt when these relationships are betrayed. Hosea depicts the relationship between God and Israel in these intimate terms: God is not only
the husband betrayed by a faithless wife; God is also the parent whose
child has stopped calling home:

When Israel was a child, I loved him, and out of Egypt I
called my son. The more I called them, the more they went
from me; they kept sacrificing to the Baals, and offering
incense to idols. Yet it was I who taught Ephraim to walk, I
took them up in my arms; but they did not know that I healed
them. I led them with cords of human kindness, with bands
of love. I was to them like those who lift infants to their
cheeks. I bent down to them and fed them. . . . How can I give
you up, Ephraim? How can I hand you over, O Israel?[27]

It was a revolutionary change in the human vision of God and it
remains a central and commanding metaphor. Over a century later,
Jeremiah explored the same theme and in the next century the Second
Isaiah and Ezekiel picked it up again. Ezekiel painted an extended
picture of Israel as a bride whom God prepares for a wedding:

I passed by you again and looked on you; you were at the age
for love. I spread the edge of my cloak over you, and covered
your nakedness: I pledged myself to you and entered into a
covenant with you, says the Lord GOD, and you became mine.
Then I bathed you with water and washed off the blood from

you, and anointed you with oil. I clothed you with embroidered cloth and with sandals of fine leather; I bound you in fine linen and covered you with rich fabric. I adorned you with ornaments: I put bracelets on your arms, a chain on your neck, a ring on your nose, earrings in your ears, and a beautiful crown upon your head. You were adorned with gold and silver, while your clothing was of fine linen, rich fabric, and embroidered cloth. You had choice flour and honey and oil for food. You grew exceedingly beautiful, fit to be a queen. Your fame spread among the nations on account of your beauty, for it was perfect because of my splendor that I had bestowed on you, says the Lord GOD.[28]

Unlike Hosea's portrait drawn apparently from personal experience, Ezekiel's picture is imagined and therefore more richly developed. But the point remains the same: Israel has repaid God's care and love with betrayal:

But you trusted in your beauty, and played the whore because of your fame, and lavished your whorings on any passer-by.[29]

It seems extraordinary that this highly personal picture of God could develop among a people who, at the same time, were working out the consequences of the commandments against the use of God's name and of carved images to avoid all direct reference to God of any kind. Thus the very same Ezekiel who can portray God so humanly as a rejected lover describes a vision in which he saw — not God, but ". . . the appearance of the likeness of the glory of the LORD":[30] Not God or even God's glory or even the likeness of that glory, but God at three removes. As against that valid understanding of God's transcendence, the prophetic commitment to Hosea's understanding of a deeply personal God is vitally important, not least for our understanding of the meaning of human marriage.

The prophets' concern was not for marriage as such, but a metaphor can work both ways. There is, of course, danger in turning it around; it would be disastrous to suppose that husbands should model themselves on God in an unrelenting pursuit and unfailing forgiveness while wives adopted the role of faithless, adulterous Israel. The passages we have quoted are not passages to be read at a wedding. But these passages do open up for us the human and personal aspect of covenant. Indeed, as they explore the comparison between human marriage and God's covenant with Israel, they transform the meaning of covenant itself so that it becomes a warmer, fuller word than contract, a word less precise, more mysterious, simply because it involves the ever-changing, indefinable, wonder-full truth of the relationships that are possible both between a man and a woman and between humanity and God.

Let's return then, to the question of covenant itself and the prevailing modern view of it as a one-sided arrangement on God's initiative. Gerhard von Rad, one of the leading Old Testament scholars of the twentieth century, tells us that covenant often deals with a "relationship between two parties of unequal status," indeed that it "is often an agreement imposed by a superior on an inferior."[31] But he also warns us to "guard against assuming that there was anything like a uniform 'conception of the covenant'" because the term "leaves room in each case for different conceptions."[32] Another scholar says that a covenant can be:

> a relationship which a superior attempts forcibly to impose upon a weaker party (1 Sam. 11.1-2) or an agreement in terms of which a superior makes promises to those under his control (Jer. 34.8); a relationship between equals involving mutual obligations (Gen. 21.27; 31.44)) or a solemn pledge of friendship (1 Sam. 20.8). It can denote a political deal (2 Sam. 3.13), a treaty between states (1 Kings 5.12) or the marriage relationship (Mal. 2.16).[33]

Clearly, if we want to base our thinking on the Bible, "covenant" is a word to be used with great caution. It is not exactly the word we need to describe our current thinking about marriage without careful qualification.

There is a passage toward the end of the Pentateuch which does not use the Hebrew word for covenant but which does summarize the terms of a two-sided covenant:

> Today you have obtained the LORD's agreement: to be your God; and for you to walk in his ways, to keep his statutes, his commandments, and his ordinances, and to obey him. Today the LORD has obtained your agreement: to be his treasured people, as he promised you, and to keep his commandments . . .[34]

The phrase "obtained . . . agreement" translates the Hebrew word *amar*, which seems to mean something like "declare" or "strongly assert." But we should note that a clear obligation exists on both sides. As to the people, they are committed to keep God's commandments — a task, they will discover, far beyond their capacity. If there is one-sidedness, it seems here to be in the other direction, for God is committed only to being who God is. The people are to be more than they can be, but God is simply to be God. If we see this agreement as one-sided, it is only because we have no way of understanding what it means to be God. But surely it is a commitment. To be the God of people like us involves, as we learn in the gospels, suffering, pain, and death.

Still "covenant" remains a word whose use is somewhat unclear and somewhat mysterious; and if that leaves us room to add our own particular emphasis, that may not be entirely bad. We need a word that can stand up to the rich potential and constant danger of modern marriage, that points toward the depth of personal fulfillment and carries with it all the limitations and opportunities of total commitment, and that connects us to both past gift and future promise. "Covenant" may be that word.

THIRD WITNESS: THE SONG OF SONGS

A long while ago a catalog came my way that offered a complete set of the writings of the early Christians, the "Ante-Nicene, Nicene, and Post-Nicene Fathers." I must have had some extra money available at the time to buy books, because I bought them — all forty volumes. They are a modern re-printing of a series of nineteenth century — "Victorian" — translations and are, as a result, a little stiff to modern ears. For years they sat on a long bottom shelf of my bookcase looking very impressive — but almost completely unread. Recently, in trying to understand the early church's view of marriage, I've spent a lot of time working my way through them: Augustine, Chrysostom, Origen, Clement, and others.

Browsing through Augustine one day I was startled to come upon a passage untranslated from Latin. Augustine had been talking about sexual matters and a footnote explained that the passage had been left untranslated "for obvious reasons." In a strict sense it isn't obvious at all unless your Latin is better than mine; I could get some idea of what was being talked about but not much of what was being said about it:

> Neque enim quia experientia probari non potest, ideo credendum non est; quando illas corporis partes non ageret turbidis calor, sed spontanea potestas, sicut opus esset, adhiberet; ita tunc potuisse utero conjugis salva integritate feminei genitalis virile semen immitti, sicut nunc potest eadem integritate salva ex utero virginis fluxus menstrui cruoris emitti . . .[35]

There are, I discovered, a number of such passages in my previously unopened forty volumes. If only I'd known! Of course, the italicized Latin simply signals the interesting sections and then you have to go off to a library to find a modern translation. Having aroused your interest, let me save you the library trip and provide a translation (with the context):

(In Paradise)...In such happy circumstances and general human well-being we should be far from suspecting that offspring could not have been begotten without the disease of lust, but those parts, like all the rest, would be set in motion at the command of the will; and without the seductive stimulus of passion, with calmness of mind and with no corrupting of the integrity of the body, the husband would lie upon the bosom of his wife. *Nor ought we not to believe this because it cannot be proved by experiment. But rather, since no wild heat of passion would arouse those parts of the body, but a spontaneous power, according to the need, would be present, thus must we believe that the male semen could have been introduced into the womb of the wife with the integrity of the female genital organ being preserved, just as now, with that same integrity being safe, the menstrual flow of blood can be emitted from the womb of a virgin.* To be sure, the seed could be introduced in the same way through which the menses can be emitted. In order that not the groans of labor-pain should relax the female organs for parturition, but rather the impulse of the fully developed foetus, thus not the eager desire of lust, but the normal exercise of the will, should join the male and female for breeding and conception.[36]

And if that doesn't shock you at all, go to the book rack in your nearest drugstore. Times have changed! Augustine himself goes on to say:

We speak of things which are now shameful, and although we try, as well as we are able, to conceive them as they were before they became shameful, yet necessity compels us rather to limit our discussion to the bounds set by modesty . . .[37]

"The bounds set by modesty" were obviously narrower in the nineteenth century than the fifth — and non-existent, apparently, in the twentieth. But one wonders what my nineteenth-century translators would have done had they lived in the time of King James and been summoned to work on a new translation of the Bible. Could they, do you suppose, have brought themselves to translate the Song of Songs, or would they have left it "for obvious reasons" in the original Hebrew?

Certain it is that this brief book at the center of the Bible has an erotic content sufficient to embarrass not only the Victorians but a good many others as well. When did you last hear it read in church on Sunday morning? Carefully selected verses from it are, in fact, often read at weddings, but even on those occasions there are not many who would be willing to read any one chapter in its entirety.

So what is this powerful evocation of erotic love doing in the Bible? How is it that the same faith that relentlessly excoriated and opposed the fertility religion of the Canaanites should at last have included in the Bible itself a text that evokes that same erotic spirit and that may itself have originated in the sacred sexual rites of Near Eastern fertility cults?[38]

There have, of course, always been those, both Jews and Christians, who would sanitize it by telling us that the poetry really means something other than what it seems to mean. It is, they would seek to persuade us, not at all about the erotic passion between a man and a woman, but about God's love for Israel or Christ's love for the church. Those who believe the poem originated in a fertility cult also would see it as having a significance beyond the love of a man and a woman. Some suggest, for example, that the poem has to do with the Tammuz cult and refers to the love of the moon goddess, Ishtar, for a young god whom she kills and restores to life.[39]

The problem with an allegorical interpretation is not only that no two commentators read the poem the same way (that is true of non-allegorical interpretations as well), but that modern readers, whether fundamentalist or radical historical critic, see the Bible in those terms. As Richard Corney puts it,

> We talk of a God who acts in history, not of a God who wrote a book. Allegory is a technique of reading, a way of getting at the true significance of what God wrote. It is the change in world view, it seems to me, that means allegory can no longer communicate with us as it did with our ancestors.[40]

Nonetheless, it did work for those of an earlier day. The earliest known Jewish commentary on the entire book tells us that Yahweh is the bridegroom and the Jewish people are the bride. In great detail it analyzes the poem in terms of Jewish history from the time of the Exodus to the coming of the Messiah.[41] Christian allegory, taking the same approach, has imagined the lover to be Christ and the beloved to be the church. Many editions of the King James Version of the Bible have chapter headings that spell out this allegory in detail. But Martin Luther saw the bride as a symbol of the state and Roman Catholics have tended to see the bride as the Virgin Mary. The difficulty is that, read as allegory, the symbols are not simply ambivalent, they are polyvalent. One Midrash interprets the phrase, "My beloved is to me a bag of myrrh that lies between my breasts" [42] as a reference to Abraham's head clasped between the Divine Presence and the angel, while an early Christian commentator locates the man's head between the Old Testament and the New.[43] If the Song of Songs is an allegory, it is a failure; it no longer communicates a clear symbolic meaning — and perhaps it never did.

But it does communicate. Any reader can recognize, even in translation, the power of its poetry; those whose experience includes erotic passion will hear within the music of the Song a resonance deeper than words. And those whose most profound experience is of divine love have rightly used the Song of Songs as an allegory for their experience as well. Though God is not mentioned, love is, and those who have known love have always known something of God.

Here then is a poem that, because of its place in Scripture, validates the human experience of sexual pleasure and enables us to look even there for knowledge of God. One scholar believes that Augustine himself had learned what he knew of the human capacity for joy in that way:

> I suspect that in spite of his loud and frequent disclaimers, Augustine learned "the deep and irreplaceable knowledge of (his) capacity for joy" from his sexual experience, and that it was precisely this experiential knowledge from which Augustine extrapolated his model of spiritual pleasure.[44]

Yes, even Augustine writing his *Confessions* (and elsewhere as well) found in this poem language to express the way in which we are drawn to God, how God speaks to us through human flesh:

> He looketh through the lattice (2.9) of our flesh, and He is fair-speaking, and hath inflamed us, and we run after his odours (1.3).[45]

We might have learned from the story of the creation that the God who created us male and female did so, in part at least, to give us a way of knowing the love of God. We might have learned from the way the prophets used the language of marriage to express the meaning of God's covenant that human love is capable of opening our understanding of divine love. But if these lessons have not commanded our attention, perhaps the stunning eroticism of the Song of Songs can persuade us that even our flawed and self-obsessed passion can draw us toward the God who seeks us so passionately. We may fear and deny that truth, but we cannot finally avoid it any more than Augustine could. Finally, the Song of Songs is perhaps the most striking evidence in the Bible that, as James Hillman put it so succinctly, "the sexual is a way the soul speaks."[46]

Or, as Grace Schulman puts it: "The more its authors sing of love, the more they whisper of God."[47]

CHAPTER FOUR

Come to the Wedding:
The New Testament

*C*hristians have often used Jesus' words in the New Testament in
an attempt to establish legal norms for the Christian life — and
for marriage. But Jesus' words, like the image of the wedding feast
in the Johannine literature and of the Body in Paul, call us back to
God's original purpose and point us forward to its fulfillment.

FIRST WITNESS: THE WEDDING FEAST

The suggestion made in the last chapter that we would need to understand Einstein to overcome a linear view of history may have overlooked
the advent of the video cassette and the television remote control. None
of us now needs to be a victim of the studio's idea of what we should
see and when we should see it. Now we can create our own sequences:
we can zap the commercials, switch channels on a whim, select our
own instant replay, freeze frame, or slow motion; we can, in short,
create our own experience of time.

Those who wrote the gospels had no video cameras but they did
have time to ponder and deepen their understanding before they sat
down to write. And therefore the events they chose to record and the
order in which they told the story are carefully designed to provide us
not with a simple, linear narrative but with a way to see deeply into the
story so that it becomes a window on God's whole plan and purpose.

The story of the wedding at Cana in St. John's telling of the gospel is
a brilliant example. All the gospels begin with stories of John the
Baptist and the call of the first disciples, but John alone then proceeds
to tell us the story of Jesus' visit to a wedding. To a modern reader, the
story may seem trivial and unworthy; what kind of messiah would begin to save the human race by providing an outlandish quantity of wine
for an unimportant wedding in a country town? But John sets this story
first and marks it "first" by telling us that this was "the first of his signs."[1]

To understand John's purpose, we need to remember how the prophets had developed the image of marriage as one way to make clear the implications of the covenant. Ezekiel, for example, provided an elaborate portrayal of Israel adorned as a bride for her marriage. If then the first sign John gives us of Christ's ministry was done at a wedding, we may well imagine that John expects us to make a connection. It seems entirely possible also that John would like us to remember a visionary passage in Isaiah about a feast — not specifically a wedding feast, but a feast for all people in the Messianic age, a feast provided with well-aged wine.[2] And certainly he was deliberately recalling the story of creation in Genesis. His gospel begins with a deliberate echo of the creation narrative, "In the beginning . . ."[3] As in the beginning of creation, so here in the beginning of the new creation, it is out of water that the rich new material is drawn.

Can we really ask one brief and seemingly trivial story to carry this weight of meaning? John seems to invite us to do so. In the very next chapter, John the Baptist confirms the meaning of the wedding imagery by identifying Jesus as the bridegroom and implying that Israel is the bride. And if we still miss the connection, the gospel tells us that the Baptist made that statement in the context of a discussion of purification. The water pots at Cana, we remember, were set there for the rites of purification. Only in those two chapters does the word "purification" occur in John's gospel.

So once again we are told a story that cannot be simply fixed at a point in linear time, but that draws us back to the beginning of creation and at the same time points forward to the messianic age. Yet it is also a rich and immediate glimpse of a real wedding in a small town in Galilee two thousand years ago. Friends and relatives have come from all the surrounding area and an awkward moment comes when the wine runs out. We can imagine the same thing happening at a party we might give. And the Lord who is always the ultimate source of our joy, though sitting apparently unnoticed at the side, makes sure that our joy is complete — though we seldom stop to recognize how God has been present for us.

But if we do recognize the implications of this story, we can see how the theme of marriage is woven all through the New Testament as an image of God's relationship with God's people. In the other gospels, Jesus refers to himself as the bridegroom and compares his time with the disciples to the time of a wedding feast.[4] If the Old Testament has compared the relationship between God and Israel with that between bridegroom and bride, then Jesus' use of that word about himself must be clear. Consequently, too, the parables that compare the kingdom of heaven to a wedding feast[5] take on a broader significance. In fact, when we discover that all the other stories of marriages in the New Testament have to do with the kingdom and the messianic age, it is almost inevitable that we will read the story of Cana in that light.

Finally, of course, in the last book of the New Testament the marital imagery culminates in the picture of the new Jerusalem "coming down out of heaven from God, prepared as a bride adorned for her husband." In this image, the relationship is made immediate and complete, for:

> the home of God is among mortals. He will dwell with them as their God; they will be his peoples, and God himself will be with them; he will wipe every tear from their eyes. Death will be no more; mourning and crying and pain will be no more, for the first things have passed away.[6]

This is, remember, not an image we are given for the sake of our understanding of marriage but to help us understand the depth of love God has for us and the fullness of the unity God seeks with us. But we must inevitably meditate on human marriage also. If the fulfillment of human existence can be imaged by my marriage to my spouse, does this tell me something about my marriage as well? Have I been missing something? If St. Augustine thought a friendship with another man was a better means than marriage for overcoming human loneliness, and if half the marriages made today end in divorce, then it must be evident that marriage as we know it falls more than somewhat short as an image of the kingdom. And that must challenge us to look at what we make of marriage and what we could make of it. The image does not exist primarily to tell us about human marriage, but inevitably it does so, and perhaps God's wisdom intended that it should.

THE SECOND WITNESS: "JESUS SAID . . ."

So far, we have, you might say, been circling the target. The biblical passages we have looked at have not dealt directly with marriage, however important they may be for guidance and inspiration. Now the time has come to ask a direct question and get a direct answer — like it or not! And however much we may think we want direct answers from the Bible for specific questions, the fact is that when we do we often find them more than a little awkward.

The gospels record only one specific saying of Jesus concerning God's will for marriage. Jesus was asked about divorce and he told them what he thought. That's where the trouble begins. Now we have what we asked for: a clear and definite answer. But when we look carefully, it seems that we have three versions of Jesus' saying. We need to spend some time thinking about this, and maybe even getting a bit technical, because this is Jesus' one direct expression on the subject of God's will for marriage and a great deal depends on the way we understand it.

St. Luke gives us the simplest version:

> Anyone who divorces his wife and marries another commits adultery, and whoever marries a woman divorced from her husband commits adultery.[7]

Some scholars think this version is closest to Jesus' own words[8] but the fact is that Matthew, Mark, and Luke have only the first phrase in common: "Anyone who divorces his wife and marries another commits adultery." Even then, Matthew adds *"causes her* to commit adultery"[9] and Mark adds "commits adultery *against her.*"[10] Both these changes show a certain sympathy for the woman's position in Jewish society. Quite apart from the morality of divorce, a man who took that step left his wife in a very difficult position. Mosaic law required that she be given a divorce certificate so that her position was clear, but, even so, she would have had great difficulty, as a divorced woman, in finding another husband and for a woman to support herself would have been very hard as well. But this is probably the least significant difference among the three versions.

St. Mark adds the reverse clause, "and if she divorces her husband and marries another, she commits adultery."[11] And here we begin to see something of what is called "development." Jewish law did not permit a woman to divorce her husband, so there would have been no reason for Jesus to add that phrase; in fact, it would have made his listeners wonder whether he were in touch with reality. Why should he say anything at all about something that couldn't happen? But Roman law did permit either partner to initiate a divorce, and by the time Mark's gospel was written down, the church was well established in the Roman world. So the relevant phrase was added.

We could stop right here and spend time discussing the significance of this move. What right does the disciple have to re-state Jesus' teaching to meet a new situation? But don't we ourselves, if we think about it, do that all the time? Day by day, as we try to apply Jesus' teaching to our own lives we do exactly what Mark did. What does the parable of the Good Samaritan require of me in a world where "my neighbor" is suffering on the other side of the world and the other side of town and maybe even next door? What would Jesus say to me about ethical conduct in my place of work or tensions in my local church or community? Again and again, I have to take what the gospel tells me Jesus said and try to apply it to my situation with the guidance of the Holy Spirit. Mark's gospel does the same thing but, since there was no written gospel before him, he could modify Jesus' words to fit the new situation. Suppose, however, the gospel had not been written down for another century or two: how far would it be legitimate to carry on that process?

The question becomes more difficult still when we see what Matthew's gospel does. Here the modification is not simply an adaptation to a new situation but a major exception to Jesus' clear command: "Whoever divorces his wife, *except for unchastity,* and marries another commits adultery." What do we make of that? Did Jesus really say it and did Mark and Luke leave it out? If so, they made Jesus' words much more narrow and rigorous than they were. But if Jesus did *not* say it and Matthew added it, what right did he have to make so major an exception to Jesus' command?

Matthew's gospel makes it clear that people found Jesus' words more than a little uncomfortable. How could Jesus really expect people to get into marriage if he left them no way out?

> His disciples said to him, "If such is the case of a man with his wife, it is better not to marry."[12]

If that was the reaction to Jesus' teaching with the exception about unchastity included, it's no wonder the church felt a need for some moderation of Jesus' words. We should be sure to notice before moving on how both Matthew and Mark show us the same thing happening that we saw when we looked at Clement, Augustine, Origen, and other leaders of the early church. Here in the gospels themselves, we see the way in which society modifies and helps shape the church's understanding of marriage. Mark modifies a saying of Jesus because Jesus was speaking in terms of Jewish law, but the church was now operating in the context of Roman law. Matthew apparently modifies the same saying in light of the distance between the standard Jesus had set and the ability of his world to accept its full implications.

Of course, again, the fact is that we ourselves do this same kind of thing all the time. We read Jesus' words about giving up everything for the sake of the kingdom and we make the little modifications that allow us to keep a reasonable balance in the bank account and go out to dinner in a world where our neighbor is hungry. Jesus also said, "Be perfect, therefore, as your heavenly Father is perfect,"[13] but we tend to allow ourselves a bit of leeway, don't we? In the same way, we are told that Matthew's exception was "a necessary step — the step of taking account of human faults in marriage."[14] Wasn't Jesus aware of human faults himself? Of course he was, and the gospel, if it is anything, is a gospel of compassion and understanding and forgiveness. But the standard to which we are called is perfection: the living out in human life of perfect love. What Jesus exemplified, we are called to exemplify also.

Presumably, therefore, when Jesus was asked about divorce, his reply was simple and clear: "Divorce is wrong." But Matthew and Mark tell us that Jesus set that teaching in a specific context: "Divorce is wrong because . . ." More important than the simple prohibition is the basic principle; more important than the basic principle is the way in which Jesus taught his disciples to seek such principles and understand God's will.

The question Jesus was asked had to do with divorce. He began his reply by asking what Moses had commanded, and he was told that Moses commanded a written divorce to be given. Yes, Jesus said, but that was because of the hardness of human hearts:

> But from the beginning of creation, 'God made them male and female.' 'For this reason a man shall leave his father and mother and be joined to his wife, and the two shall become one flesh.' So they are no longer two, but one flesh. Therefore what God has joined together, let no one separate.[15]

So here we are back again at that same passage in Genesis with which we began our study of the Old Testament, a passage that we said should be seen as drawing us forward toward a future fulfillment. Yet in quoting it here Jesus is inviting us to go back to the beginning and to God's original purpose. What human beings have done in the time between now and then is always an accommodation, and accommodation may be necessary but accommodation is not the goal. The goal is the fulfillment of God's purpose and that purpose is seen as clear and bright on the last day of creation as on the first. Jesus is reminding us that time may be a linear progression but the kingdom, like God's eternal purpose, stands outside of time and in judgment over it.

Given three versions of Jesus' words, how can we know exactly what he really said? The short answer is that we can't. But what we can do is see the early church grappling with Jesus' words, as we have to do, in the midst of the reality of their own lives, trying to find a way to be faithful both to his words and to his Spirit. As St. Paul says:

> Not that we are competent of ourselves to claim anything as coming from us; our competence is from God, who has made us competent to be ministers of a new covenant, not of letter but of spirit; for the letter kills, but the Spirit gives life.[16]

Perhaps we can try to understand our story in those terms. Jesus did not come to deliver a new law but to call us back to the perfection of creation, to point us forward to the kingdom in which that perfection will be restored, and to offer us the forgiveness without which we could never dare set out on the journey. The story we have to follow is one of repeated failure to understand but also a story of repentance and renewal and growth.

THE THIRD WITNESS: A PROFOUND MYSTERY

"Submit yourselves"

When my wife and I began to plan our wedding service, the Book of Common Prayer provided only two readings: the gospel story of the wedding at Cana and the passage from the letter to the Ephesians that says, "Wives, submit yourselves unto your own husbands, as unto the Lord. For the husband is the head of the wife, even as Christ is the head of the church . . ."[17] We didn't know at the time that this reading has been used for centuries in the Coptic Rite, the Byzantine Rite, the Roman Missal, and innumerable other liturgies; we only knew that we didn't want it read at our wedding, and it wasn't. Since the wedding was scheduled for a day in Easter week when other readings were provided, we decided to use the readings for the day rather than those for a wedding. What ever other ages may have felt about this passage, it no longer commended itself to us at first glance. The Book of Common Prayer no longer even suggests that passage from Ephesians as an option, presumably because most couples can be expected to react to it as we did and reject it without a second look.

In recent years, studying the letter to the Ephesians more objectively, I have come to believe that that instinctive rejection was unfortunate because no other New Testament passage says something so revolutionary. If any one passage provides a charter for a radically new way of understanding marriage, this is the one: the tension between what we find in the world around us and what God calls us to be is nowhere more evident than here.

What we need to understand first, I think, is the position of the church in the first century of the so-called "Christian era." The term implies a predominant Christian influence on society, and that may have been the case in the Middle Ages, but it was certainly not the case in the first three centuries after the resurrection. Christian witnesses went out into a world with a highly developed civilization and a political system which had achieved a level of peace and security unknown before that time. Greek philosophy and Roman law had combined to produce a structured and ordered society. It had its flaws, but not many of those who lived under its protection were prepared to risk their security in an attempt to correct them.

The foundation stone of this structure was understood to be the individual household. The ancient Roman religion made each husband not only the head of the household but the chief priest in the domestic religion. When a woman married, as we have said, she was "converted" to her husband's faith and carried across the threshold of his house as a symbol of her entrance into this new religion.

This Roman religious perspective was powerfully reinforced by Greek philosophy. Aristotle had laid it down that the household was the foundation of the state:

> Seeing then that the state is made up of households, before speaking of the state we must speak of the management of the household. . . . Now we should begin by examining everything in the fewest possible elements; and the first and fewest possible parts of a family are master and slave, husband and wife, father and children. We have therefore to consider what each of these three relations is and ought to be: I mean the relation of master and servant, the marriage relation . . . and thirdly, the procreative relation . . .[18]

Step by step, Aristotle proceeds to analyze carefully the proper management of a household, distinguishing between the use made of slaves and the use made of animals and between the royal rule that a man exercises over children and the constitutional rule he exercises over his wife. "There may be exceptions to the order of nature," Aristotle suggests, but "the male is by nature fitter for command than the female."[19]

What matters to us is the fact that the pattern Aristotle established was so widely adopted and respected. Four centuries later, as the Christian church began establishing itself throughout the Greco-Roman world, the so-called "household code" remained a familiar pattern. There were religious movements — Christianity among them — that appealed especially to slaves and to women, but they bore a heavy burden of suspicion since they seemed to question, indeed to undermine, the stability and good order of the community. Judaism was among the groups that incurred such suspicion, not because it held radically different ideas about slaves or women but because Jews would not take part in the public cult of the emperor or offer sacrifice to the gods. Leading Jewish writers of the first century, men like Philo and Josephus, made a determined effort to persuade a Gentile audience that Judaism also believed in good order, obedience to the law, and households in which each member knew and accepted the role assigned them. The careful elaboration of the Mosaic law provided them with a solid foundation for this effort. Josephus, for example, wrote:

> The woman, it [the Law] says, is in all things inferior to the man. Let her accordingly be obedient, not for her humiliation, but that she may be directed; for God has given authority to the man.[20]

And Philo agreed that:

> Wives must be in servitude to their husbands, a servitude not imposed by violent ill-treatment but promoting obedience in all things.[21]

To imagine otherwise, they agreed, would be detrimental to the state as well as to the individual household.

It was only natural, then, that Christians also would attempt to show that their beliefs were not subversive. The evidence of that effort is present in several books of the New Testament itself. The epistles, as letters of advice to new Christian communities, frequently contain adapted versions of the household code, and Christians are advised to obey them specifically so that they will put to rest the negative rumors about their faith: "For it is God's will that by doing right you should silence the ignorance of the foolish."[22]

Once again, then, we find the church adopting or commending a standard of behavior not entirely because of its own deep convictions but because of the need to survive as a small minority group of dubious reputation in a world where minority rights and religious freedom were completely unknown. To present a positive image was important for survival and important also to a church with a mission: How could the gospel be heard by people who had heard nothing good of those who proclaimed it? Therefore the epistles urge that Christians respect the authorities and, if we arrange the statements in a generally agreed time sequence, it would seem that the pattern commended becomes less distinctive — more like Aristotle's — as time goes on.

In an early letter, St. Paul had written to the Galatians:

> There is no longer Jew or Greek, there is no longer slave or free, there is no longer male and female; for all of you are one in Christ Jesus.[23]

Galatians is a passionate letter, written in the white heat of anger and not carefully weighed and considered. What Paul says here about the relationship of male and female would seem to come, then, from his deepest conviction about the transformation in human life which has taken place in the church. In later letters, responding to questions about specific circumstances or pondering how best to commend the faith to those outside, Paul speaks differently. But in those letters he speaks to issues; here he witnesses to the ideal. We need to remember that when we search the scriptures for an ideal for our own lives on which to base practical conduct in our time, we are apt to find the practical first-century instructions for which the letters were written and miss the fundamental ideal which may be glimpsed only in the occasional un-guarded moment. Large parts of Paul's correspondence dealt not with eternal ideals but with immediate realities. So, perhaps a generation or more later, we find the first letter of Peter taking that same approach:

> Wives, in the same way, accept the authority of your hus-bands, so that, even if some of them do not obey the word, they may be won over without a word by their wives' con-duct, when they see the purity and reverence of your lives. . . . Husbands, in the same way, show consideration for your wives in your life together, paying honor to the woman as the weaker sex, since they too are also heirs of the gracious gift of life — so that nothing may hinder your prayers.[24]

Notice again the motive: not because the gospel commends such behavior but so that others "may be won over."

Our passage from Ephesians, then, must be understood in that con-text. The author is not setting out to provide us with a straightforward statement on the nature and meaning of Christian marriage; rather, he is working from a tradition of household codes, writing to a people who need to commend their behavior to others, and within those limits attempting to show how different Christian marriage is. He does it with enormous skill. We can still see how he selects his materials and weaves a finished picture that, for all its difficulties for us, still speaks — even to us — with beauty and power.

Why does he address the three relationships of husband and wife, parent and child, slave and master? Because, as we have seen, there is a tradition going back to Aristotle that these relationships are founda-tional. The question is not what relationships he will choose but what he will make of the guidelines he has inherited. And first of all, he sets them in a relationship of worship and praise. The modern translations fail to show accurately the development of the author's thought. Earlier in the chapter he had been speaking of the contrast — like that between darkness and light, he says — between those who belong to Christ and those outside the church. He begins to focus his thought on marriage by speaking first of worship and praise:

> Do not get drunk with wine, for that is debauchery; but be filled with the Spirit, as you sing psalms and hymns and spiritual songs among yourselves, singing and making melody to the Lord in your hearts, giving thanks to God the Father at all times and for everything in the name of our Lord Jesus Christ.[25]

We have a succession of participles, "singing . . . making melody . . . giving thanks," which continues straight on, though the new translations generally make a complete break and begin the next verse with a new paragraph and an imperative: "Be subject to one another..."[26] But there is no such break in the author's thought: "singing . . . making melody . . . giving thanks . . . submitting to one another in the fear of Christ." The picture he gives us is that of a community of believers, filled with the transforming Spirit and unconcerned any more with rank or distinction or priority. Aristotle's careful analysis of political relationships is bound to undergo a sea-change in that context. The author intends it to.

By constructing his sentence in this way, he is able to modify the traditional "wives obey your husbands" by leaving out the verb entirely and treating the relationship as simply one example of the mutual submission all Christians should give each other. "Submitting to one another," he writes, "wives to their own husbands as to the Lord." He offers it as an illustration of his theme and immediately turns the attention back to the relationship between Christ and the church:

> For the husband is the head of the wife just as Christ is the head of the church, the body of which he is the Savior. Just as the church is subject to Christ, so also wives ought to be, in everything, to their husbands.[27]

He has kept the feel of the original household code but set it in a transforming context. And the extent of the transformation is clear when he moves on to speak to husbands:

> Husbands, love your wives, just as Christ loved the church and gave himself up for her . . .[28]

You won't find that in Aristotle!

So what do we have here? The long tradition from Aristotle to Philo and Josephus gave a pattern of household codes that established a fixed hierarchy of relationships, the state in microcosm. Everyone either rules or is ruled and that's the end of it. But that is not the vision here. Though the formal structure remains the same, the spirit has been radically changed. Now the issue is no longer structure and order, but a self-sacrificing love that takes no more thought for prerogatives than did Jesus in washing his disciples' feet and dying on the cross. Nor is that all.

Moving on, and shifting the focus constantly back and forth between the husband-wife relationship and that of Christ to the church, the author picks up the covenant/marriage language that was developed in the Old Testament. Ezekiel had portrayed Israel as a bride whom God had prepared for marriage with elaborate care, washing and adorning her and lavishing rich gifts on her. So the author of Ephesians portrays Christ and the church:

> as Christ loved the church and gave himself up for her, in order to make her holy by cleansing her with the washing of water by the word, so as to present the church to himself in splendor, without a spot or wrinkle or anything of the kind — yes, so that she may be holy and without blemish.[29]

But notice that in that last phrase the author has gone beyond the language of Ezekiel who, for all the washing and adorning he spoke of, never described Israel as "holy and without blemish." So where does that language come from? It comes from the richly erotic poetry of the Song of Songs, which proclaims: "You are altogether beautiful, my love; there is no flaw in you."[30]

Once again, we are weaving together various times and visions: the practical and prophetic, the prose of everyday life and the poetry that inspires that life.

But the Song of Songs does more than add the passion of poetry to the picture being created here. J. Paul Sampley, in an important study of this passage, points out a further wealth of meaning in the phrase "there is no flaw in you." There is, in the first place, a tradition in rabbinic literature that a man can divorce his wife if he finds anything repulsive in her.[31] Clearly the bride of Christ must be flawless — and the author of the letter to the Ephesians tells us that Christ will make the church flawless and worthy of himself. But the word used in the Song of Songs connects us not only to marriage law but also again with Leviticus and the requirements for priesthood. The priest, too, must be without blemish[32] and the same Hebrew word sets that requirement.[33] Indeed, as the word "blemish" (Hebrew *mum*) connects priesthood and marriage negatively, so the same Hebrew root *(k-d-sh)* connects priesthood and marriage in terms of holiness. "You shall be holy . . ," God said to Israel in Leviticus[34], and rabbinic literature used the same root to describe the espousal of a bride, since she was considered to be "set apart" for her husband.[35] So it is precisely the priesthood of Christ and the marriage of Christ with the church that this passage in Ephesians is describing by weaving together the various strands in the tradition to create simultaneously a picture of Christian marriage and the church espoused to Christ.

"One flesh"

For half a dozen years my family and I lived in Japan, where my primary ministry was in the foreign community. I learned enough Japanese to get around but never reached a level that might be called "conversational." My understanding of the country was largely filtered through the medium of the English language. So it was a major benefit to me that for most of my time in Japan I had the privilege of serving as "advisor" to the Tokyo Intercollegiate Debate League, an organization that sponsored debates *in English* between students from the colleges of Tokyo. The level of debate was not always very high, but I used to wonder how successful American students would be in conducting debates in Japanese. The duties of the advisor were not especially demanding but I was often asked to judge debates and that gave me a chance to hear Japanese students speak about some of the major issues of the time. Again and again I was struck by their use of the phrase "we Japanese." After a while my Japanese reached a level at which I recognized the phrase in Japanese also: "watakushitachi Nihonjin wa . . ." I don't remember often hearing someone say "we Americans."

There is, it seems to me (and such generalizations, I know, are generally dangerous), a different sense of the individual in Japan from that in the United States. Japanese workers, we noticed, usually take their vacations together, the men who work in a factory or office unit going off together to a resort — without their wives and families. This pattern, as I observed it, seemed to me rather biblical. There was a sense of corporate unity, of belonging to one another. Western society on the other hand, American in particular, has a highly developed sense of individualism which may not only create obstacles to our understanding of the Bible but may also create unnecessary tensions within our society and within ourselves.

Toward the end of his instruction to husbands and wives, the author of the letter to the Ephesians cites, as Jesus did, the creation story in

Genesis as the ultimate authority for his position. Thus we are taken back again to beginnings and faced once more with those powerful words: "the two will become one flesh."[36] Coming, as these words do, in the first pages of the Bible, cited as foundational by Jesus himself, reinforced by this vitally important passage in Ephesians, these words have shaped the Christian theology of marriage from the very beginning. They have, as a result, also shaped the foundations of the Western legal system concerning marriage: "the husband and wife are one person in law."[37] Words that have held such influence need to be looked at very carefully before we move on.

It seems to me that the phrase "one flesh" means both more and less than we have generally assumed. The words come to us, first of all, out of ancient Judaism and reflect an understanding of human nature that is significantly different from our own. In that world, it was the people corporately who mattered far more than the individual. There was, in fact, no familiar word in biblical Hebrew for the individual human body.[38] There were words for the various parts of the body and a word for the flesh which we have in common, but no word equivalent in meaning to the Greek word *soma* or the English word "body."[39] The sources of the mythical "American individualism" have been a source of some debate. Some believe it is inherited from the philosophers of the Enlightenment and mediated by transcendentalism, while others trace its roots to the frontier experience and its emphasis on individual survival skills. Whatever the source, it stresses very different characteristics from those valued in the nomadic experience of the Jews, in which survival depended on the unity of the tribe and the willingness of each to subordinate their interests to the needs of the group. It may be enough to note that contemporary societies offer abundant opportunities for individuals to pursue their own goals without immediate reference to the good of society. That was not the case in the world of the Bible, and consequently we may be less able than first-century Jews — or twentieth-century Japanese — to understand St. Paul's frequent and extended references to the church as the body of Christ. When he writes that "we are members one of another,"[40] he means more than common membership in a neighborhood association. To say that we are "one flesh" evokes a deep sense of human unity beyond what we may be easily able to understand. But that sense of unity pervaded every human relationship, not simply that of marriage. When the people of Israel came to make David their king, they said to him almost exactly what Adam said to Eve: "Look, we are your bone and flesh."[41]

But what could a world that thus understood human unity have been able to add when it came to the unity of husband and wife? If Adam and Eve were "one flesh" by creation, as all human beings are one flesh, what could be added to that by marriage? Given the realities of the Hebrew language and experience, it would be difficult to express anything more than that even if there were a desire to do so. The treatment of women and marriage in Mosaic law would indicate that it was not understood to carry very great weight. Polygamy was accepted; divorce was accepted; and a woman's role was primarily to preserve the tribe by producing new members. Failing to do that, as we have seen, she could be dismissed. The unity of husband and wife was not seen as indissoluble.

We should be careful, then, to avoid reading too much into the use of the phrase "one flesh" by Jesus or Paul. No doubt they intended to stress the unity that marriage creates, but we need to study their usage carefully and in context. Their age knew something about human unity that we have almost forgotten — and we are aware of divisive forces in human society and personality that were almost unknown to them.

We are, in any event, dealing throughout this passage with metaphorical language. When we speak of the church as the "body" and "bride" of Christ and ourselves as "members" of his body, we are attempting to express an invisible reality, one that may challenge and shape our everyday experience but which cannot be touched and witnessed in the same way. Likewise, the term "one flesh" appears to be used here as an attempt to speak of a reality beyond the immediate and physical, perhaps more real and true than that immediate experience, but needing to be understood in a different way. Both Jesus and the letter to the Ephesians would seem to be giving the term a new weight of meaning. As we move on to see how the church's understanding of that meaning and of marriage has continued to evolve, we will need to think carefully about these words and how best to interpret them in our own situation.

"A great mystery"

There was a nineteenth-century revival preacher, so the story goes, who was greatly offended by the way women, in response to current fashion, had begun combing their hair into elaborate topknots. It seemed to him a dangerous kind of vanity, and he preached against it using the text, "topknot come down." When people asked him about the location of the text, he cited Matthew 24.17: "Let him which is on the house*top not come down*." It's an extreme case of reading more out of a text than was ever meant to be there.

The word "mystery" in this fifth chapter of Ephesians has suffered something of the same fate, though altogether by accident. In the fourth century, when Jerome translated the Bible into Latin, he used the word *sacramentum* to translate the Greek word *musterion* or mystery. Perhaps at the time it was a good choice. The term came from Roman army use where it had to do with a soldier's oath and had come to mean something sacred as that oath was sacred. But about this same time the term also began to be used for certain Christian ceremonies such as the eucharist and baptism. Over time, as the theology of these "sacraments" developed, the word took on a growing weight of meaning. So, when Christians looked at the fifth chapter of Ephesians, they not only read about marriage but they also found the words "this is a great sacrament." It seemed that the passage was endorsing the fully developed sacramental understanding of Christian marriage. Ephesians was not talking about sacraments with the weight of meaning attached to that word in the Middle Ages, but it became a primary "proof text" for the idea that marriage is a sacrament.

We will trace that development later, but we need to begin our study of this text by putting out of our minds all such later meanings. And we need also to notice that the word "mystery" here does not necessarily refer to marriage at all.

We began by saying that no passage is more revolutionary in its impact on our understanding of marriage. I would go further and say that no passage is more important. But the revolutionary genius of this passage is in the way it teaches about marriage by analogy with the relationship of Christ to the church. The prophetic insight was that we could better understand God's relationship with Israel by seeing what happens in human marriage. A marriage of failed and frustrated relationship can help us understand how God is offended by the faithlessness of the people God has called. Likewise the joy of a human wedding can help us think about the joy of the unity with God to which we are called. Other New Testament passages follow that same thought pattern, but here the focus is on marriage — this is part of a household code, instructions for family life — and the analogy is turned right around. If we can learn about God's relationship with us by looking at a human marriage, so too we can learn about marriage by understanding better God's relationship with us. It is in this reversal of imagery first of all that the uniqueness of Christian marriage lies. Marriage is a natural human relationship, evolved, if we choose to put it in that context, out of the mating patterns of animals. Human marriage has to do with the social structuring of a basic biological need. It is what human beings have made of it in different ages and cultures. We can understand it better (as we set out to do in chapter two) by looking back and looking around, by asking where we have come from and what others do. But Christian marriage looks forward or upward: it is drawn toward a given image, the relationship of God with God's people, that of Christ with the church. We are given not only a tradition but a vision. And this is what we are told is "a great mystery."

Now we need to understand that word in context: it is the fifth time it has been used in this epistle and it is used once more later. We have, in other words, a good deal of context out of which to understand the word "mystery" when it is used here, and the first thing to notice is that wherever we find it in Ephesians — except here — we find the words "to understand" or "make known" in the same sentence. A mystery, in other words, is not something forever hidden and unknown but something God now enables us to understand and even proclaim. For the point is that the age-old human wondering about the meaning and purpose of life, the "mystery" of God's plan in creation, has now been opened to us through the life, death, and resurrection of Jesus Christ.

Perhaps the central mystery proclaimed in this epistle is that of the relationship between Jews and Gentiles. Jews must often have wondered why it was that God had chosen them and separated them. Now, says this epistle, the plan has been revealed: "that is, the Gentiles have become fellow heirs, members of the same body, and sharers in the promise in Christ Jesus through the gospel."[42]

The unity of Jew and Gentile in the church is a major theme, and the marriage theme in the fifth chapter is simply an aspect of this larger mystery. It is that larger theme to which the author returns at the end of the chapter. The focus has swung back and forth between the husband and wife relationship and that between Christ and the church with the focus on what the latter means for the former. So verse 29 states that a husband should love his wife as he loves himself: "For no one ever hates his own body, but he nourishes and tenderly cares for it, just as Christ does for the church, because we are members of his body."[43]

Christ's care for the church is our example. So the focus shifts again to the church and from that focus we are referred to the "one flesh" passage in Genesis and through that passage to the mystery:

> For this reason a man will leave his father and mother and be joined to his wife, and the two will become one flesh. This is a great mystery, and I am applying it to Christ and the church.[44]

The author leaves us so dazzled by his switching back and forth that we are not quite sure at the end where the focus is. We might read it as saying that our membership in Christ's body is the reason husband and wife become one flesh, that Genesis can only be understood in the light of Christ's relationship with the church, that the mystery is in creation and the church is revelation. Or we can read it as simply bringing both creation and church to bear on the mystery of marriage. But the larger theme of the epistle is God's eternal purpose of bringing all creation into unity.[45] It would seem that here, having expounded the way in which Christ's love for the church serves as a model for human marriage, the author draws that imagery back into the larger theme, applying the particular mystery of human marriage to the larger theme of the church and the even greater unity of God's whole purpose. Our own immediate purpose, however, is to see how human marriage is given a model and vision. However obvious it may seem to us now, it was — and still is — a demanding and revolutionary insight. From this point the story of the evolution of the institution of Christian marriage begins.

CHAPTER FIVE

All Are One In Christ:
The First Millennium

*R*eluctant though it was to "get involved," the Church found itself
increasingly responsible for the institution of marriage. Its
approach was practical: beginning with inherited folkways, the
church was prepared to make exceptions when necessary and
gradually moved towards an institution shaped to some degree by
Christian beliefs.

We need to trace now the long process through which Christian
marriage came to be what we know today. The biblical vision is one
thing; what Christians actually did is another, for this was shaped by
their society as much as or more than by the vision. That shaping process begins in the New Testament itself and in the writings of St. Paul.

It is interesting to reread the books about marriage and family that
were written in the era after World War II. We've come a long way in a
short time. The first generation after World War II were the new families
that populated the suburbs (creating behind them the urban problems
we have inherited) and built a way of life that seems already to be
heading towards obsolescence.

The people who married in those years were members of the generation that designed communities centered on the automobile, but the
"auto-mobile" is not actually self-moving — someone has to drive it,
and most often it was the wife. She it was who drove her husband to
the station and her children to school, and to scout meetings, and to a
myriad other activities. She it was who served as chauffeur to a generation of husbands and children in the first communities not designed
for walking. At first, no doubt, it provided a great sense of freedom and
accomplishment. But children grow up and move away from the suburb
in which they were raised. What happens then?

If St. Paul had written letters to the churches of that generation, perhaps he, too, would have written the sort of letters and books that were written by and for that first generation of suburban families. He, too, might have written about family life and Christian nurture. He might have encouraged wives to get involved in church and community activities. He might have urged husbands to set aside "quality time" for their families.

But now, a generation later, the issues are radically different. Women are no longer willing to spend the best years of their lives as chauffeurs. Many have spied the land of equal career opportunity and even established some settlements. Others, raising families alone or simply to help pay the bills, work outside the home because they have no real choice. St. Paul would need to write very different letters to churches today. How would he suggest we staff a church school when so many families are away so many weekends? How might we keep a volunteer organization going when there are so few volunteers? How can the church support men and women in their marriages when so many other forces in society tend to drive marriages apart?

And suppose your whole knowledge of the Christian church depended on the literature produced by one of these last two generations or even both of them. How clearly do you suppose that literature would explain the fundamental principles of Christian marriage? Could those principles be derived from books about sexual harassment in the workplace, about how to survive divorce, about developing communication skills? These are the books we write, but what fundamental principles or assumptions lie behind them, and would those principles apply equally to both generations and to the Victorians, the Puritans, and societies in Asia and Africa as well?

The Bible, as we have seen, holds up a vision, but that vision is somewhat clouded for us by the difference between the world from which it comes and the world in which we live. Gates of pearl and streets of gold are all very well for an age that traveled mostly on foot and knew nothing of biophysics, but heaven for us might be a matter of self-sustaining biosystems and computer intelligence and nonpolluting sources of energy (if any place could be counted on for a source of energy cleaner even than solar power, heaven must be that place!). Beyond even that sort of problem, however, lies the fact that the vision, inspiring though it may be, remains simply a vision until we can reduce it to practical terms, drawing specific guidelines from it that help us live in our own surroundings.

But the Bible provides not only a vision; it also provides practical guidelines for people who were living at that time and in that world.

Sometimes those guidelines need no updating at all; at other times they, too, may seem far from relevant to us and our particular problems. Yet behind those guidelines, relevant and seemingly irrelevant alike, there are usually important and fundamental principles. We have looked at the vision and will return to it. We need also to look at the practical guidance given for the first Christians to see what they made of the vision and whether we can glimpse behind their guidelines some fundamental principles from which we might draw guidelines to suit our own need.

Our earliest source of practical advice for Christian marriage is, of course, the New Testament and, especially, the letters of St. Paul. Fortunately, St. Paul had visited Corinth, a city at the crossroads of the world, filled with conflict and controversy — a city, in that respect, rather like many of our own. St. Paul had all he could do to give the church in Corinth guidelines not only for marriage but many other problems as well. What were those guidelines, and what assumptions and principles lay behind them?

At first glance, what we find is a series of specific directions on practical matters. Paul is scandalized to hear that a man is living with his father's wife and directs that the offender be removed from their community.[1] Paul warns against prostitution;[2] he endorses monogamy;[3] he warns against long periods of sexual abstinence;[4] he repeats Jesus' condemnation of divorce[5] but suggests on his own authority that while a Christian could continue to live with an unbelieving spouse, he or she should not resist if that partner chooses to leave;[6] he suggests that the unmarried should remain so if they can and marry if they cannot;[7] he rules that a widow is free to remarry, but "only in the Lord."[8] Is there, behind these unconnected rulings and preferences, any foundational understanding of what marriage is from which other guidelines could be drawn to answer other questions?

What we may notice first as we begin to look for such basic principles is that Paul refers again and again to one underlying issue that shaped his thinking far more than it might shape ours: he thought that the end of the world was just around the corner. Even in one short passage, he puts this concern in several different ways. He speaks of "the impending crisis" and says "the appointed time has grown short;" "the present form of this world," he writes, "is passing away."[9]

Now, those who think that the mortgage rates may go down next week don't take thirty-year mortgages; those who believe the end of the world is imminent don't give thirty-year mortgages. Such thinking is likely to have a powerful influence on the way we behave and the advice we give. And this notion dominated Paul's thought at the very moment when he was giving advice about marriage in the seventh chapter of the first letter to Corinth. The biggest scriptural source of practical guidelines on marriage for Christians is set in terms of the imminent end of the world.

We need to recognize that St. Paul was writing about marriage with very different assumptions from ours. Nearly two thousand years later, we assume a need to make long-term plans — and marriage should be a long-term plan.

Are you considering marriage? Paul advises against it. "Those who marry will experience distress in this life, and I would spare you that."[10] It's as true today as it was then that those who marry "will experience distress," but many of us, being less concerned about the imminent end of the world, will decide that the distress is worth it. Even in his day, Paul knew that there would be some for whom the Last Day would not come soon enough to save them from distress, and he had advice for them also: "it is better to marry than to be aflame with passion."[11]

Paul also tells the Corinthians that marriage is a distraction:

> I want you to be free from anxieties. The unmarried man is anxious about the affairs of the Lord, how to please the Lord; but the married man is anxious about the affairs of the world, how to please his wife, and his interests are divided. And the unmarried woman and the virgin are anxious about the affairs of the Lord, so that they may be holy in body and spirit; but the married woman is anxious about the affairs of the world, how to please her husband. I say this for your own benefit, not to put any restraint upon you, but to promote good order and unhindered devotion to the Lord.[12]

See how our situation has changed! Today the unmarried man and woman are more likely to be anxious about getting married than about pleasing the Lord; typically it is marriage that turns people's minds back to the church after years away. Married people and widows fill the pews of our suburban churches, while the singles (validly) complain about the difficulty of finding a place for themselves. So can we still learn anything useful from this passage? We can if we can focus on underlying principles rather than on the immediate advice based on them. Those who look only to the immediate practical advice come away thinking Paul was opposed to marriage. But that isn't what he said. What he said is pastoral, not theological. He would spare them from distress and free them from anxieties — in view of the short time remaining. Paul was not negative about marriage as such: he simply thought it was relatively unimportant in view of the imminent end of the world. That is a value judgment we might make too if we felt ourselves to be in the same situation. But to opt against marriage does not mean that marriage is evil; it simply means God comes first in our lives and all other concerns must be seen in that context. Perhaps more marriages would be successful if more people thought that way. So that may be one basic principle of enduring value.

Paul's judgments were pragmatic and practical: human beings have certain biological needs, and, though these will vary from one individual to another, they are not to be ignored: "Each has a particular gift from God, one having one kind and another a different kind."[13] Therefore Paul advises that not everyone may be able to remain single, and "if you marry, you do not sin."[14] However grudging an endorsement of marriage that may seem to be, it is in fact an important minimum statement that the church has not always found it easy to endorse. Other philosophies, other religions, even pressure groups within the church have tried to persuade Christians that if you marry you do sin, and Christians have been strongly tempted to agree with them. Paul's bottom line has saved the church from that.

Thus we have three principles already: God comes first; biology must be taken seriously; and marriage is not sinful. These are valuable principles and just as useful to our society as that of the early church. But notice that this letter nowhere refers to the New Testament vision of Christ as the bridegroom and of Christ's union with the church as a model for Christian marriage. It seems as if Paul is simply making ad hoc moral judgments and letting his pastoral judgment take precedence over his theology. When Paul rules against divorce, for example, he simply refers to Jesus as the authority for his judgment without grounding that judgment, as Jesus did, in the "one flesh" statement in Genesis. And when he turns to the relationship between a believing husband or wife married to a pagan, no notion of "one flesh" seems to be involved. Although Paul suggests that the Christian partner should not separate from the other, indeed that the Christian partner may be the means of the non-Christian's salvation, he is quite ready to allow the nonbeliever to leave if he or she so choose. In that case, the believer should let the other go, for "it is to peace that God has called you." Like many a pastor today, high principles of marital unity may evaporate quickly when faced with the actual circumstances in which people live. I don't believe in divorce, but how much abuse should a woman be asked to tolerate? What happens to the vision of "one flesh" then? Clergy do not normally expect to recommend divorce, but what alternative is there when the spouse is in physical danger? Clearly Paul, too, believed that peace takes precedence. Perhaps one could argue that Paul sees the vision of Genesis as applying only when both partners are Christians, yet when Paul does refer to that passage, he uses it not to speak of husband and wife as becoming "one flesh" in marriage but to provide a rationale for avoiding prostitution:

> Do you not know that your bodies are members of Christ? Should I therefore take the members of Christ and make them members of a prostitute? Never! Do you not know that whoever is united to a prostitute becomes one body with her? For it is said, "The two shall be one flesh."[15]*

So here Paul extends the significance of Genesis not only beyond Christian marriage but to all sexual relationships. The non-Christian partner may be allowed to depart and somehow "one flesh" does not become an issue, and yet the momentary liaison does raise it. Is there a consistent principle at work here or not? This is a question we will have to look at more carefully later.

One further principle underlies Paul's practical instructions to the Corinthians: In discussing conjugal rights, he says:

> For the wife does not have authority over her own body, but the husband does; likewise the husband does not have authority over his own body, but the wife does.[16]

The operative principle here is clearly that the husband and wife have a fundamental equality in their relationship. We have seen already that Paul stated that principle even more directly in his letter to the Galatians. Given the realities of the societies in which it existed, the church did all too little to develop that principle and make use of it, but it did continue, as we shall see, to influence the church's teaching and practice.

Pressing against this principle of equality were those aspects of Jewish and Greek tradition that gave the husband dominance in the marriage relationship. Elsewhere in the New Testament we find these traditions reflected rather uncritically.[17] The church felt a need to show itself as respectful of the society surrounding it. The revolutionary principle of equality, which seems implicit in Jesus' conduct and teaching, and which seems to underlie St. Paul's teaching though sometimes overshadowed by competing values, would not emerge as a controlling principle for centuries to come.

---

*Notice that St. Paul makes no distinction here between "one body" and "one flesh," but treats them as if they mean the same thing.

Perhaps, then, we are now in a position to sketch a preliminary picture of the first-century church in relation to marriage: In its writings, not yet canonized as scripture, there is, on the one hand, the transforming vision of marriage we have looked at earlier, based on the "one flesh" standard of Genesis and aspiring to the model provided by Christ's love for and union with the church itself. On the other hand, there is practical advice for immediate situations, advice that seems sometimes to pay more attention to the standards of pagan society than to the vision of Christian writings.

Why this split personality? I think we need to recognize that the entire tradition inherited by the early church was of marriage as a secular reality. Judaism had explicitly rejected the sacred marriage customs of paganism; the Greek philosophers had regarded marriage as a social institution to be placed in a rational order; and Roman society had come to treat marriage as a simple matter of personal choice. Ordinary Roman men might still carry their brides over the threshold and induct them into the household cult, but this was a private matter in which the state had no interest. In none of these cultures was there a pattern of marriage as a matter of central importance to religion. Rather, it had to do with personal morality, and Christians apparently felt that they could adapt themselves to a great extent to the moral standards of their neighbors without unduly compromising their faith.

Even where the new faith differed from the old on sexual matters, the difference was sometimes only a matter of degree. Christian teachers stressed continence for both men and women, but Greek philosophy and pagan religious practice also saw a need to separate sexual intercourse and spiritual endeavor. The Vestal virgins of Rome were not dedicated for life, but they ordinarily retired from their religious duties only when they were past the childbearing years. Pagan temples often excluded those who had recently had sexual relations, especially adulterous ones. The public cult in Pergamon toward the end of the second century before the time of Christ demanded a day's abstinence after sex with one's wife and two days abstinence after sex with someone else's. But continuous, lifelong abstinence widely practiced was a new phenomenon.[18] Sexual abstinence, most contemporary medical writers maintained (though not without opposition), was beneficial not only to the soul but also to the body. Christians were far more concerned with controlling the body than promoting its health, but in a world that saw both physical and spiritual value in virginity, the Christian difference may not have surprised people as much as it would today. Athenagoras, a late second century Christian, writing a defense of the faith for a pagan audience, could say, "of course virginity brings a man nearer God," and expect his audience to agree.[19]

But all of this is not to suggest that Christianity did not make a significant difference in sexual matters or that Christians always preferred compromise to confrontation. Christians did hold up new standards in many ways, some that resulted directly from the vision they had been given and some that set them completely outside the law. The demand for fidelity, for example, sprang from the "one flesh" doctrine and the vision of marital union as being like that between Christ and the church. Roman sexual practices made no such requirement. We are told, for example, of "the normal genital whimsy of the Roman husband, for whom wife-stealing and wife-trading were common enterprises, and for whom the call at the neighborhood brothel was almost as usual as the business lunch of today.[20] But Christians equated adultery with murder and fornication with apostasy.[21]

Christians also held up a new standard in the area of divorce and re-marriage. Jesus had so shocked his hearers by pronouncing against divorce that his own disciples said, "If such is the case of a man with his wife, it is better not to marry."[22] The only controversy over divorce within Judaism was over how easy divorce should be. Roman citizens had always divorced as freely as they married, by mutual consent. Augustus, at the beginning of the Christian era, had tightened the law to require seven witnesses, but that was simply to provide some clarity in a situation that might otherwise have been dangerously uncertain. Since he had also ruled that only children of a recognized marriage could inherit, it was important to know who was married and who was not.[23] Christian influence brought about a gradual shift so that by the fourth century specific reasons for divorce were required and punishments were instituted for those who divorced without such reasons. By the sixth century the Emperor Justinian (527-65) had so tightened the restrictions that the guilty partner in a divorce was condemned to join a religious order.[24] Whether the religious orders were grateful for this new source of members we are not told.

In one other way the marital behavior of Christians set itself apart from that of their neighbors: Christians paid little attention to class distinction in a world rigidly divided by class. Those of different social class were not free to marry under Roman law, though a man of one class could take a concubine of another. Church membership drew heavily from the slave and lower-class population but also included a relatively high percentage of upper-class women. Since such women found it difficult to marry, concubinage was the socially accepted solution — and the church did not object. Because there was no specifically Christian form of marriage at that time, the difference between marriage and concubinage was not a matter of ceremony or sacrament, but the implications for our understanding of the meaning of "one flesh" and for sexual relationships in our own day merit further consideration.

While the church could accept concubinage, the empire could not accept marriage between slaves and citizens. Slaves, in fact, were not allowed to marry each other. A kind of common-law relationship between slaves could be permitted by owners, though it could also be ended at any time. Children born of such a relationship were considered illegitimate and could be kept or killed at the owner's pleasure. All slaves, male and female alike and whether involved in such a relationship or not, were nonetheless always available for their master's sexual pleasure.[25]

From the beginning, the church was willing to break the law by allowing slaves and freedmen to marry citizens. These marriages were kept secret to avoid exposing those involved to legal action or a master's fury. Pope Callistus I (217-22) was even criticized by other Christians for permitting such marriages. Permission from the bishop was apparently expected in such situations. Was it a working out of the "one flesh" doctrine that led the church to treat all its members equally in this respect, or was it Jesus' example of caring equally for rich and poor? Perhaps the two standards came together and bore witness to that fundamental human unity, restored in Christ, that St. Paul emphasized when he told the Galatians: . . . There is no longer Jew or Greek, there is no longer slave or free, there is no longer male and female; for all of you are one in Christ Jesus.[26]

Of course, what the right hand gives is sometimes taken away by the left. Slaves seeking freedom found an interesting dichotomy in the church's views. On the one hand, what had been "antiquity's most travelled route to freedom" was now closed to them. Sexual interest in a male or female slave on the part of the *pater familias* frequently led to freedom for the slave. To Christians, such extra-curricular interests were strictly forbidden and that route to freedom was closed. On the other hand, married converts to Christianity were required to give up their concubines before being baptized and if the concubines were slaves, they would often be set free.[27]

Aside from these moral issues, we need still to ask the very practical question: how did Christians marry in the first place? Many of the first converts were already married, as Peter was, but other converts would obviously have been single, widowed, or divorced. When Paul wrote to the Corinthians, he was already being asked whether such Christians should marry or not. And when he ruled that marriage was not a sin, a flood of questions must have followed: what should the service be like? where should it be held? who should be invited? These questions Paul ignores. And not only St. Paul. Once again, it is sometimes the most obvious areas about which we feel the least need to make records. Whatever

Christians did, it was not, apparently, different enough or controversial enough to leave any traces on the record.

In legal terms, there was very little problem: with the exception of class distinctions, Christians could recognize the laws of the empire. An explicit ruling to this effect was made by a church council in 306, even before the empire had recognized the church.[28] But what do we know about the church's internal customs?

The experts differ sharply on this subject. The Dutch theologian Edward Schillebeeckx, citing a document from the early second century which says that Christians "marry just like the whole world," believes that Christians continued to do whatever they had been accustomed to doing. Taking that as a reference to marriage customs and knowing that marriage was primarily a family affair both among Jews and Romans, Schillebeeckx argues that Christians who married in spite of St. Paul's advice followed the customs of their neighbors; the church had no special role to play at that point in their lives.[29]

The leading English authority on Christian marriage, Kenneth Stevenson, on the other hand, while recognizing that honesty requires us to say that we do not know how early Christians married, nevertheless believes we can make an educated guess on the basis of the evidence available.[30] Admittedly the evidence is fragmentary, but some tentative conclusions may be justified.

It would seem obvious, to begin with, that a faith that objected so strongly to divorce would also take an interest in the initial formation of the marriage. St. Paul's negative advice on entering a marriage indicates that, and so does his advice that a widow should remarry "only in the Lord." In the next generation, Ignatius of Antioch gives similar advice, writing that "... it becomes both men and women who marry, to form their union with the approval of the bishop, that their marriage may be according to the Lord, and not after their own lust."[31] Ignatius is often suspected of claiming more authority for bishops than was typical of his age, but his policy would not seem radically out of line with Paul's policy in Corinth. We know that a hundred years later, the bishop of Rome required slaves, catechumens, and clergy to have the bishop's permission to marry, so the marriage of Christians evidently had a certain significance. We know also that bishops customarily arranged the marriages of orphans within the community and that some bishops even served as "marriage brokers" for church members. Augustine, justifying his reputation for wisdom, refused to serve in that capacity on the grounds that not all marriages are successful and that the one who arranges can be the one who is blamed.[32]

Stevenson suggests that we can also make some assumptions about the early development of Christian marriage liturgy. Since we know something about the way in which marriage was celebrated in Roman and Jewish families, and since we know something about Christian marriage from the records of later centuries, it seems reasonable to conclude that the first Christians would have entered into marriage in ways consistent with the customs familiar to them on the one hand and the perspective of their new faith on the other. The few brief pictures we have indicate that this is so. Before as well as after the final expulsion of Christians from the synagogues, Christians would have followed the Jewish sequence of a betrothal, then a formal agreement, and finally the marriage. The marriage would have centered on a feast and the bride would have processed to the celebration in a special robe, wearing a veil or a crown, with her attendants. Stevenson also argues that Christians would have adapted the traditional Jewish Seven Blessings and that these would have been recited by the bridegroom or, perhaps, a local minister.[33]

Truly reliable evidence is not available until late in the second century when we find, for example, a picture of a marriage in an apocryphal Syrian document called *The Acts of Thomas*. The story is told of how the apostle came to a city where the king was celebrating the marriage of his daughter, and how he was prevailed upon to give his blessing to the happy couple. The wedding feast with its flute-players and other music, its wine, crowns, and ointment, was undoubtedly typical of marriage in the Roman world in the first centuries of the church's life. We can imagine that Christians were married in that same way with a blessing from a minister if one were available. On the other hand, this was *not* a Christian wedding and the story goes on to tell how Jesus appeared to the couple after Thomas' prayer and persuaded them to "refrain from this filthy intercourse" in their marriage.[34] Obviously this is not in the main line of development, but from such faint traces we must construct our picture.

In a somewhat similar way, we can draw large or small conclusions from a rhapsodic description of marriage offered by Tertullian toward the beginning of the third century:

> What words can describe the happiness of that marriage which the church unites, the offering strengthens, the blessing seals, the angels proclaim, and the Father declares valid?... What a bond is this: two believers who share one hope, one desire, one discipline, the same service! The two are brother and sister, fellow servants. There is no distinction of spirit or flesh, but truly they are *two in one flesh*. Where there is one flesh,

there is also one spirit. Together they pray, together they prostrate themselves, together they fast, teaching each other, exhorting each other, supporting each other. Side by side in the church of God and at the banquet of God, side by side in difficulties, in times of persecution, and in times of consolation. Neither hides anything from the other, neither shuns the other, neither is a burden to the other. They freely visit the sick and sustain the needy. They give alms without anxiety, attend the sacrifice without scruple, perform their daily duties unobstructed. They do not have to hide the sign of the cross, or be afraid of greeting their fellow Christians, or give blessings in silence. They sing psalms and hymns to one another and strive to outdo the other in chanting to their Lord. Seeing this, Christ rejoices. He gives them his peace. For where there are two, he also is present; and where he is, there is no evil.[35]

Beautiful; but what does it mean? When we speak of a marriage which "the church unites, the offering strengthens, the blessing seals, the angels proclaim, and the Father declares valid" we might well imagine a solemn ceremony in Westminster Abbey with an archbishop, state trumpets, and everyone using the same Prayer Book, but Tertullian lived in a time of persecution when such trimmings were obviously not available. Was there a specifically Christian service, or does he mean simply that when two Christians are married, the Christian community supports them in their new life? To be honest, we do not really know. Even the fact that Tertullian condemns the ancient use of garland-crowns at marriage as idolatrous can be read as evidence of his opposition to elaborate ceremonies or simply his aversion to pagan customs.[36] There is much about which we can only speculate.

Look, for another example, at the fragments of information to be gathered from the contemporary writings of Clement of Alexandria (c. 150 - c. 215). He writes that "each of us is free to betroth himself lawfully to the woman he wants," and that seems to imply that Christians followed the two-stage Greek custom of that time, which included a betrothal and separate wedding. That a blessing was given at Christian weddings is implied in the way Clement pours scorn on the brides who wore wigs; it must be the real hair of the bride, he insists, on which the priest lays his hands.[37] But the first undisputed reference to the blessing of a marriage comes from the end of the fourth century: when we learn that the church's blessing cannot be given to a *second* marriage, we can safely assume that such a blessing was now customary for a *first* marriage.[38] So indirectly does our information come.

With the fourth century, the situation changed radically; now the church could go about its business in public. Moreover the increased interest in Christianity brought about by imperial favor created a need both to explain Christian practices and to defend against the intrusion of inappropriate pagan customs. John Chrysostom (347-407) was one of the most eloquent voices of the time; interpreting Christianity to a largely pagan society, he dealt with a broad range of issues both of teaching and practice. He had much to say about how to choose a wife, about the way husbands should conduct themselves toward their wives, about what he considered women's excessive concern for adornment, and about the behavior that was common at wedding feasts. We can gather from his sermons that the feasting, like that of first-century Judaism, went on for seven days, and that the pagan tradition of crowning had become so much a part of Christian custom that it had taken on a specifically Christian meaning. Chrysostom argued that it symbolized the couple's victory over passion.[39] When he inveighs against unnecessary expenditure on the wife's adornment or the wedding celebration, he is one of those rare witnesses in whom concern for personal morality is deeply related to a concern for social justice, and whose words may be as relevant now as they were then:

> When you prepare for a wedding, don't run to your neighbors' houses borrowing extra mirrors, or spend endless hours worrying about dresses. A wedding is not a pageant or a theatrical performance. Instead, make your house as beautiful as you can, and then invite your family and your neighbors and friends. . . . Don't hire bands or orchestras; such an expense is excessive and unbecoming. Before anything else, invite Christ. Do you know how to invite him? "Whatsoever you do to the least of my brothers," He said, "you do to me." Don't think that it is annoying to invite the poor for Christ's sake.[40]

Behavior at wedding feasts was obviously a problem long before the twentieth century. Chrysostom is particularly eloquent on the subject:

> Marriage is a bond, a bond ordained by God. Why then do you celebrate weddings in a silly and immodest manner? Have you no idea what you are doing? You are marrying your wife . . . what is the meaning of these drunken parties with their lewd and disgraceful behavior . . . Camels and mules behave more decently than some people at wedding receptions! Is marriage a comedy? It is a mystery, an image of something far greater. If you have no respect for marriage, at least respect what it symbolizes . . . It is an image of the Church, and of Christ, and will you celebrate in a profane manner? "But then who will

dance?" you ask. Why does anyone need to dance? Pagan mysteries are the only ones that involve dancing. We celebrate our mysteries quietly and decently, with reverence and modesty . . . . you give marriage a bad name with your depraved celebrations.[41]

Nor was Chrysostom alone in feeling that the situation was getting out of control. The celebration of weddings was a public event involving songs and dances with a sexual reference that left little to the imagination.[42] Both within and without the church procreation was strongly emphasized, and the man and woman being married were not left in doubt as to what was expected of them. Clergy were not often present on these occasions, and they were advised to leave early if they came. A church council at Laodicea at the end of the fourth century forbade Christians to dance at weddings and ruled that clergy must not "witness the shows at weddings, but before the players enter they must rise up and depart."[43] Further details on the nature of these performances might be very interesting! Nevertheless, the Council of Laodicea did not solve the problem: five centuries later a French bishop felt it necessary to forbid his clergy to participate in nuptial ceremonies at all.[44] It seems likely that the negative attitude of the church toward sexual matters was, in part at least, simply a reaction to the graphic, crude, and public sexuality of a still largely pagan society.

Gradually, however, the church began to play a larger part in the shape and conduct of the marital events. The fact that neither Jewish nor Roman customs involved specifically religious ceremonies but were centered so largely on the family made the transition easier. Clergy were probably invited to the weddings of friends and church members and asked to add their prayers — as the apostle Thomas is supposed to have done. Then, what began as something special would have become expected, and the prayers of the clergy would have gradually evolved into specific marriage ceremonies.

We can almost see this happening when we read the words of Gregory of Nazianzus:

Let the father (of the bride) impose the crowns, as he desires. It is this we have decided, when we have occasion to assist at these weddings: that to the fathers belongs the imposition of the crowns and to us the prayers . . ."

Obviously Gregory was being invited to weddings and being asked to "do something religious." The ancient custom of placing crowns on the heads of those being married, whatever its pagan associations and implications, seemed to him best left to the father of the bride who would otherwise have conducted the entire ceremony. Yet, only a generation later, John Chrysostom could attribute a religious meaning to the custom, and priests had taken over the placing of the crowns.[45] Today the placing of the crowns remains a central ceremony in the liturgies of the Eastern churches.

In a similar way, other ancient folk customs were simply absorbed and have become part of the tradition of the Eastern churches. So today it is the custom of betrothed Armenian couples to exchange crosses, while the Maronite couple is anointed and the East Syrians mix water, ash, and wine in a chalice for the couple to drink.[46] East and West chose to absorb different customs and give them different prominence. Although the veiling of brides and the crowning with laurel had been practiced both in West and East, the Roman church gave prominence to the veiling while the Orthodox chose to emphasize the crowning.[47] The wedding ring, which had been a betrothal symbol in the Roman pagan customs, remained associated with betrothal in the East, while the Western church eventually made it central to the wedding itself.[48]

Given the general division of the marital process into the two stages of betrothal and nuptials, the Christian clergy found their natural role in the second part of that process. Betrothal was generally the more solemn and formal occasion since it involved the exchange of pledges between the families. The later marriage celebration tended to be less formal and would have provided a natural opportunity for a member of the clergy to play some small and informal part. For Christian families, however, the clergy prayer, once requested, would soon become a familiar and expected part of the ceremony — and eventually, the central feature of it. No church service was required for Christian weddings — except, by decree of the bishop of Rome, for those of the clergy and candidates for baptism — until well into the Middle Ages, but it seems evident that clergy participation in Christian marriage ceremonies had become common even during the age of persecution, and that this role grew significantly when the persecution came to an end. In subsequent centuries, the variety and extent of Christian marriage ceremonies continued to grow and develop.

But what have we here? A church that taught that marriage is an institution only for those not able to respond to the higher calling of sexual continence and that sexual relationships have been corrupted by the fall and are redeemable only by procreation found itself increasingly involved in and even responsible for the shaping of that same somewhat suspect institution. As if it had found an unwanted baby on the doorstep, the church found itself raising the child and training it and directing its life and development. By the ninth century in the East, the church had been given full control of the process: those who wished to be married had to go to church; there was no alternative. In the West, the priest's role grew more slowly, but steadily nonetheless, from the status of a guest in the wedding hall to that of one who blessed the wedding chamber, then to blessing the couple in the church porch, and at last to the altar itself in an elaborate nuptial mass. But it almost seems as if marriage was shaping the church rather than the other way around. Or perhaps what was taking place was an inevitable recognition that marriage has an inherent sacredness, an ability to reveal the love of God that not even the church could deny.

Nonetheless it was a difficult baby to manage from the very first. Would it be blasphemous to suggest that it was easier to be Jesus and hold up a vision than to be the members of the church who tried to live with the vision? A vision is wonderful, without it we perish, but with it we never escape the problem of reconciling the vision of perfection with our all-too-imperfect humanity. "Be ye perfect" requires either a drastically remodelled humanity or a system for dealing with failure. "One flesh" is an equally intractable standard; taken seriously, it allows of no exceptions, for if exceptions are made, how is the vision to be taken seriously? But if exceptions are not made, how can the church exemplify the forgiving love of God revealed in Jesus Christ? In fact, if exceptions are not made, how many members can the church expect to find? Torn, then, between the vision of marital unity and the vision of a loving God, the church has found itself again and again making concessions to human weakness.

The beginning of that process can be seen in the gospel itself. We have already noticed how St. Matthew's version of Jesus' teaching on divorce includes an exception for *porneia* or unchastity. The specific translation of that word — it is sometimes rendered, for example, as lewdness — is less important than the fact that the church so early in its life felt it necessary to make an exception to a standard that allowed no exceptions. "One flesh" either is or is not one; there can no more be a "partly one flesh" or an occasionally divisible one flesh than there can be a slightly bad egg or a woman who is "a little pregnant."

Nonetheless an exception was made, and St. Paul, in allowing the pagan spouse to depart is, if not creating an exception, at least narrowing the reference. Jesus did not limit the standard he held up to Christians, but Paul felt free to exempt non-Christians — and Christians married to non-Christians — from the standard for the sake of peace. A pattern of exceptions, as the United States Congress has discovered with the tax code, is hard to control once started. As time went on the church found ever more interesting reasons to make exceptions.

Consider, for example, the problems presented to Leo, bishop of Rome, in the middle of the fifth century. Attila the Hun was raging on the northern frontier and had taken a large number of captives in one of his forays into the crumbling empire. The spouses of some of those taken captive, assuming they would never see their partners again, re-married — and then were faced with the problem of what to do when their assumptions proved wrong and some of the captives returned home. They went to Nicetas, the bishop of Aquileia, for advice, and he, having learned nothing about such dilemmas in his theological training, turned for wisdom to Leo. Leo had an answer: goods abandoned in time of war must be returned to the rightful owner at the war's end; the wives must go back to their first husbands. Leo further ruled that those husbands who did not want their property back were free to remarry.[49] Such a ruling may have more to do with the development of the law of property than with the law of marriage, but it was one way to resolve the problem, and throws some light on Leo's understanding of the relevance of Jesus' teaching.

Leo also was asked to rule on the question of a man who had lived for some time with a concubine and now sought to marry someone else. Whatever the Council of Toledo may have meant by giving formal recognition to concubinage, Leo ruled that a relationship with a concubine could be dissolved and the man was free to marry.[50] "One flesh" apparently has its limits.

But then, what of the man whose wife was too sick to perform her marital duty? Boniface, the missionary bishop of Mainz in the Rhine-land, wrote to inquire of Pope Gregory II in 726. If it is "better to marry than to burn with passion," is it also better to marry a second time when the first marriage has not eliminated the problem? It seemed to Gregory that it was, though he did advise that the man must remain responsible for his first wife. In a missionary situation like that of Boni-face, Gregory may have remembered the suggestion Augustine had made in his *Reply to Faustus:* "A plurality of wives was no crime when it was the custom; and it is a crime now because it is no longer the custom." What is unclear is whether Augustine, and Gregory in his time, felt that the verse in Genesis could be amended to read "and the three (or more) shall become one flesh." Of course, Augustine, as usual, was thinking in terms of lust and argued that lust was only involved when a man's appetites went beyond what was customary — and what was lustful was wrong.[51]

Like the first disciples who exclaimed in wonder at the vision Jesus offered, the church continued to see a need for exceptions. The "penitential books" that provided guidance to the clergy of the Middle Ages developed longer and longer lists of those who could be permitted to divorce and remarry — though often, it must be noted, after severe penances. Those who might be granted such opportunity included:

- both spouses after adultery by one of them

- the husband maliciously abandoned by his wife

- the wife of a man condemned to slavery

- the spouse who obtained freedom while the other had to continue in slavery

- the spouse of one who was taken into captivity

- the spouse who converted to Christianity while the other remained in paganism

- the wife of a man who was impotent (not merely infertile).[52]

The Eastern church, traditionally less given to the rigidity of law than the Roman church, was no less willing to recognize exceptions. In various rulings, the Byzantine emperors allowed divorce of a partner who contracted leprosy and of partners who had attempted to murder their spouses. Second marriages, however, took on a penitential character and were not to be celebrated as first weddings were. Third marriages were not unknown but entailed canonical punishment; it is against divine law, said St. Basil, but better than wholesale fornication. But if you marry a fourth time, said the saint, you are behaving like a pig.[53]

In both the East and West, the church provided one other means of escape from the bonds of marriage: if a partner took monastic vows, or, in the East where the marriage of priests continued to be acceptable, if a man were elected a bishop, the other partner was free to remarry.[54] Apparently the church believed that one who was called to such a status could be counted dead to ordinary life, life in the flesh. The partner, like a widow, was free to go on with life in the flesh.

The developing list of exceptions to the rules is enough to raise an eyebrow or two, but it is important to remember that exceptions are only needed when standards are high and the opposition is strong. There would have been no need for exceptions if, in spite of the difficulties, the church had not held, however dimly and distantly, to a standard it would not surrender, to a vision of human marital union in "one flesh." Exceptions can always be modified and eliminated, but they are there to enable a standard to be maintained. The church held to that vision, and the very existence of exceptions is evidence that the vision did challenge society to change.

And society did change. In spite of the all-consuming need to civilize barbarians and Christianize pagans, in spite of the compromises necessary to wage that battle, the church did exert a transforming influence on marriage and family life. To begin with, the church was deeply unwilling to recognize divisions of class. Slaves could marry each other in the church, and they could even marry those who were not slaves. If law and tradition prevented the legal marriage of people of different class, then the church would tolerate concubinage. "In Christ there is neither slave nor free," said St. Paul, and the church took that seriously. The church made no significant effort to end the institution of slavery, but it would not recognize within its society those divisions the world had created; in time, that would make a difference.

Nor is there "male and female, for all are one in Christ Jesus." The church also made little direct effort to change the status of women; in fact, it taught what society taught: husbands are to be obeyed and women are to be obedient. It did more than that: it reinforced the norms of society by teaching them as scriptural commands. But the church's refusal (with whatever exceptions) to recognize divorce did give women a security they had not had under Roman law or Jewish. And the church protected the widowed and divorced by insisting that no marriage could be made without a dowry, a fund to which the bride had title and which could not be diminished during the marriage.[55] The requirement of mutual consent to marriage, previously unknown to the Germanic tribes, the insistence that the woman had rights before the law, the limitation of the father's power of life and death over his children — all these also can be cited as results of the church's influence in reshaping the society in which it existed. [56] Our world, quite rightly, expects and insists on much more than that, but the medieval church was not dealing with our world, and the bishops and theologians of that church, themselves the children of that society, were as limited as we are by the fears and prejudices of the world around them.

All this is a very sketchy picture of the developments that took place through the first thousand years of the church's life. The records from which a picture can be drawn are frustratingly incomplete and inadequate. The glimpses we are given reveal a church struggling with the enormous task of transforming a chaotic and largely pagan society and bringing to that task a set of beliefs based partly on the gospel and partly on Jewish, Greek, Roman, and even pagan beliefs and customs. Whatever the source of its standards, however, the church worked steadily at the task of imposing them on its world, and by the end of its first millennium bishops and synods were regularly issuing decrees concerning the requirements of marriage and opposing adultery and divorce. Germanic and Roman custom, however, still made divorce easy — for the husband — and marriage remained as much a matter of families as of individuals. Children were still married in the cradle, and parental consent remained an essential ingredient under most circumstances.[57] Marriage was still primarily a matter of families and folkways rather than of liturgy and theology. It is, in short, a mixed picture, though there are positive notes to be found. At the end of the millennium we have still nearly a thousand years to travel to reach our enlightened world, which, without resolving all the problems of the past, seems to have created new ones as well.

CHAPTER SIX

The Spires of Chartres: The Twelfth-Century Revolution

S eeking to bring order to a chaotic world, the church developed a legalistic doctrine of marriage and the sacraments. Still uncomfortable with the fleshly reality of marriage, the church continued to accept the political and economic realities of the world around it. Society and the church continued to shape each other.

CANON LAW

In the early years of the twelfth century, Peter Abelard, one of the most brilliant theologians in the history of the Christian church, was asked to tutor the niece of one of the canons of the Paris cathedral. The canon's name was Fulbert and his niece was Heloise. It wasn't usual in those days for a woman to get much education but Heloise was a good student and Abelard enjoyed working with her. In fact, he enjoyed working with her so much, and she with him, that the relationship between tutor and student moved beyond theology and became quite personal. To make a long story short, they had a child. Then they got married. Then the trouble began. Canon Fulbert was more than slightly displeased at the result of his efforts for his niece's improvement. Fearful of his wrath, Heloise withdrew to a convent. She was right to fear her uncle's anger; Fulbert sent agents who castrated Abelard.

So the marriage came to an unhappy ending — but the story went on. From her convent, Heloise wrote to Abelard and a correspondence developed which gives us valuable insights into the ideas and customs of the time and especially those concerning marriage. In her letters, Heloise accepted the fact that their marriage was over. All marriages end with legal action or death, but love does not. The love she had known with Abelard had not ended with their separation; indeed she had incorporated her love for Abelard into her love of God in a way that preserved it. In fact, she established a new religious order with love as an integral part of it; and she wrote to Abelard that she could not think of him without remembering the physical joy that had made them one flesh. Love is eternal, she wrote, but marriage is not.

From the beginning Heloise had felt that her love for Abelard could not be limited by the definition of marriage. She was familiar with human marriage as it was institutionalized in the twelfth century, and it had little to do with her relationship with Abelard. Heloise wrote to Abelard later that she would rather be his mistress, concubine, or whore than wife to the greatest emperor. Marriage, to Heloise, was (as the church taught it was) a matter of contract and childbearing. All too often it was corrupted by those who sought from it money or title. Therefore it seemed to Heloise that the pure and selfless love she had for Abelard could only be diminished by the formality of marriage.[1] Many of those who live together today without benefit of marriage will say something similar; having very likely grown up as children of loveless marriages they would prefer to share a marriageless love.

"Love and marriage," an old song tells us, "go together like a horse and carriage . . . ," but the century that began by developing the horse-less carriage is coming to an end by making a specialty of love without marriage — though we could hardly claim to have invented that. As for marriage without love, that has an even longer history. The point about the story of Abelard and Heloise that needs to be pondered is this—after a thousand years of Christianity, two highly intelligent and committed Christians could feel that their love had little if anything to do with marriage. We should also ponder the fact that after nearly one thousand years more of Christianity, more and more people seem to be coming to the same conclusion.

There is a tragic dichotomy between the scriptural vision of human love and marriage and the institution of marriage shaped by the church and society. If the patristic period remains the seed bed of our theology of marriage, the period from the twelfth to the sixteenth century is the formative time of the institution. The twelfth century in particular was a time that crystallized the legal forms that have shaped our world ever since. The law-making and institutionalizing energy of that time even took control of theology and gave the church's teaching an enduring structure that even now may be more congenial to lawyers and bureau-crats than to mystics.

Harold Berman describes the events of the twelfth century as a revolu-tion, "the Papal Revolution," and he shows that what took place meets the standard of a true revolution: it was rapid, it was violent, it was total, and it endured.[2] Georges Duby and Henry Adams, on the other hand, dis-cuss the twelfth century in terms of building.[3] Mont Saint-Michel, which, in Adams' view, rises out of the eleventh century as a harbinger of the twelfth-century will to order, stakes out its claim to dominate, to impose its power, at the place where earth, sky, and ocean meet. And Mont Saint-Michel is a symbol, too, of the overweening ambition of the time: One tower fell in 1300, the whole facade began to give way three hundred years after that, and in 1776 (Americans will note the significance), the facade and almost half the nave were pulled down in order to save the rest.[4]

Yet no tourist today will ever forget how what is left still dominates the landscape and draws people, whether pilgrims or tourists, in admiration. We may not share the faith it symbolizes, we certainly have no desire to share the way of life of those who built it, but it remains a structure we have to admire and ponder, whose power we have to acknowledge. So likewise the twelfth-century achievement in relation to marriage: from the Middle Ages until our own day, how many couples ever questioned the need to obtain civil permission to marry? How many men and women planning to marry have stopped to ask whether there were an alternative to a church wedding? How many theologians doubted for a minute that marriage was a sacred matter? But until the twelfth century, these ideas were far from being generally accepted. Still today it is true that for the longer part of the history of the church Christians needed no civil permission to marry, did not come to church for their weddings, and had no idea of marriage as a sacrament. All this and more is our inheritance from the revolution of the twelfth century. Some of what they built in those days has fallen or been pulled down, but much remains and continues to dominate our landscape.

What was it that gave the people of the twelfth century such creative energy? If we continue the analogy of building, the time between the age of Constantine and the twelfth century might be seen as a slow-motion film in which we can watch one building, the Roman empire, gradually crumble and fall and then watch a new one, modern Europe, begin to rise. The barbarian invasion of the Roman empire not only brought about the collapse of that once powerful structure but left Europe paralyzed in chaos. By the time Charlemagne took the first great step toward erecting a new structure, the Saracen invasion of Spain and southern France had brought a new threat, and when that danger began to recede, Christians began to wonder whether the year 1000 might not bring the end of the world. With attention centered on that mystical date, Europe remained still in a state of near-paralysis until it was safely past and its population could breathe again. And then, with a giant breath, a great burst of creative energy was released: Agriculture began to prosper, towns came alive, roads were filled with traffic, armies were gathered to surge eastward to the Holy Land, an economic system took shape, new nation-states began to form, and the cathedral spires thrusting upward on every side symbolized this reawakening and rising up.

Look from the side at the silhouette of the great Norman cathedrals that remain from that time; look at the twin towers or spires on the Western end and the spire rising above a central tower, and perhaps you will see it, as Henry Adams did, as the very profile of a Norman knight on horseback with his spear held aloft.[5] The solid mass of the Norman cathedral and the armored knight on his horse represent the age's new-found ability to control the chaos people had endured for centuries and to impose order and pattern on human lives. No part of this pattern was more important than the institution of marriage.

Bourchard, bishop of Worms in the early eleventh century, is one of those who began to assemble the materials for the cathedral builders and society shapers of the next century. A highly educated and sophisticated man, Bourchard felt a need for clear guidelines in his pastoral work. So he drew down volumes from his shelves, talked to other bishops and monks, and produced at last a set of twenty books mapping out the road from earth to heaven. A century later, a monk named Gratian would use it as a primary source in the construction of his definitive "cathedral" of church law. An interesting aspect of Bourchard's work for us is that the sections on marriage are quite separate from the sections on sexual matters. Apparently marriage was understood to be a part of the social structure, a matter of fundamental relationships between families and individuals and the state; sexual passions were something separate which might endanger that structure but were not essential to it.[6]

Looking at marriage this way, Bourchard could provide a certain flexibility. Marriage was intended to build society, and if a marriage failed to prove useful, there had to be some means of escape or the structure of society would only be weakened. If guidelines were too strict, laws would simply be ignored, so bishops needed to exercise some discretion and they needed an array of precedents from which to choose. Impotence was an obvious reason for dissolving a marriage, since marriages were intended to produce heirs. Adultery, too, indicated a fundamental flaw and could be used to void a marriage when necessary. The close quarters of the medieval castle threw people together while, at the same time, providing very little privacy for protection against witnesses. Adultery under such circumstances might be readily provoked and also easily witnessed or suspected. Attempted murder of one's spouse was also grounds for dissolution: A revealing comment on a society where marriages often were not a matter of choice, where men might grow impatient with wives who gave them no heir, and where women might not always be willing to demonstrate patience under male authority.

Marriage might be indissoluble, but there were clear reasons for deciding that a marriage did not exist.

Bourchard's *Decretum* gives us a first glimpse of a church attempting to take control of society. If Augustine's primary concern was control of the lusts and passions that overheat the human body, the concern of the post-millennial church was to control the lusts and passions that shake the body politic. Women seemed to the men who shaped that world to symbolize those disorderly passions; their orderly exchange, "moved from square to square like a pawn,"[7] held society together, but they had an exasperating tendency to slip away from control and entice men with them into disobedience as Eve had done to Adam in the Garden.

Medieval men were afraid of women. Perhaps they had reason to be afraid — as slaveholders had reason to be afraid of slaves. Men were trained to the military arts through which, in orderly array, with armed companions and following the agreed patterns of conflict, battles were won and order created, while women were socialized to the communal arts and skills of domestic life. The knight was required to come home from the understood chaos of battle and impose his rule on a domestic scene which his wife ruled in his absence and where he found himself alone, indeed naked, on foreign soil. He knew little about what went on in the women's quarters, but he knew that those who spent their time in that area talked together and understood each other and did not always accept his authority. Georges Duby paints a vivid picture of the consequences:

> Contemporary chronicles are full of princes who were supposed to have been poisoned by their wives, and of allusions to "female intrigues," "pernicious wiles," and spells of all kinds cooked up in the women's quarters. We can imagine a knight of the eleventh century lying trembling and suspicious in his bed every night, beside an Eve whose insatiable desire he may not be able to satisfy, who is certainly deceiving him, and who may be plotting to smother him under the bed covers while he sleeps.[8]

To balance this domestic insecurity, the male of the medieval species was given more indulgence outside the marriage bond. "If people wanted to play," says Duby, "they should do so outside marriage." The penitentials are understanding of the sexual escapades of squires and knights who rescue fair maidens and enjoy their reward. Energy needed to be siphoned off if marriage were to provide a stable base for the social order.[9] A good psychology of control leaves room for steam to escape.

But the driving conviction of the age was that men must control women and the church must control marriage. Until this time, the church had been content to let the civil law shape marriage while the church provided guidance on moral issues. The growing stability of the social order, however, enabled popes and bishops to dream of a day when the church might impose unity on the whole of society. Popes like Alexander III (1159-80), who had been an eminent jurist, found that scholars like Gratian in canon law and Peter Lombard in theology were beginning to provide the tools they needed to bring the dream to reality. Fundamental to their vision was the establishment of a coherent doctrine of marriage, and that was to prove an almost impossible task.

There was in the first place a discrepancy between the church's Roman heritage of marriage as the union in free consent of husband and wife and the church's scriptural vision of lifelong monogamy. The church could affirm the idea of a freely undertaken commitment in God's presence, but the Roman version of free consent included free consent to separate, and how could the vision of lifelong union be fulfilled if the partners were free to divorce and remarry at their discretion? So vision turned to rulings and rulings turned to law; the internal disposition of the marriage partners was important — but not so important as the institutional unity of marriage. Feelings could not be legislated, but monogamy could be — and was. Still the church found itself in a quandary: If free consent were the essence of a marriage, what could prevent a love-stricken pair of young people from exchanging their vows and binding themselves for life against the wishes of their elders? What to do about "clandestine marriages"? The church could legislate against clandestine marriages, but it could not and would not repudiate the notion that free consent made a valid marriage. Yet how could a stable social order be built if the possibility remained that two young people might escape their parents' control simply by committing themselves to each other, even without witnesses? That issue was not resolved for centuries.

Behind the chaos and creative energy of the age there was also a deeper conflict between two wholly different theories and systems of social order. The Germanic tribes might have destroyed the Western empire, but they had been gradually civilized by the church which survived in the ruins, and the church still carried within itself the inheritance of Rome. In a stable world in which scholars could recover the learning of the past, that heritage was being not only preserved but renewed. Monasteries were finding books on long-forgotten shelves and making copies of them. The Saracens had brought other books from the East and these, too, were read and copied. So not only Augustine and Ambrose were being recovered but even Plato and Aristotle. In making their massive compilation of canons, Gratian and his colleagues also rediscovered the classical structures of Roman law. But the Roman law of marriage emphasized free and competent consent; Germanic law — we might better speak of Germanic folklaw or custom — emphasized the consummation of the marriage. And the Germanic folklaw was the familiar inheritance of the new nations shaping themselves in Germany and France.

Not only marriage law was at stake, of course; what Gratian and his twelfth-century colleagues achieved was the imposition of a new pattern (a renewed Roman pattern) of law on Europe. Berman calls it a "revolution":

> The Western legal tradition was formed in the context of a total revolution, which was fought to establish 'the right order of things'. . . a new division of society into separate ecclesiastical and secular authorities, the institutionalization of the ecclesiastical authority as a political and legal entity, and the belief in the responsibility of the ecclesiastical authority to transform secular society.[10]

The Germanic folklaw which it superseded was something very different from the formal, logical structure of Roman law. Berman describes it as less an objective code than "an expression of the unconscious mind of the people, a product of their 'common conscience'. . . rather than primarily . . . a deliberate expression of conscious reason or will. It was, in that respect, like art, like myth, like language itself."[11]

It was, in other words, a living law which reflected community values and was derived not from the written letter of legal texts but rather, in the words of Francis Kern, ". . . out of the creative wells of the subconscious." This customary law of an earlier period of European history was often "vague, confused, and impractical, technically clumsy," but it was also "creative, sublime, and suited to human needs."[12]

The shift from this way of defining community life to the clearer, cleaner — but less human? — Roman pattern has controlled Western society to our own day. Berman believes that it has now run its course and that we are beginning to realize its limitations and look again for a pattern more responsive to human needs. This is a suggestion we will return to later. For the present, our concern is limited to the conflict between the Germanic and Roman ways of understanding marriage and the church's attempts to reconcile the two. The contest between these two ways of forming a society had been brewing for some hundreds of years before it came to a climax in the midst of the twelfth-century revolution.

From the early days of the empire, the Roman approach had defined marriage as a relationship dependent on the free, competent consent of the two parties or of their parents or others with authority to make an agreement on their behalf.[13] Such an agreement defined the status of the partners in the eyes of the law but was not considered a contract because it involved no legal obligations. Christians, for many years, had been content to accept this definition: marriage was a state of life, a calling, not a contract under what was, after all, a pagan code of law.[14] This view of marriage was stated in the ninth century with the authority for the first time of the pope himself. Nicholas I (858-67) proclaimed that a true marriage comes into being with the consent of the parties and that even sexual intercourse is not sufficient to make a marriage without such consent.

The reforming jurists of the twelfth century learned that Roman contract law included a consensual model eminently suited to their understanding of marriage. It came into being by consent alone, as marriage did, and included, as marriage also did, a well-defined structure of rights and obligations.[15] Thus marriage could now be defined as a contract that was entered into at a specifiable moment, that could not (with whatever exceptions might prove the rule) be undone at a later date, and with a set of obligations that could be dealt with in a legal procedure. What more could anyone ask?

The difficulty was that an entirely different theory of marriage, based on the German folklaw model was already widely accepted in Northern Europe. The tribes which were now rapidly developing into the modern nation-states of Europe had brought with them the belief that marriage was the result of a process that began with negotiations between two families, developed with the exchange of gifts, was inaugurated with a formal betrothal, and was consummated at last in the marriage bed.

At the very time that Nicholas was proclaiming the Roman theory of marriage as consent, Hincmar, bishop of Rheims (805-82), was defining marriage in the Germanic way. Asked to answer the question "what makes marriage," Hincmar spoke of how both the solemnization and the consummation played a part in perfecting marriage. If a marriage was properly solemnized and consummated, he ruled, it should not be dissolved, but if it could not be consummated, then it might be ended. Hincmar was the first to state clearly that a marriage, once consummated, gained a new status, for now it represented the union of Christ to his church and therefore could not be dissolved. In Hincmar's view indissolubility is intimately linked to consummation.[16] Important, too, in Hincmar's analysis was the betrothal promise in which consent to the union was initially given.

From the church's point of view, Hincmar's theology had much to recommend it. Was not physical union, after all, a clearer way to represent that total union between Christ and the church of which St. Paul had spoken? Bishops had pointed to that analogy for some time. And yet there was a problem lurking in this otherwise useful picture: Mary and Joseph, the church had taught, had never consummated their relationship, yet who could deny that their marriage was a model for every human marriage?[17] Indeed, the very lack of a physical consummation made their marriage a splendid example of that control over the power of lust which the church's teachers had been so anxious to urge on the faithful. But if Mary and Joseph had no physical relationship, how could consummation make a marriage?

Consent or consummation? The skillful theologian avoids the dilemma and finds a way to give value to both. Gratian found a way out by arguing first that there must indeed be a physical union *(copula carnalis)* before the sacrament was complete. But at the same time he found a place for the element of free consent, including consent to the physical union. Eventually canon lawyers discovered three stages in the development of the marital relationship:

(1) an exchange of promises to be married in the future which constituted a contract of betrothal, that could be broken in certain cases by either party and could always be dissolved by mutual consent;

(2) an exchange of promises to be married in the present, which constituted a contract of marriage;

(3) consent to intercourse following the marriage, which constituted consummation of the marriage.

The contract was formally completed with the words of consent in the present, but it remained vulnerable to dissolution until it had been consummated.[18] But what about Mary and Joseph: Was their marriage less than complete? Of course not! The solution to that dilemma lies in the fact that the canon lawyers spoke of consent to intercourse, not the act itself. Mary, they claimed, gave Joseph the right to intercourse in perfect confidence that he would never exercise that right. And that makes a perfect marriage.

What the lawyers had now constructed was the basis not only of a useful tool for controlling the institution of marriage, but something on which to lay the foundation of certain elements of the modern law of contract. Consent must be given freely, without coercion or duress, without fear or fraud or mistaken identity, and both parties must be competent to make the agreement between them.[19] Such a definition would be as useful to banks giving mortgages and to corporations planning mergers as to young couples trembling on the edge of adulthood.

Once it was clear that what was at stake was the legal definition of a contract, innumerable refinements could always be added. Not long after the twelfth century was over, the English theologian Duns Scotus spelled out exactly what the contract was for: the spouses made a contract for certain rights, the most important being the *jus ad corpus,* the right to the body of the spouse primarily for the purpose of procreation. It seems a rather cold-blooded description of what remains a very warm-blooded business, but sometimes, no doubt, such sacrifices must be made by theologians for the sake of clarity and control.[20]

And now the necessary exceptions could find their place in a coherent structure and additional requirements could be tailored to local circumstances. A minimum age could be set according to local customs, marriage with a heathen, a heretic, or an excommunicated person could be banned or allowed, the marriage of priests could be declared void. A world could be constructed with a proper provision for every situation and heavenly order given to earthly human lives.

A few loose ends remained to be tucked into place: the matter of clandestine marriages continued to be troublesome. The church's efforts to impose order on the unruly marital affairs of the nobility were accepted largely because the nobility, once safely past the millennium, began to be more concerned for an earthly future and the orderly transmission of their names and their estates. It was helpful to have one legitimately recognized heir or a clear succession of such heirs if necessary, and the church's solemn recognition of valid marriages was a valuable step toward that goal. Yet if the church insisted on recognizing clandestine marriages, the whole system stood in constant peril; young people besotted by love could tear down the walls of the castle. But the church had a heritage it would not lightly abandon. Even if the principle of free consent had come from Rome and not from Scripture, it had been accepted for a thousand years and seemed to resonate with certain scriptural principles. The evangelists and St. Paul had spoken of freedom and, though the full impact of that word could scarcely be imagined in those days, the church, concerned though it was for control, seemed reluctant to abandon those traces of freedom it possessed. For three more centuries the battle raged, until at last the Council of Trent required that all free consent must also be witnessed by a priest. Society did have a stake in the success or failure of the marital enterprise and must have a say in the matter from the outset.

THE SACRAMENT

Three spires piercing the horizon are the first glimpse of the cathedral at Chartres as you drive south and west from Paris. Gradually the spires rise higher and at last the whole cathedral comes into view. If you think of it, as Henry Adams suggested, as a model of the Norman knight on horseback with his spear held upright, you will see the church setting out to impose its will on society as fully as the cathedral dominates the surrounding landscape of the Loire valley.

Perhaps, however, we can also think of the three-spired cathedral as an image of the structures the church created in the twelfth century to shape its life. The two west towers control the approach to the church, and they are striking both in their similarity and in their differences. The older of these two, the southern tower, which has been called "the most perfect piece of architecture in the world,"[21] comes from the twelfth century almost unchanged. The northern tower, taller and more ornate, is almost four centuries younger. When the original north tower had to be replaced in the sixteenth century, the architect had no compunctions about making his distinctive contribution to the ancient landmark. Re-create it? No, he would deliberately overshadow it, yet do it so subtly that at first glance it might not even be noticed. In fact, you could even argue that by raising his tower above the late thirteenth-century, the later architect had only restored the original vision by enabling his tower to stand free as it was meant to do.[22]

Think of these two towers as the canon law and the sacraments. Strikingly similar in the way they set out to order lives, both were first developed into complete structures in the twelfth century. Think next of the central tower at the crossing as representing the liturgy, the formal worship of the church, its chief act of praise rising up toward heaven. We have already talked about the canons; now we need to put its balancing tower in place. Then we will need to say something about the liturgy as it reflects changing ideas of marriage. And finally, before we move on from our analysis of this creative era, we will try to look behind the stone and stained glass at the people within the church, whose lives were shaped by the building they themselves erected.

The genius of the Norman cathedral builders lies in the way they managed to transform a four-sided tower into an octagonal spire in such a way that the transition is almost invisible. The tower represents the four-cornered earth, while the number eight has always represented heaven. So the towers symbolize the movement of God's people from earth to heaven, and the church's role is to help people make that transition as smoothly as possible. Canon law and sacraments were elaborated in the twelfth century with the deliberate purpose of shaping a church and earthly kingdom from which the transition to the heavenly kingdom could easily be made.

But let us further adapt the building metaphor for our own purposes to suggest that the canon law and the sacramental theology of marriage also rise up through history in a natural development and then are suddenly and almost seamlessly transformed in this era into something very different. The secular traditions of marriage, for example, emerge almost overnight as the "sacrament" of Holy Matrimony with a complex theological form, just as the traditions and accumulated rulings of popes and bishops now emerge suddenly as a formal body of law.

The foundations for these structures, however, had been laid in a far earlier time than those of the cathedral. The transition may have been sudden and rapid, but the foundations had been constructed long before. Perhaps the cornerstone for the structure of sacramental theology had been set in place in the fourth century when Jerome and Augustine chose the word *sacramentum* to translate St. Paul's word *musterion* in Ephesians 5.32. When we discussed this earlier, we noticed that the word has to do with a soldier's oath of loyalty. Why would such a word be chosen? Because the central actions of the Christian church, baptism and eucharist in particular, also have to do with commitment, with God's faithfulness to us and our faithfulness to God. In fact, from at least the second century, baptism itself was often spoken of as a "contract."[23] So *sacramentum* expressed that formal relationship and also conveyed some sense of the life-changing importance, the holiness, of such a contract. Implicit in the term from the very beginning, then, is the notion of contract which later came to dominate the theology of marriage and, at the same time, gave it such a striking resemblance to the understanding of marriage in canon law.

Augustine, once again, was a prime mover in this early stage of development. He, more than anyone else, laid the foundation for the developed structure of sacramental theology.[24] But Augustine did not design the completed tower. His use of the word was very broad and general: "symbolical actions of former and present times, because of their pertaining to divine things, are called sacraments."[25] So, in his view, the term could be applied to the Creed and the Lord's Prayer, to salt, ashes, and the baptismal font.[26] So also there were sacraments in the Old Testament such as circumcision — and marriage. But because Augustine spoke of marriage as a sacrament he gave it both a theological category and a title with distinctive overtones. If the same language could be used of marriage that was used of baptism and eucharist, then definitions would have to be framed alike for all of them and, perhaps, for others as well. All of these rites would also, because of the origins of that word *sacramentum,* have the aura of something legal, something precisely definable — perhaps even a tool with which the church could order and control the lives of its members as the soldier's life is controlled by the army to which he has sworn his obedience.

Augustine may have laid the foundation for this development, but in the chaotic years that followed, no building was erected on it. Indeed, Augustine's work itself almost disappeared from view until Charlemagne, four centuries later, began encouraging scholars to copy books and expand libraries. If sacraments were spoken of at all in the early Middle Ages, Isidore of Seville (d. 636) summed up the general approach by speaking of them as involving a mysterious presence of the Holy Spirit.[27] Even in the twelfth century, Hugh of St. Victor (d. 1141) could speak of sacraments as including not only baptism, the eucharist, and marriage, holy water and the sign of the cross, but also sacred vessels and vestments, vices and virtues, death and judgment, and the future state of things.[28] Yet within ten years of Hugh's death, Peter Lombard set in train the completion of the structure of sacramental theology by listing seven and defining the sacrament of marriage as depending entirely on consent.[29]

It is still surprising, however, to find marriage in such exalted company. A manner of life involving sexual acts that were only considered excusable if soberly undertaken to preserve the human race now found itself called a means of grace at a time when theologians like Peter Damian were still repeating some of Jerome's harshest language about women in general and sexual relationships in particular. "The thought in the back of everyone's mind," as Edward Schillebeeckx put it, was "How could marriage, which involves 'you know what'(!), be a sacramental source of salvation?"[30] Perhaps again Augustine provides the key. He listed three "goods" of marriage: the procreation of offspring, marital fidelity, and the sacramental bond.[31] The second of these, marital fidelity, was valued because it served as a preventive against uncontrolled human lust. As Cranmer so plainly stated in the sixteenth century, marriage was instituted "as a remedy against sin and to avoid fornication": a negative kind of "good," perhaps, but important nonetheless. Hugh of St. Victor treated marriage as a medicine that the clergy are to administer to the laity.[32] If marriage could heal human sinfulness, it had at least the same claim to sacramental status as penance.

Peter Lombard still held back, however, from speaking of marriage as transmitting grace; when it came to marriage, symbolism was still primary and the symbolism of Ephesians 5 still held enormous power. As husband and wife are united through the "consent of souls and the mingling of bodies," so Christ is united with the church both by will and by nature.[33] Marriage remained, nevertheless, a rather negative sacrament, a protection against sin, not yet a source of life.

But the twelfth century was replete with talented builders; what Peter Lombard was not yet ready for would be pushed ahead by others. Abelard, for example, a few years earlier than Lombard, had listed six sacraments, including (no surprise!) marriage and omitting (significantly?) ordination. Roland Bandinellis, who became Pope Alexander III and helped give the new theology of the sacraments approval at the highest level, named seven sacraments and said that marriage was the oldest, having been instituted by God in the Garden of Eden.[34] Cranmer would reflect these earlier theologians when he wrote in the Book of Common Prayer that marriage was "instituted by God in creation." But Bernard of Clairvaux, meditating on the Song of Songs, made the strongest statement on love and marriage when he compared human love to God's love and spoke of the equalizing power of love.

> Love neither looks up to nor looks down on anybody. It regards as equal all who love each other truly, bringing together in itself the lofty and the lowly. It makes them not only equal but one. Perhaps up till now you have thought God should be an exception to this law of love, but anyone who is united to the Lord becomes one in spirit with him.[35]

If marriage had that power, how could it not be listed among the chief means of grace? So, when the century was over, and Thomas Aquinas in the early thirteenth century summed it — and all creation — up, marriage was firmly defined as one of seven sacraments and not only a sign of God's love but a cause of grace. For how, Aquinas asked, could God require sanctity in marriage and not supply the means to achieve it?[36]

But still Aquinas added marriage grudgingly and explicitly named it as the lowest and least:

> Matrimony according as it is ordered to animal life, is a function of nature. But in so far as it has something spiritual it is a sacrament. And because it has the least amount of spirituality it is placed last.[37]

And why, Aquinas asked himself rhetorically, should we need a special remedy for lust when no special remedy is provided for the other cardinal sins? His answer reveals a man still as concerned for the supremacy of mental control as were the first Christian theologians: A special remedy is needed against lust "because of its vehemence which clouds the reason."[38]

If, then, for the theologian and canon lawyer alike, the issue remains control, they would inevitably build almost identical structures. Can you tell the difference between Duns Scotus the theologian and Gratian, the expert on canon law?

> Marriage is an indissoluble bond between a man and wife arising from the mutual exchange of authority over one another's bodies for the procreation and proper nurture of children. The contract of marriage is the mutual exchange by a man and wife of their bodies for perpetual use in the procreation and proper nurture of children.[39]

> It is not intercourse that creates a marriage, but consent that does so . . . This is to be understood in the following way: intercourse without the consent to contract a marriage, and the deflowering of a virgin without the exchange of consent, do not create a marriage. But an antecedent intent to contract marriage and the exchange of consent have this effect, that in the losing of her virginity, or in her intercourse, a woman is said to marry her husband, or 'to celebrate her marriage.'[40]

The former is Scotus the theologian and the latter is Gratian the canonist; the correct answer entitles you to free admission to the seminary or law school of your choice.

So notions of consent and contract became embedded in the church's teaching on marriage, and marriage itself remained what it has been in most societies: a means of establishing order. The theologians of the early Middle Ages, like the earliest theologians, sought to define and control partly to clarify Christian teaching in response to heresy and partly to provide security in a rapidly changing world.

Dualism under a new name, the Albigensian heresy, had unleashed a new attack on marriage. Drawing converts throughout central Europe in the twelfth and early thirteenth centuries, the Albigensians denounced all fleshly pleasure as sinful. They believed that souls are eternal and exist happily in heaven until, doomed to earthly existence by procreation, they are "dragged down into the misery of the flesh."[41] That was too much for orthodox theologians to accept. The theologizing of the twelfth century and the high Middle Ages was, at least in part, the reflection of this struggle for the soul of society; a reaction to a challenge, not a product of security and peace.

Rapid social change and the resultant feeling of insecurity also brought a response. The massive pile of a Norman cathedral seems anything but insecure — until you think of it as a fortress. The appearance is of a church strongly in control and dominating society, but the reality may be rather different: strong walls may speak of an institution under siege. Walter Kasper, for example, suggests that the whole twelfth-century development reflects a process of secularization that began to separate the secular and spiritual realms.[42] Indeed, in reading the history of the twelfth century we learn about a consuming struggle for control between pope and emperor which came to a climax in 1302, in the claim of Boniface VIII that every human being must be subject to the pope in order to be saved. But what sounds like the moment of triumph has been characterized as "the desperate last shout of a defeated man."[43] Not the pope but the emperor and the rising national states of Europe would define the future, and the church would gradually find itself segregated within its cathedral walls, caring for spiritual things while the business of the secular world paid ever less attention to its mandates. No specific theology of the sacraments and marriage was needed as long as they were an integral part of life and all of life was understood to be lived in God's world. But in this newly divided world, self-understanding was a high priority. So the theologians and canonists built their fortress towers to define their aspect of a world no longer peacefully united within those imposing walls. Indeed, by the very act of building the walls, they helped create a lasting division.

CHAPTER SEVEN

Divorcing the Sacrament: The Reformation

R *eacting to the legalistic view of marriage dominant in their day, the reformers attempted to treat marriage as the early church had done: as a secular matter of no particular theological concern. Though Luther affirmed marriage, the reformers still tended generally to see it as a "remedy for lust." While the reformers rejected a legalistic understanding of marriage and sacrament, the Roman church responded by tightening that approach.*

THE REFORMATION

Looking back at the Reformation from the vantage point of the twentieth century and the ecumenical movement, the Reformation that occurred in the sixteenth century looms up as a major watershed in the history of the Christian church. In its own day, and, more accurately, it may be considered not so much an event in its own right as a reaction to the events of the twelfth century which we have just discussed.

In terms of the evolution of Christian marriage, the Reformers' views are difficult to see clearly except against the background of twelfth-century developments. Martin Luther, John Calvin, and the other leaders of the Reformation were not so much staking out new ground, or even recovering old ground by returning to scripture, as they were challenging the adequacy of the twelfth-century structures. Indeed, structures which claimed so much for themselves would almost inevitably evoke a reaction; it is only surprising that the reaction was so long delayed.

The reaction, when it came, came from people who spoke a language similar to, if not identical with, the language used by their twelfth-century predecessors. On the whole, they preferred to build with the same stones their predecessors used. Perhaps the major revolutions are always essentially civil wars, fought between siblings. It was as true of the American, French, and Russian Revolutions as it was of the Reformation. They were fought out on common ground and with similar weapons. In relation to marriage — only one segment of a long line of battle — the issues were the definition of a sacrament, the requirements of the marital contract, the meaning of Ephesians 5, and the value of human sexuality. Neither Luther nor Calvin, for example, rejected the sacraments totally, but they used the same fundamental definition of a sacrament and applied it strictly: it must include a sign given by Christ himself and it must have a specific promise of grace. Peter Lombard might have disagreed in detail, but it was the same debate he had participated in during his own century. Thus Luther could not accept marriage as a sacrament, "because there is no evidence that Christ determined any special ceremony for its making, or gave any special promise of grace to one who takes a wife."[1]

As to the marriage contract, Luther revealed his German roots by insisting on parental approval; lacking that, even if the marriage had been consummated and even if children had been produced, parents and authorities should be able to declare the union null and void.[2] In post-Reformation Augsburg, obedience to parents was required by law, and in fourteen of sixteen cases over a ten-year span, the court voided the vows that had been made without parental consent. Gratian had dealt with the same problem almost three centuries earlier, but he had emphasized the free consent of the marriage partners and over-ruled the Germanic customs. So Luther's position here was reaction, not reform. In the long debate between the German and Roman views of marriage, Luther upheld, not surprisingly, the traditional German view. On this point, at least, his position had nothing to do with either Scripture or faith or other Reformation principles.

A critical text for the church's teaching on marriage as a sacrament was, of course, the fifth chapter of Ephesians. We have seen already something of the issue surrounding the translation of the Greek *musterion* into the Latin *sacramentum*. Luther and Calvin have much to say on the subject, but the issue is more one of knowledge than of faith. In the sixteenth century the knowledge of Greek and Hebrew was being revived and people were looking at the original language, not at the translation. Calvin understood very clearly what the issue was:

> The reason why the ancients used this word in this sense is clear enough. For wherever the old translator wished to render into Latin the Greek word *musterion,* especially where it refers to divine things, he translated it "sacrament." . . . And from this it came to be applied to those signs which reverently represented sublime and spiritual things.[3]

Calvin was right. The choice of a word in translation had played a major role in helping to develop a whole system of theology. "Sacrament" had come to mean something very different from what *musterion* means in Ephesians, and the use of Ephesians as proof of that developed meaning was completely invalid. But no one knew that until the revival of learning. There was no deliberate deceit, but Luther was outraged by the discovery and proceeded to question not only the proof text but the theology as well:

> [T]hey understand [the passage] as spoken of marriage, whereas Paul himself wrote these words as applying to Christ and the church, and clearly explained them himself by saying: "I take it to mean Christ and the church" (Eph.5.32). See how well Paul and these men agree! Paul says he is proclaiming a great sacrament in Christ and the church, but they proclaim it in terms of man and a woman! Christ and the church are, therefore, a mystery, that is, a great and secret thing which can and ought to be represented in terms of marriage as a kind of outward allegory. But marriage ought not for that reason to be called a sacrament . . . You see, he would have the whole passage apply to Christ, and is at pains to admonish the reader to understand that the sacrament is in Christ and the church, not in marriage.[4]

Calvin has marvelous fun attacking such use of the allegory:

> . . . it is, they say, the sign of a sacred thing, that is, of the spiritual joining of Christ with the church. If by the word "sign" they understand a symbol set before us by God to raise up the assurance of our faith, they are wandering very far from the mark; if they simply understand "sign" as what is adduced for a comparison, I will show you how keenly they reason. Paul says, "As star differs from star in brilliance, so will be the resurrection of the dead." There you have one sacrament. Christ says, "The Kingdom of Heaven is like a grain of mustard seed." Here you have another. Again, "The Kingdom of Heaven is like leaven." Behold a third . . . There is nothing that by this reasoning will not be a sacrament. There will be as many sacraments as there are parables and similitudes in Scripture. In fact, theft will be a sacrament, inasmuch as it is written, "The Day of the Lord is like a thief" . . . I admit that whenever we see a vine, it is a good thing to recall what Christ said: "I am the vine, you are the branches" . . . Whenever we meet a shepherd with his flock, it is good that this also come to mind: "I am the good shepherd." . . . but anyone who would classify such similitudes with the sacraments ought to be sent to a mental hospital.[5]

Calvin neglects to notice that the similitude between a human marriage and Christ's relationship with the church has a longer history and deeper implications, but the heat of battle can easily distort one's perspective. Luther and Calvin — and contemporary scholarship — warn us rightly against a simplistic analysis of the mystery of marriage as a metaphor, but there is more to be said.

A recent biographer of Martin Luther finds it "astonishing [how] Luther spurned everything the Middle Ages held sacred."[6] That seems like an overstatement in view of the fact that Luther remained a Christian. But in considering three aspects of marriage the reformers did break new ground or, at least, turn in a new direction: in their assessment of human sexuality, in their acceptance of a new relationship with the secular state, and in their teaching about divorce. The first was in marked contrast with the church's reluctance for a millennium and a half to find good things to say about sexuality. The second reflected an understanding of the modern world that the Roman church has been very slow to accept. The third claimed to be based on Scripture, but it could be argued that it was based as much on the medieval understanding of marriage as a contract.

In contrast to the general consensus of church teaching until his time, Luther's "assertion that sexual drives were a divine force or even God's vital presence"[7] is, indeed, something new, although Calvin attacked the issue with greater vigor:

> There is also another absurdity in their dogmas. They affirm
> that in the sacrament the grace of the Holy Spirit is conferred;
> they teach copulation to be a sacrament; and they deny that
> the Holy Spirit is ever present in copulation.[8]

That may not be quite fair since it was Origen who denied the presence of the Holy Spirit in the sexual act but not Origen who classified it as a sacrament. And even Augustine, who did speak of marriage as a sacrament, did not speak of it as conferring grace. That was a development of the medieval theologians. Revolutionaries are not always fair and balanced in their judgments; but neither, of course, are their opponents. Luther and Calvin laid about with sword and cudgel — or at least with well-sharpened pens — and their opponents responded in kind. The sadness is that such a set-to leaves scars that are not easily healed when passions have cooled.

Luther based his understanding of human sexuality on the book of Genesis and found it good. "This is the Word of God," Luther said of Genesis, "by virtue of which . . . the passionate, natural inclination toward woman is created and maintained. It may not be prevented by vow and law. For it is God's Word and work."[9] Note that Luther speaks of an attraction *maintained* by God's word where earlier theologians were concerned that it be *contained.* Marriage, Luther said, "is a divinely noble business."[10] "Whoever is ashamed of marriage," he wrote, "is also ashamed of being human."[11] Christians four and a half centuries later would cheerfully endorse these phrases, but Luther was not, we should remember, a late-twentieth-century Christian. In his day marriage remained a matter of family more than individuals and of procreation more than sexual equality. In respect to marriage and sexuality, Luther is perhaps more nearly an echo of the Old Testament than a prophet of the modern world.

But it was, undoubtedly, the reformers' rejection of the whole legalistic approach to the sacraments which marked their sharpest break with the church in their day. The very structures that had been built to defend the church seemed to Luther and Calvin the church's greatest weakness. The church's concern for control became a weapon they used to attack its domination. In Calvin's mind, the whole business was simply an attempt by the church to gain secular power:

> Thus, you may say that they sought nothing but a den of abominations when they made a sacrament out of marriage. For when once they obtained this, they took over the hearing of matrimonial cases; as it was a spiritual matter, it was not to be handled by secular judges. Then they passed laws by which they strengthened their tyranny, laws in part openly impious toward God, in part most unfair toward men. Such are these: That marriages between minors contracted without parental consent should remain firm and valid. That marriages between kinsfolk even to the seventh degree are not lawful, and if contracted, must be dissolved. They forge the very decrees, against the laws of all nations and also against the ordinance of Moses that a man who has put away an adulterous wife is not permitted to take another; that godparents may not be coupled in matrimony; that marriages may not be celebrated from Septuagesima to the Octave of Easter, and in the three weeks before the nativity of John, and from Advent to Epiphany; and innumerable like regulations which would take too long to recount. At length we must extricate ourselves from their mire, in which our discourse has already stuck longer than I should have liked. Still, I believe that I have accomplished

something in that I have partly pulled the lion's skin from these asses.[12]

Luther and Calvin alike were prepared to turn the whole matter over again to secular authority. "Marriage is outside the church," said Luther, ". . . it is a civil matter, and therefore should belong to the government . . . we have enough work in our proper office."[13] But to draw a line between the church and marriage was not so easy to do. Luther had had the experience of giving advice that only created further problems, and undoubtedly he wanted to avoid such involvement if he could. But the pastoral responsibility, the desire for guidance, that led to the canonical development in the first place could not be easily escaped. Luther, for example, was asked about divorce, and he said he detested it so much that he would prefer bigamy to it. When Philip of Hesse was dissatisfied with his wife and sought another, Luther gave him exactly that advice: If you are determined to marry another, at least you must not divorce the first. Like Pope Gregory in an earlier day, Luther insisted on a continuing obligation to the first wife and found bigamy preferable to divorce. He set great store by the verses in Genesis that defined God's purposes in marriage, and yet he believed it possible to make exceptions in a particular case — although he was troubled by the matter and had hoped to keep it secret. Luther thus found himself making exceptions to rules exactly as the bishops of Rome had done; he "distinguished between the inflexible law and the Gospel of grace" which "sees the individual and seeks his welfare in the maze of moral obligations" and "risks unconditional love."[14]

An impartial observer might find it difficult, however, to tell the difference between Gregory's law and Luther's "obligations." The church's law had often been found to be far from inflexible, and the distinction between it and "the maze of moral obligations" would seem to lie primarily in the fact that the latter remained unwritten and therefore dependent on the individual conscience — Luther's or Philip's — rather than on an agreed and accepted standard — and the judgment of the pope.

For all Luther's insistence that marriage is a worldly business and not a sacrament, the Reformation did not result in a return to biblical or patristic times when marriage was a worldly business, nor did it result in a renunciation of responsibility. In their stress on procreation, indissolubility, and the obedience owed by the wife to the husband, the reformed rites present a picture of marriage that would have been as familiar to Augustine as to Aquinas.[15] Far from handing marriage over to the civil authority, the steps taken by the reformers seemed better calculated to give the church a more complete control. Indeed, Calvin and Knox seem to have regretted delegating power to a civil authority so weak-principled that it would let adulterers escape with their lives.* In the reformed churches of Germany, the service previously conducted in the church porch, on the boundary between the sacred and the secular, now came into the center of the church.[16] In Luther's service rings were used, and the pastor "spread forth his hands" over the couple and prayed. There was no nuptial eucharist, but that was a relatively new feature of church weddings and far from universal in any event. Luther and Calvin both made much use of Scripture, and both stressed the essential goodness of marriage. Luther concluded the biblical readings with a citation from the Book of Proverbs: "Therefore, Solomon also says: 'Whoso findeth a wife findeth a good thing . . .'"[17] And who would have known that better than Solomon? But Luther still hoped that most Christians would be satisfied with one.

So the careful construction of canon law and sacramental theology intended to bring order to people's lives had been renounced by the movement for reform, but somehow the newly reformed church still stood in nearly the same place saying almost the same things. Luther and Calvin both found it easier to reject Aquinas than Augustine. When Calvin refers to marriage as "a necessary remedy to keep us from unbridled lust"[18] or commends virginity but adds, "let every man abstain from marriage only so long as he is fit to observe celibacy,"[19] we seem to hear the Bishop of Hippo speaking in Geneva. The same concern for legitimate offspring and the transmission of property that had dominated twelfth-century theology still dominated that of Calvin:

> [H]usbands who have had illicit intercourse with unmarried women have not been subject to capital punishment; because that punishment was awarded to women, not only on account of their immodesty, but also of the disgrace which the woman brings upon her husband, and of the confusion caused by the clandestine admixture of seeds. For what else will remain safe in human society, if licence be given to bring in by stealth the offspring of a stranger? and to transfer to them property taken away from the lawful heirs? It is no wonder, then, that formerly the fidelity of marriage was so sternly asserted on this point.[20]

---

*Knox wrote: "If the Civil sword foolishly spare the life of the offender, yet may not the Church be negligent in their office, which is to excommunicate the wicked, and to repute them as dead members, and to pronounce the innocent party to be at freedom, be they never so honourable before the world." ("First Book of Discipline" in John Knox's *History of the Reformation in Scotland,* vol. 2, 318 (1949 ed.) Calvin wrote: "The Law of God commands adulterers to be stoned. Before punishment was sanctioned by a written law, the adulterous woman was, by the consent of all, committed to the flames. This seems to have been done by a divine instinct, that, under the direction and authority of nature, the sanctity of marriage might be fortified, as by a firm guard . . ." *Commentaries on Genesis,* vol. 2, 286 (commentary on Gen. 38.24-25).

Indeed, even as marriage was declared to be a secular matter, the popular wedding customs, rowdy processions and revelry and feasts, were put down as inappropriate; the pipes and drums were banned in favor of the church organ. And Martin Luther, inveighing against young people who "act so disgracefully at weddings, making fools of themselves with laughing, jeering and other nonsense,"[21] echoes John Chrysostom preaching in Constantinople a thousand years earlier. Is there, we are bound to ask, something about marriage that continues to elude the grasp of the church? Is it finally the people, more than lawyers and theologians, who make marriage what it is?

Finally, a word must be said about the teaching of the reformers on divorce. Luther detested it and Calvin wrote:

> [T]he bond of marriage is too sacred to be dissolved at the will, or rather at the licentious pleasure, of men . . . God binds them by an indissoluble tie that they are not afterwards at liberty to separate.[22]

Nevertheless both Calvin and Luther allowed grounds for divorce. Indeed, it might be argued that the teaching of Luther, Calvin, and their followers opened the floodgates for the modern ease and frequency of divorce. The scriptural basis for divorce after adultery was easily discovered in Matthew 9.9; abandonment was also easily found on the basis of St. Paul's teaching in 1 Corinthians 7.15. Luther, Calvin, and their followers all allowed divorce for adultery and desertion. And having opened the door, they widened it: Melancthon, Zwingli, and Calvin among them included divorce also for cruelty, poisoning, plots against life, violence, treason, imprisonment, and "persistent refusal of what is due." Bucer, Calvin's colleague and successor, added "if he beat her" and "if she frequents theaters and sights, he forbidding."[23] Their logic was that Jesus and Paul had intended to provide relief for the forsaken and suffering, and therefore whatever was similar in causing such pain ought to be included.[24] Contagious and incurable diseases, leprosy in particular, were not to provide grounds of divorce "relief in such a misery being one of the ends of marriage."[25]

Unanimously the reformed theologians agreed that the innocent party in any divorce should be allowed to remarry rather than suffer for the sins of another or be subjected to temptation; as in the medieval church, marriage was seen as a way to avoid fornication.[26]

Most significant, of course, is the fact that the reformers, by eliminating the sacramental nature of marriage, left themselves, essentially, with marriage as a contract. They spoke of it as a "divine ordinance" and referred to scripture as discussing "rules" and "cases." If grounds of divorce are discovered in scripture, the reformed theologians proceeded like a lawyer with a precedent. They felt free to decide what purpose lay behind the words of Jesus or Paul and then applied that purpose to other situations. The result was not a wave of divorces; marriages were held together by economic and social forces that could not be dissolved by theology. But if marriage is not a sacrament, if it does not constitute a fundamental change in the very nature of the couple, then indeed marriage becomes a matter for the secular state to deal with in whatever way is practical. When the social and economic realities of people's lives changed in the late nineteenth and twentieth centuries, the civil authorities in Protestant countries had become accustomed to looking at marriage in that light and felt free to proceed accordingly. As for remarriage, an age trained in the psychological evaluation of human conduct finds it difficult to determine an "innocent" or "guilty" party and so to deny remarriage to anyone.

THE COUNTER-REFORMATION

If every action creates, as the scientists say, an equal and opposite reaction, it is hardly surprising that the twelfth century created the Reformation and that the Reformation, in its turn, created the counter-Reformation. When the leaders of the Roman church came to the small Italian city of Trent in 1545, they had, in one sense, a single agenda item: to respond to Luther and Calvin. That they traveled north from Rome almost to the northern border of Italy and the southern border of the Swiss and German states emphasized their hope that not only German bishops but leaders of the Reformation would be present. In spite of concessions made, those hopes were not realized. Some 270 bishops attended the Council at one time or another, but only two of them were German.

That broader issues than those of faith and the nature of the church were at stake was obvious even at the time. The fact that the bishops met in national groups to articulate their positions made it clear that matters of faith could not be separated from issues of nationality. But we may be able to see the Reformation and Counter-Reformation more broadly than those involved in it. We may be able to see it in terms of economics and politics and deep-seated ethnic difference. Ever since the Germanic peoples had become Christian, they had struggled to preserve their social patterns in a church that assumed the patterns of the Mediterranean world. The Reformation can be understood as the ultimate failure of that attempt. Germanic and Mediterranean Christianity could not, at least for a while, live together in one church.

Marriage matters serve, then, simply as one aspect of a larger issue: will a Germanic manifestation of the Christian faith be allowed? It seemed obvious to Luther and his supporters that it would not be. To them, the handing over of the bride by her father or guardian was the basic criterion of the validity of a marriage. Luther saw the Roman rejection of this element (made explicit at Trent after Luther's death) as evidence of immorality,[27] although, like the matter of parental consent discussed earlier, what was at stake was simply ethnic custom.

Trent, on the other hand, was concerned both to codify Roman tradition and to remove ancient sources of difficulty. The tradition of free consent as the basis of marriage was so strong in the Mediterranean church that all through the Middle Ages, the church had accepted the problems caused by clandestine marriages rather than modify the tradition. Finally and reluctantly, the Council of Trent changed the long tradition: now a marriage must be witnessed by a priest and two or three others or it was not valid. For the first time, a legal form had been defined as essential to a sacrament.

Thus the church from the sixteenth century onward followed two separate paths. The Roman church, driven to narrower definitions by the impact of the Reformation, found itself defending a view of marriage in which law and sacrament were bound together. Not only marriage but the sacrament of marriage was defined as a contract, and the contract was defined by consent and consummation. The quality of the relationship was not an issue: neither heresy, cruelty, nor adultery was adequate grounds for divorce.[28] The Reformed and Lutheran traditions, on the other hand, began with a definition of marriage as a secular matter, to be controlled by the state not the church. In this as in other secular matters, the church's role was simply to exhort its members to moral behavior. Neither path was free of problems: if Rome could fall into legalism, the Reformed churches could lapse into moralism. If Rome could bind partners together against all reason, the Reformed churches could be rather casual about divorce on the one hand and polygamy on the other. Today both sides are beginning to recognize that the other may have a point. We need to look at the way society has changed in the intervening centuries to complete the story of how we got where we are so that we can also begin to make suggestions for the future.

CHAPTER EIGHT

Love and Marriage:
Toward the Next Millennium

*T*_{*he rapid social changes that began to transform Western Europe*} *and America after the Reformation were reflected in marriage practices also. Though the separated churches attempted to maintain control of marriage patterns through canon law, secular law, or parental authority, folk customs developed that enabled both marriage and divorce to take place apart from such authority. By the latter part of the twentieth century, the Christian ideal of lifetime monogamy was being widely ignored, but now marriage could be valued apart from economic necessity and legal constraint; for the first time, marriage could, potentially, be shaped primarily by Christian faith.*

It was a pleasant midsummer evening in 1549 and John Cotgreve, Alice Gidlowe, and a group of friends had spent a festive day together. They were walking home across the Cheshire fields when they came to an abandoned house and John suggested to Alice that they might go in and make love. Alice was too sensible a woman to do so without certain precautions, and so they asked their friends to gather around while they exchanged promises. When they had made their vows and sealed them with a kiss, John asked his friends if they would "goe a littel before towarde Saltney" while he and Alice explored, among other things, the abandoned house. He and Alice, he told them, "wold shortlie come after."[1]

The naturalness of the scene and the fact that John Cotgreve was a clergyman of the Church of England help illustrate how radically marriage customs have changed over the years. What one age takes for granted is shocking to another. We are, in addition, very prone to place religious significance on matters that seem important to us whether they are directly connected to our faith or not. To tell the difference between patterns dictated by social circumstances and those essential to faith has never been easy.

Too much has been written about sex and marriage over the last four centuries for us to do more than attempt a brief summary of that period of time. Our concern is still to observe the changing shape of the institution of marriage and to notice the ways in which "Christian marriage" was shaped by social and economic forces as well as by specifically Christian beliefs. The patterns that concern us include (a) the institution of marriage in its setting, (b) the shape of the family, and (c) Christian teaching and practice. We will center our attention on Western Europe and the United States since those areas have done most to shape the experience and expectations of those who might read this book.

MARRIAGE IN CONTEXT

Underneath the ecclesiastical tumult of the Reformation — and helping to produce it — enormous changes were taking place in some of the basic patterns of human life. The increasing specialization of life, for example, led to a pattern of lengthy apprenticeship which, in turn, seems to have produced a later age for marriage. In the early seventeenth century, the average age at marriage reached an unusually high point: twenty-eight for men and twenty-six for women. That seems to have been the highest average age for marriage in the last five hundred years[2] and it reflects the fact that marriage had become an economic as well as a physical milestone. For the man, marriage marked not only the beginning of a family but also his coming of age economically. Marriage marked the significant rite of passage from dependence to independence.

Marriage under these circumstances was, first of all, an economic partnership and important to parents who cared about an orderly transmission of their property. Though the Reformation had insisted on the goodness of marriage, it also reasserted parental control of marriage — and parents, with the wisdom of hindsight, have different priorities from those of young people. The secular states, having been urged to take control of the marriage process, showed themselves to be, if anything, more narrow-minded in this respect than the medieval church. Sensitive to the needs of those with large possessions, the civil authorities had always wanted tighter control of property and heredity than the church was willing to provide. Now they had their chance. Even France, which remained within the orbit of the Roman church, felt it necessary to impose more stringent regulations on marriage than the church was willing to establish. When the Council of Trent failed to establish a minimum age of consent, the king forbade the publication of the Tridentine decrees in France. Laws were then created that remained in force into the twentieth century and that set the minimum age of marriage without parental consent at thirty for men and twenty-five for women.

Parental control was especially important for those with considerable possessions, but those of the merchant and artisan class would also want to be sure that a young man made an appropriate choice. Love had its place, but the primary consideration was the suitability of the woman to the man's estate or as a helper in the man's trade. We hear of one Hans Amman, a weaver, whose wife Margaret had died leaving him with two very small children. Amman applied for permission to marry an elderly servant woman, "because I am of the comfortable hope that she will faithfully help me to bring up my children for me, will profit my nourishment, and help me in my craft."[3]

In this case, it was the man himself, not his parents, who made the choice, but he had been married once already and gained a parent's perspective. At its core,

> marriage was a bargain in which a man agreed to provide for a woman financially while she undertook to bring up his children, keep house and provide some assistance in the work of his craft.[4]

Those without property might have the same concern for economic partnership, but the young people had almost complete freedom in their courtship. Parents lacked the economic resources to exercise effective control, and, in any event, the young people would have left home for positions as farm hands or domestic servants before sexual maturity began to produce an interest in the opposite sex.[5]

Where economic factors did set the priorities, marriage placed the groom, not the bride, at the center. It was he, more than she, who was acquiring a new status. Her role continued to be one of dependency, while his became one of position and authority. Marriage, then, was the groom's day more than the bride's, and it was he who was on center stage during the celebration.[6]

Of course, when economic factors become controlling and marriage is long delayed, sexual needs may have to be met in other ways. The medieval church had urged an early age for marriage as a means of controlling the sexual drives; as the age of marriage rose, a betrothal period with sexual rights was a solution offered in the Northern European countries affected by the Reformation. The informal promises declared by John and Alice were the accepted way of becoming betrothed, and betrothal in that time and place carried with it a full sexual relationship. Until a separate home was established, a "full sexual relationship" would naturally have only a limited opportunity to develop. An abandoned house might not be available, but "bundling," spending the night together in the sitting room or bedroom of one parental home or the other, was common in England, Scandinavia, New England, and elsewhere in the seventeenth and eighteenth centuries.[7] France, on the other hand, offered publicly supported brothels until the church took action against them after the Council of Trent. But the increased difficulty of becoming established in a trade resulted in a later age of marriage, and that, combined with a growing movement of population to the cities and the elimination of brothels, led to a breakdown of the traditional social patterns and a rising rate of illegitimacy and pre-marital pregnancy.[8] The opportunity for marriage may not be easily available because of economic and social conditions, but where it is not, alterative solutions, good or bad, will be sought and found.

MAKING COMMITMENTS

Betrothal has been a critical stage in the marriage process in many cultures. As a formal ceremony, however, it had almost disappeared from Northern Europe by the end of the Middle Ages. As the church's role in marriage became increasingly important, the church centered its attention not on the betrothal ceremonies with their future commitment but on the marriage celebration with its focus on the present. The vital importance of present consent led the church to shift the focus from the betrothal exchanges to the marriage promise. As the marriage promises gained primary importance, the betrothal exchanges were largely absorbed into the marriage itself and betrothal, if it remained, became in many areas an informal arrangement between those planning to marry. Even today, many church services still include a relic of the betrothal promise in the preliminary commitment, "I will," (a future promise, not a present "I do") in addition to the exchange of marriage vows.

A transitional time between single life and marriage seems to be a psychological necessity even if it is not a social or religious one. In the England of John Cotgreve and Alice Gidlowe or in post-Reformation Germany, betrothal had become a customary opportunity for young people to move into a deeper relationship before marriage itself. An exchange of promises would be made in words similar to those of the familiar church service and often in the presence of witnesses. The ceremony might take place in an open field, in a tavern, or in a home, but it was considered to be a binding commitment, often for a specified period of time. Though it was not indissoluble, the breaking of the betrothal was a very serious step, since it was intended to provide protection to those involved. If pregnancy resulted, the man was obligated to support or marry the woman, yet there was no commitment of property, and, if the couple found they were incompatible, they could break the relationship — again before witnesses — before entering an indissoluble marriage.[9]

The felt need for more flexible social patterns resulted in similar "home-made" remedies in relation to marriage itself. In some parts of England and the United States, marriages could be made as freely and informally as a betrothal. What percentage of the population felt themselves to be married by "jumping over the broom" is hard to determine, but "besom" marriages did take place in parts of Wales, Yorkshire, Shropshire, and other rural districts of England.[10] In the American South slaves adopted this custom since they were unable to enter into legal marriages. More frequently, men and women formed "common law" marriages simply by arranging to live together and becoming known as husband and wife to their neighbors. In England, where neither civil nor religious reformation of the medieval marriage law had occurred, the validity of simple consent was still recognized and at least at the lower end of the social scale informal marriages, with or without witnesses and parental approval, continued as a very real option.[11] Though the courts often rejected such arrangements, the claim to be "married in the eyes of God" was widely accepted by the public.[12]

Many couples were apparently anxious to avoid the expense of a wedding, the opposition of parents, the criticism of friends, or simply the publicity of a public reading of the banns and the ribald customs associated with formal marriage. A widely used alternative for them was provided by clergy (and pseudo-clergy) who were willing to conduct a marriage service with few questions asked. Such weddings might be contrary to law, irregular, and without effect on the transmission of property, but they remained valid in the eyes of the church and attractive to large numbers of people. Though a number of clergy were jailed for failure to conform to legal requirements, they were often able to turn a profit on the situation by arranging to be transferred to the Fleet prison in London, where they could continue to ply their trade quite profitably in the prison chapel. At its height, in the early 1740s, some 15 percent of all the marriages in England were being conducted "within the Rules of the Fleet."[13] This trade was finally stopped only by the marriage reform act of 1753 and a provision that clergy continuing to perform such marriages would be exiled to America for fourteen years. When a few unhappy clergy were actually sentenced to this dreadful fate, the practice came to a halt.[14]

Finally, two centuries after the Council of Trent, the Parliament reluctantly accepted what the Church of Rome had accepted with equal reluctance two centuries earlier. The Hardwicke Act of 1753 attempted to reform British marriage law by requiring that the wedding be held in a church before witnesses.[15] The need for alternative services remained, however, and it was quickly discovered that they were still available in Scotland. Gretna Green, just over the border on the main road north, became the rendezvous of choice for young couples eloping, opportunists, bigamists, and more established and respectable people as well. Lord Brougham claimed in 1835, though with doubtful accuracy, that "it is well known that at one time the Archbishop of Canterbury, the Lord Chancellor and the Lord Privy Seal were all married at Gretna Green, and had issue after marriages contracted there."[16] In short, the situation of marriage in England between the Reformation and the nineteenth century was, as Lawrence Stone sums it up very simply, "a mess":

> The root cause was that there was no consensus within the society at large about how a legally binding marriage should be carried out. Popular custom took one position, the church another, and the state and the propertied laity a third. Village opinion seems to have been satisfied by the outward signs and gestures of marriage, without enquiring too closely into the hard evidence of a legal ceremony. The church was satisfied by a mere verbal contract, if properly witnessed, but the common law denied that these had any effect on the transmission of property. . . .[17]

ENDING COMMITMENT

As for divorce, though it was prohibited in English law until 1857, there were, in addition to a few narrowly limited legal routes to that end, several informal procedures as well. Legally, the only options available were a separation decree from the church courts without the right to remarry or a full divorce with the right to remarry by special act of Parliament. These were expensive and time-consuming processes available only to those of means. Lawyers could also draw up separation agreements but these did not technically end the marriage. For those without access to those procedures, desertion was often the best route available, though it might lead to a new life in a distant part of the country or another country entirely.

As a final resort, folk liturgy came to the rescue in divorce as in marriage. If no institutional provision for these transitions was available in a particular area, people would design their own. Since a public exchange of vows and rings in a home or tavern was thought to make a marriage, an equally public return of the ring in the same setting was thought to undo it.[18] In the same way, those who had jumped over the broom to begin a marriage would jump back over a broom to end it.[19] Those with a preference for something even more dramatically satisfying might find that "wife-sale" was the answer. By prior arrangement with a third party (with whom the wife might already be living), a man would lead his wife to town on market day with a rope halter around her neck and conduct a public auction. Apparently all three parties would normally have worked out the arrangements in advance and would often retire afterwards to a tavern for a celebratory drink.[20] The church taught that marriage was a contract, and everyone knew how to make and break contracts for the ownership of property; what could be simpler or more satisfactory? The state felt bound to disagree and prosecuted some of those involved, but the practice continued in areas both of England and North America. The last recorded "sale" took place in the twentieth century.[21]

Methods like wife-sale, without legal standing but acceptable to certain communities, were for those without influence and property. The wealthy man might obtain a special act of Parliament or simply confine an unwanted wife in a tower, a distant estate, or even a madhouse. The law, which understood marriage as a contract and the man as the owner of property, provided very little relief. In a Chancery ruling of 1718, the court declared that a husband had a right to his wife's custody and could therefore — a subtle distinction — confine her but not imprison her. When Mr. Head, in 1744, attempted to seize his admittedly unstable wife and place her in a madhouse, Lord Hardwicke ruled that this was "not such an act of cruelty as to be ground for an absolute and perpetual separation" and said she must return home.[22]

Settlers in the North American English colonies brought with them the heritage of English law, but since many of them had come to the New World to escape that very thing, they felt free to improvise in many respects and establish new patterns of government. The New England colonists, drawing their principles in large part from Calvin's Geneva, allowed divorce and their laws were not overruled by the English Privy Council. The records indicate that women took advantage of these laws more often than men.[23] But opportunity to divorce did not mean that the family was less important. The well-known French visitor Alexis De Tocqueville said, "There is certainly no country in the world where the tie of marriage is so much respected as in America, or where conjugal happiness is more highly or worthily appreciated."[24]

On the other hand, a later French visitor, Auguste Carlier in 1860, noted that the value placed on conjugal happiness did not always result in freedom:

> Hence, we need not wonder at seeing in the primitive laws of the New England colonies, where the religious sentiment was so intimately associated with the idea of family, the most severe penalties pronounced against violations of conjugal life.[25]

Ideas of what makes for freedom and happiness do change. Carlier tells us in one sentence that marriages in colonial America were "contracted under the eyes and with the approbation of the head of the family, and consecrated by the pastor in accordance with the imperative prescriptions of the law, but always in obedience to a recognition of religious duty." And in the next sentence he is able to say without any awareness of incongruity, "Nothing but their own happiness influenced the choice of the espoused."[26]

But the diversity of state governments in the United States did allow for a variety of laws and perhaps also for various kinds of happiness. Pennsylvania passed a divorce law immediately after the Revolution[27] and the newer Western states enacted laws that, in the opinion of one commentator, rendered marriage little more than "temporary concubinage."[28] Carlier listed the causes for which divorce might be granted in the United States and found that they ranged from adultery and bigamy to the slighting of conjugal duties. He felt the list lacked only Cicero's excuse of needing a new dowry to pay his debts.[29] Governments were, at any rate, beginning to take more seriously the Reformation ideas about dissolving marriage. After a long struggle and with severe restrictions still in place, England passed a divorce act in 1857, and France took the same action in 1894.

THE FAMILY

At the beginning of the modern period, the marriage relationship was still dominated by economic considerations. The very terms "husband" and "wife" signified first of all a certain position or set of responsibilities but not necessarily married persons. A "husband" (house-bond) was the head of a household, who might be married or not. A "husband" could also be a farmer, in which case it was not redundant to say "husbandman." The word "wife" originally meant simply "woman," but came to mean one engaged in some practice or the sale of some commodity, as a "fishwife," "ale-wife," "midwife," or "housewife," who might well be a single woman or widow. In widowhood, a woman might "husband" a farm (even today a woman can "husband" her resources) and a widower might "wyfe" a house.[30] The married man and woman, then, were "husband" and "wife"[31] not simply because of their marriage, but because of a position they had acquired — though the two were so closely linked as to have become almost synonymous.

Normally a couple would not be able to marry unless they had acquired the appropriate position and were able to sustain themselves in it. In post-Reformation Augsburg, the city council would examine a couple planning to be married, and, if they were not from Augsburg and lacked sufficient means, they would be made to leave the city.[32]

"Family" in that period and under those conditions did not mean what it has come to mean in the last two centuries. It is said that before the eighteenth century, no European language had a word for the parent-child grouping which we know as "the nuclear family." (The very fact that we use such a phrase implies that we have some memory still of another sort of family.) The Indo-European root of the word "family" meant "house," and from the Latin *familia* down to recent times it retained that significance, meaning "those who live in one house." Those who live in one house, however, often described a rather diverse group of people, including servants and slaves, the majority of whom might not be related at all. The conjugal unit which we know as "family" did not need a name, since it had no separate existence.[33]

It is also true that the conjugal unit was far less stable than it is now. Divorce may affect modern families, but death was a greater factor in earlier times. In mid-seventeenth-century Bordeaux, less than a quarter of the brides entering a first marriage had both parents living. More than half the young men (ages fourteen to twenty) entering apprenticeships had lost their fathers, and more than a third had lost both parents.[34] The conjugal family unit was thus in a constant state of flux even within itself: a parent would die and be replaced by a step-parent, children would be orphaned and adopted by uncles and aunts. A mortality rate of one-third to one-half among children under the age of five — with a high birth rate to compensate — meant that they, too, gave the family a constantly changing aspect.[35] Only when the falling rate of mortality finally gave the conjugal unit sufficient longevity and changing economic circumstances enabled that unit to be more self-sufficient did the word "family" come to mean first of all only a married couple and their children.

As the mortality rate fell and the separation between home and work increased, a distinction began to appear between marriage as a public institution and marriage as a private relationship. That separation came earliest for the middle class, those working in the new sectors of the economy, without a skill to hand on like the peasants and craftsmen or inherited wealth and property like the aristocracy.[36] The turmoil — and resultant increase in freedom — of nineteenth-century society was expressed in a wide variety of experimental patterns ranging from the celibacy of Shaker communities to the free love advocated, and practiced for a while, by followers of Robert Dale Owen. Throughout the century there were complaints about the laws of marriage which so often deprived women of independent status before the law and placed their property, children, and person under their husband's control. When Owenite experiments revealed that the lack of marital status often made women more helpless, not less, some resorted to writing their own marriage contracts. Lucy Stone and Henry Blackwell, for example, wrote a contract for themselves in 1855 and added:

[W]e deem it a duty to declare that this act on our part implies no sanction of, nor promise of voluntary obedience to such of the present laws of marriage as refuse to recognize the wife as an independent rational being, while they confer upon the husband an injurious and unnatural superiority.[37]

The Reformation had questioned marriage as a sacrament but not as a contract; now people were beginning to challenge the terms of the marriage contract. They were not yet ready to question the idea of contract itself.

LOVE AND AFFECTION

What did love and affection mean to people three or four hundred years ago? Did they weep real tears when a family member died? Did their eyes light up when their best beloved came back from a journey? In short, did the early modern family know the sort of emotional involvement between wife and husband, parent and child, that we know — or think we ought to know? To paraphrase Shakespeare, "Hath not an early-modern man or woman hands, organs, dimensions, senses, affections, passions? If you prick them, do they not bleed? If you tickle them do they not laugh? And if they fall in love, does it not involve them as fully as it does us?"[38]

The answer to this question, however obvious it may seem, is not obvious. Scholars, as they often do, have found evidence on both sides. When parents choose the marriage partner, when economic considerations are dominant and the marriage is seen as a partnership for survival, when many women die in childbirth and a high percentage of children die in infancy, when life is relatively short and the average marriage may last only ten or fifteen years — under such circumstances we might well wonder whether men and women could commit themselves to each other and to their children with deep affection? We have seen the same question asked about the Middle Ages, and the same debate goes on, although there I have already given the edge to those who argue for love. When we come to the seventeenth and eighteenth centuries, Lawrence Stone has made a strong case against the presence of strong affectional ties:

As for life itself, it was cheap, and death came easily and often. The expectation of life was so low that it was highly imprudent to become too emotionally dependent upon any other human being. Outside court circles, where it flourished, romantic love was in any case regarded by moralists and theologians as a kind of mental illness, fortunately of short duration; the latter advised that even affection should be prudently limited by the prospect of the early death of its subject. Of course by no means everyone heeded this advice, but for this and other reasons affective relations seem generally to have been cool, and those that existed were widely diffused rather than concentrated on members of the nuclear family. As a result, relations within the nuclear family, between husband and wife and parents and children, were not much closer than those with neighbors, with relatives, or with 'friends' — that group of influential advisors who usually included most of the senior members of the kin. Marriage was not an intimate association based on personal choice.[39]

The element of personal choice would, as I have said, have been greater for the poor, but the burden of effort required for mere survival might have served to dampen affections at this level of society also. Stone cites a report on the peasantry in eighteenth-century northern France that says:

> [P]assion plays little role in alliances. People want wives simply to have children, to have a housekeeper who can make good stew and bring something to eat out to the fields, and who can spin for the shirts and mend the clothes.[40]

Citing death rates among children in the late eighteenth century, Stone remarks that "to preserve their mental stability, parents were obliged to limit the degree of their psychological involvement with their infant children."[41] He goes on to create a long list of disincentives to strong emotional ties, ranging from the lack of personal cleanliness and of opportunity for intimacy to the dangers of childbirth and the cost of raising a large number of children. Stone sums up the early-modern period in this way:

> The family . . . was an open-ended, low-keyed, unemotional, authoritarian institution which served certain essential political, economic, sexual, procreative and nurturant purposes. It was also very short-lived, being frequently dissolved by the death of husband or wife, or the death or early departure from the home of the children. So far as the individual was concerned, it was neither very durable, nor emotionally or sexually very demanding. The closest analogy to a sixteenth-century home is a bird's nest.[42]

But how much do we really know about the love life of birds?

A study of the family and sexual life in French history finds considerable support for Stone's position. It suggests that the negativity of the post-Tridentine church toward sexual expression even within marriage

reinforced a widespread feeling among the laity that sex was a force potentially destructive of the marriage system itself with its concern for
proper family ties and inheritance:

> Primarily it led young people to form unsuitable attachments
> and led them into alliances without parental consent; but by
> the same token, within marriage itself, it could result in the
> generation of more children than the parents could afford, and
> could thus endanger the social position of the entire kindred.

The authors of this study note how Lawrence Stone found a change
toward greater acceptance of the role of sexual pleasure in marriage and
emotional ties between husband and wife in seventeenth-century England.
They observe the emphasis on romantic attachment and "love" in both
England and America in the early twentieth century, but these, they say,
are absent as statements either of reality or an ideal in French society.[43]

So there is evidence to support the claim that emotional life in the
early-modern period was less intense and central than in more recent
times. Certainly we find it hard to imagine the existence of a satisfying
emotional relationship under those circumstances. On the other hand,
it is always hard to read the inner life of others. Why would the shortness
of life reduce the emotional content? Love affairs are often described as
"brief and tempestuous" but does that make them less real? The shortness of life might well have added a zest to the brief flowering of love
which we will never experience. American social historians Peter and
Carol Stearns point out that we cannot "assume without proof . . . that
people in the past shared our emotional experience," but neither can
we assume that their emotions were "as different as vocabulary and
child-rearing and courtship behaviors suggest to the modern researcher
. . . Or affection may have been more dispersed . . . but no less real."
The Stearns have proposed a new discipline that they would call,
"emotionology," to study the matter further.[44]

The difficulty of assessing emotional ties accurately is illustrated by
the advice given in a women's magazine in 1774:

> The intent of matrimony is not for man and wife to be always
> taken up with each other, but jointly to discharge the duties
> of civil society, to govern their families with prudence, and
> educate their children with discretion.[45]

But why was this advice necessary unless the writer felt that a good
many husbands and wives were, in fact, "always taken up with each
other" and needed to be calmed down?

Even when the evidence is carved in stone it can be misleading. Wander through any old cemetery and study the emotional outpourings of a century ago: "Dear husband, thou hast left me in this world to mourn . . .Great is the loss that we sustain . . . think of me and pity take on my dear child for my sake."[46] Then look at the recent stones: "John Smith, 1924 - 1985 . . . Mary Jones, 1910 - 1978 . . . William Green, 1914 - 1989." Students of the subject a few centuries on could well see us, on this evidence, as the least emotional, least loving people ever to walk the earth.

What we can say without much fear of contradiction is that the premodern marriage at most levels of society did have a variety of common concerns — work, food, the extended family, the community — that are seldom shared in a modern marriage. Did these preclude the possibility of deep affection, or reinforce it? At this distance, it is hard to tell. Church and society, however, were working together in ways that would, over time, lead to the development — and some would say, the ultimate disappearance — of the modern family: a union of husband, wife, and children bound together primarily by a deep personal affection.

CHURCH TEACHING

The Reformation on the whole rejected the strain of Christian doctrine that held sex to be a danger if not an evil. The further rejection of celibate monasticism led almost necessarily to an affirmation of marriage and family. Luther's exuberant affirmation of sexual relations (he is quoted as saying in relation to what the medieval church called "paying the marital debt," "If the wife will not, call the maid.")[47] had an impact and was reflected in a new affirmation of the goodness of family life. Not everyone was as positive as Luther, of course. Calvin could still cite St. Ambrose approvingly for saying that "the man who has no regard for shame or honorableness in his marriage [is] an adulterer toward his wife."[48] Cranmer still listed the procreation of children and a remedy against fornication as the first two purposes of marriage while he warned against acting "like brute beasts that have no understanding." But Cranmer did add "mutuall society, help, and Comfort" to the list of purposes for which marriage was ordained. So the relationship between husband and wife had a value of its own. The Presbyterian Richard Baxter went further and placed the spousal relationship first.

Beyond that, the fact that people were now urged to make the marital decision a matter of prayer inevitably undermined the authority of those who would make a decision for others.[49] If young people were to make their choice a matter of prayer and enter a relationship intended for mutual help and comfort, then their views had to be heard and respected. It was not the intention of the reformers to undercut parental authority, indeed, the Reformers' emphasis on family was intended to re-enforce parental authority, even to enshrine the father in each family as the priest — but these other aspects of their teaching inevitably cut in that direction. Insofar as the final appeal was to the individual conscience and to Scripture and prayer as the primary source of guidance, the individual was directed toward freedom from all external human authority. Parental authority cannot compete effectively with the will of God.

A further change of the greatest significance was the fact that clergy now were often married themselves and were preaching and teaching from their own experience. If that experience was positive, their teaching would and did reflect it. Jeremy Taylor in a mid-eighteenth-century sermon said:

> The first blessing God gave to man was society: and that society was a marriage, and that marriage was confederate by God himself, and hallowed with a blessing . . . it is a thing pure as light, sacred as a temple, lasting as the world.

Taylor also points out that Adam spoke of Eve as

> "The woman thou gavest to be *with* me." He says not "The woman thou gavest *to* me," no such thing; she is none of his goods, none of his possessions, not to be reckoned among his servants; God did not give her to him so; but "the woman thou gavest to be with me," that is, to be my partner, the companion of my joys and sorrows, thou gavest her for use, not for dominion.[50]

John Milton, though his own marriage was unhappy and he wrote to urge the restoration of divorce, nevertheless could ask, "What thing more instituted to the solace and delight of man than marriage?" And Milton also pointed out that God had created marriage first for "the cheerful conversation of man with woman" and only afterwards mentioned procreation.[51] Praised in this way, marriage cannot for long be considered simply a convenient but unemotional economic partnership dedicated first to the begetting of children. A monument inscribed to Catherine, the wife of the Honourable George Mordant, who died in 1714, made clear that something more was involved:

> With unavailing tears he mourns her end,
> Losing his double comfort, wife and friend.[52]

Toward the end of the eighteenth century, a French visitor noted with surprise how Englishmen went everywhere with their wives and how husbands and wives seemed to enjoy each other's company. It was as unusual, he observed, for an Englishman to be out without his wife as for a Frenchman to be seen in company of his.[53]

Whether the role of emotional attachment in marriage is assessed as a rising tide (albeit with some seasonal ebb and flow) or a constantly present factor (albeit more prominent in some eras than others), most commentators agree that the distinctive nuclear family bound by strong emotional ties gradually emerged over the last three centuries. If the teaching of the Reformation endorsed the phenomenon, economic developments created the conditions in which it could thrive.

SOCIAL FORCES

Whatever the church might be teaching, changing social conditions also made their impact on the affectional aspect of marriage. The first impact of the industrial age certainly had its negative side. Men, women, and children who worked long hours in the mills and factories cannot have found it an experience that warmed and deepened their emotional lives. Yet the factories that drew them away from the larger social communities of an earlier rural day also made each conjugal unit more closely dependent on its other members. It was a demand many could not meet, of course, and the pubs and taverns provided an escape for the men — and, indirectly, for wives as well. Where no satisfactory emotional bond existed, at least there was a way to be separated.[54]

But factory work also gave women a separate income and with that, perhaps, sufficient emotional distance from home and husband to think in a new way about their rights. At the same time, the increased emphasis on education brought women into the work force as teachers. Indeed, the ideals of the new republic created a series of female academies in the United States, and graduates who began to articulate an alternative vision of women's role.[55] Still others began to create a new place for themselves in the world of literature. And if the first group had little ability to speak for themselves, the latter two were well equipped to articulate their views. In England, for example, at the end of the eighteenth century, Mary Wollstonecraft moved from being a governess to being a school teacher and then to earning her living through her writing. Her *Vindication of the Rights of Woman* suggested that only if women had equality in education and rights could they fulfill their potential; otherwise

> they must, from being treated like contemptible beings, become contemptible. How many women thus waste life away the prey

of discontent, who might have practised as physicians, regulated a farm, managed a shop, and stood erect, supported by their own industry, instead of hanging their heads surcharged with the dew of sensibility, that consumes the beauty to which it at first gave lustre. . . . How much more respectable is the woman who earns her own bread by fulfilling any duty, than the most accomplished beauty.[56]

Wollstonecraft's appeal was, at its root, an appeal for a new type of relationship between men and women in which affection was based on true equality and mutual respect:

But, we shall not see women affectionate till more equality be established in society, till ranks are confounded and women freed, neither shall we see that dignified domestic happiness, the simple grandeur of which cannot be relished by ignorant or vitiated minds; nor will the important task of education ever be properly begun till the person of a woman is no longer preferred to her mind. For it would be as wise to expect corn from tares, or figs from thistles, as that a foolish ignorant woman should be a good mother.[57]

The next half-century saw a few modest changes in response to such appeals before a conservative reaction set in. Divorce laws were enacted in some states and, in 1857, in England, and the property laws that gave married women no entitlement began to be modified. The following hundred years have been called "The Era of Mandatory Marriage."[58] Why it should have been so is difficult to say. On the one hand, mines and factories produced a plethora of jobs requiring minimal skills while not providing an adequate income for marriage. Jobs for women in industry were declining in number so that for a third of the young women in England, even in 1930, domestic service was the only opportunity available. And such work made saving for marriage slow and difficult.[59] On the other hand, opportunities for education were increasing and women were finding — however slowly — increased opportunity for significant employment. In the latter half of this period, two world wars brought increased numbers of women into the work force, where they learned new skills and acquired a feeling of self-confidence, while the first stages of the welfare state provided benefits to war widows which were not available to those without a marriage license.[60] Whatever it was, something in this combination of social factors led to a general feeling that marriage was essential; and that marriage must be the "traditional" kind that had just been invented, with formal attire for the men, a long white dress for the bride, the wedding marches of Wagner and Mendelssohn, and a honeymoon at Niagara Falls. In England, even the reading of the banns at last became popular.[61] It was the calm before the storm.

AND NOW . . .

The last half century of the story began with enormous optimism. The Second World War had ended and a new era was beginning; new communities were growing up around family, school, and church. Every convenience was available to make home life more comfortable. Women were freed from much of the drudgery of an earlier time — though often they found themselves free only to serve as chauffeurs for their children.

Nonetheless, there was tremendous optimism about the role of the family. The bishops of the Anglican Communion assembled at Lambeth in 1958, looked out at the state of the family and found it good. They were especially hopeful about the fact that couples were no longer compelled to see their sexual relationship solely in terms of procreation. "The new freedom of sexuality in marriage," they said,

> is also, and equally, a gate to a new depth and joy in personal relationships between husband and wife. At a time when so much in our culture tends to depersonalize life — to erode and dissolve the old, clear outlines of human personality — Christians may well give thanks for the chance given us to establish, in marriage, a new level of intimate, loving inter-dependence between husband and wife and parents and children, freed from some of the old disciplines of fear.

"It will happen," they added, "only when we deliberately choose it, and pay the cost of it in self-discipline . . ."[62] Society as a whole, however, may not have been prepared to make that payment; a great many people seemed — and still seem — to be rather far from the bishops' ideal in marriage.

To take the time to analyze all the trends and counter-trends that have shaped human marriage in the last half of the twentieth century would be to risk drowning in a sea of statistics. There is also the real danger of identifying one or two trees as representing the forest. It is far from easy to analyze past centuries with all the benefit of hindsight and the advantage of a limited amount of data available; far more difficult for our own, in which the available data seem infinite. Past centuries lend themselves to sweeping generalizations. We can speak about the twelfth century or the High Middle Ages as if life over a hundred years or several hundred years had all been lived according to one pattern. We know our own times too well for that, although we still like to generalize about decades as if in the sixties everyone had lived one way and in the eighties another. Human life is far too diverse and change too constant. Generalizations, as we said earlier, are generally simplistic —and often simply wrong.

Having said that, we will go ahead and attempt to frighten ourselves with some statistics and pretend to enough wisdom to make some generalizations. Take it with a grain of salt.

What is happening to marriage? We were told in the sixties that it was dying out; in more recent years that it was returning to favor. The statistics, however, show a steady decline. *The World Almanac and Book of Facts* provides as solid a statistical base as we can find and gives us the following information for the United States. Between 1900 and 1990, the marriage rate remained steady, between 9 percent and 10 percent, while the divorce rate increased nearly sevenfold, from 0.7 percent to 4.7 percent (down from a high of 5.2 percent in 1980). The number of married couples fell, as a result, from 74 percent of the population in 1970 to 69 percent in 1980, 64 percent in 1990, and 63 percent in 1991. Meanwhile, the number of people between twenty-five and thirty-four described as "nonfamily householders" — presumably including people living together without benefit of church or state certification — rose by decades from 1960 to 1990 as follows: 600,000, 1,200,000, 4,400,000, 5,600,000. The percentage of children not living with two parents increased from 15 percent in 1970 to 28 percent in 1991. This last is far more common among black and Hispanic people than white, but the rate of increase is greater among children of white parentage.[63]

The pattern is similar elsewhere. In Great Britain, the divorce rate increased twentyfold between 1900 and 1957 and sixfold between 1960 and 1987.[64] The proportion of couples giving a common address when registering for marriage rose from 3 percent in 1966 to over 20 percent twenty years later. The proportion of children born of unmarried parents is now about 20 percent but the proportion of those births in which both parents registered their parentage increased from 38 percent in 1966 to 66 percent in 1986. In other words, a far higher percentage of couples are living together without being formally married and are treating it as a normal manner of life.[65] A recent English study found a very large number of couples living together and not even considering the possibility of marriage. "Having seen a lot of married couples and their carryings-on over the years made it seem irrelevant," said one woman. "Everyone in my family that has married are divorced. To me, it's a lot of pain getting married and then breaking up," said another.[66] The birth rate outside of marriage has gone from 12 percent to almost 30 percent in less than ten years.[67]

Does all this represent a trend? In the short term of a century or so, it seems to, but by one estimate the number of people living together without church or state blessing in the early eighteenth century was similar or higher: a quarter to a third of the population.[68] Again, it is estimated that in the 1950s only a third of the women under twenty had had intercourse but that the proportion now is closer to that of the nineteenth century.[69] Perhaps what is happening today is not a trend away from what we think of as "normal" but a trend back to what is, in fact, a more typical pattern of human behavior.

Consider, for a more extended example, the question of divorce:

> Two generations ago divorce was so scandalous and out of the ordinary that it was scarcely even contemplated as an alternative to conventional misery within a respectable marriage. Divorce was for millionaires, aristocrats, film stars — the lucky few who no longer had to care about what other people thought of them and were powerful enough to enjoy the publicity. At the other end of the scale, the socially invisible poor simply lit out for the Territory, leaving deserted wives and children to chase them for maintenance. But for the vast majority in between — the various shadings of middle class, from upper to lower — divorce was not a thinkable option. Even one generation ago, after the epidemic of rash marriages and morning-after separations provoked by World War II, it was still a grave social misdemeanor, agonizing, suspect and against the moral grain. It damaged Adlai Stevenson's presidential chances in the 1950s and Nelson Rockefeller's in the sixties. Yet within a dozen years, Princess Margaret was divorced, America had a divorced president, while another presidential hopeful did not even bother to marry the lady he travelled with. Nobody notices because everybody is divorcing. It is now rare to meet anyone who has not been through it, or who is not married to someone who has been through it, or who is not, at the very least, yearning or plotting to go through it at any moment. The figures are overwhelming and rising.

> They are also misleading.[70]

They are misleading because the claim can be made that the average marriage today lasts longer than those of past centuries. The average marriage at mid-twentieth century lasted thirty-one years before death or divorce while in early nineteenth-century England nearly a third of the marriages were ended by death in fifteen years; in France at that time and earlier, peasant marriages lasted an average of twelve to seventeen years.[71] Rising life expectancies have made it possible for a marriage today to last fifty years and more. Seventieth wedding anniversaries now take place. Fifty to seventy years provides lots of time to rethink a situation, whereas a marriage ended after ten or fifteen years by the death of one partner provides very little. The short-lived marriages of earlier times had no opportunity to face the emotional trauma of "the empty nest" or of retirement. The prospect of having to endure a partner's annoying quirks for ten years is one thing, fifty years quite another. Lawrence Stone suggests cheerfully that "it looks very much as if modern divorce is little more than a functional substitute for death."[72] So even the divorce rate may not represent as much of a change in behavior patterns as it appears to do at first glance.

But the point is not to shrug our shoulders and murmur about "nothing new under the sun," however biblical that attitude may be;[73] nor is it simply to accept the fact that changing social circumstances tend to push the Christian understanding of marriage one way or another — whether in acceptance or reaction — though this certainly occurs. The challenge is rather to look for the opportunity to gain new insights in a given situation.

Changing circumstances tend to throw light on different aspects of Christian teaching and practice. It would seem better to look carefully at whatever is being currently illuminated for our potential growth than to continue to examine an aspect that, however interesting it may once have been, is no longer as important or relevant. The American civil rights movement of the sixties, like the industrial revolution in the nineteenth century, forced churches and church members to think carefully about the biblical meaning of ideas like "justice," and about the requirements of a Christian social conscience. Not everyone wanted to do that, of course, and those who resisted forced the rest to think more carefully and articulate their position more clearly. Both viewpoints played an important role, but it is those who respond positively to such challenges who are likeliest to grow. So, too, today the challenge is neither to affirm nor to deny what so many people are doing, but to attempt to understand, respond intelligently, and come as a result to a deeper knowledge of God's purpose in creation. That is what the second part of this book is all about.

It should be noted in the first place that there are many aspects of this social change that we are far from understanding. The rate of divorce, for example, seems to be far higher among those at the lower end of the income scale than among professional people.[74] Is this because the less educated tend to marry younger without sufficient self-under-standing and emotional maturity? Or is it because the strain of building a family with fewer financial resources is greater? What about the other radical social changes in the last half-century: the increased opportuni-ties for women, for example, with the necessary shifts in the pattern of home life? Will the divorce rate recede as new patterns emerge and men, in particular, come to understand that they cannot expect to conduct themselves as their fathers did? Will other compensatory patterns emerge with time? Or will the breakdown accelerate as more people become accustomed to think of divorce as a convenient remedy for marital difficulties? These are questions we simply cannot answer at present.

Two further points need to be made before we move on: one about the exterior circumstances of marriage in this century and the other about the interior conditions.

For all the surface appearance of an age in which marriage was held in honor and almost universally affirmed, the "Era of Mandatory Mar-riage" was, in fact, an age in which many marriages were very far from the ideal. It may be, in fact, that the urge to marry and idealize marriage represented some sort of wide-spread self-deception: "We're all having a great time, aren't we now?" In fact, a great many people were not having a good time at all. This was an age of enormous and constant change, an age in which significant change in the speed of communi-cation and travel occurred for the first time since the horse was tamed and the wheel invented. First the railroad, then the automobile, then the airplane made quantum leaps in the speed and accessibility of travel. Gas light and then electric light radically transformed working condi-tions and living conditions. Telegraph, telephone, and television created the so-called "global village." Atomic energy and the computer are the latest seismic shocks to the way we live. At the beginning of the era, factories had drawn men and women away from the farms and homes where most work had always been done; at the end of the era, the growth of suburbs had further separated the home and place of business. In the face of these and other transformations, it is hardly surprising that a "traditional marriage," a calm center in the eye of the storm, may have seemed enormously appealing.

But the reality was rather different. Factory work and office work had defined perimeters from which a man returned home, like the medieval knight,[75] to a strange environment. Insecure in his own home, he could retreat to a beer hall or pub, or stay home and fight it out. One historian sums up the resultant violence of a late nineteenth-century London weekend:

> From Saturday afternoon, when wages had been paid, till
> Monday morning the court was often a field of battle and
> bloodshed, and Sunday was a pitiful day. . . men kicking their
> wives round the court like footballs, and women fighting like
> wild tigers![76]

Were other communities and societies so dramatically violent? Whether
they reached that level of conflict or not, there were many marriages
that endured more by habit and convenience than by deep affection.
Television reduced the number of beer halls and pubs but did little to
improve communication. One anti-poverty program in the 1960s found
that divorce was the subject of 84 percent of the calls on legal services;
more than help with landlords and debts, the poor wanted relief from
their partners.[77] The rising tide of divorces and the young people fearful of entering a marriage because of their own negative experience of
their parents' marriages are evidence enough that the "Era of Mandatory
Marriage" was not a success story.

While this was observable from the outside, the more important shift
was taking place inside the institution of marriage with the steadily
increasing emotional demands made on each other by husband and wife
as communities became less stable and the other functions of marriage
fell away. The age of the motor car and the expressway had broken up
the stable communities of the nineteenth century so that a great many
couples were attempting to build a relationship without the support of
long-time friends and nearby family to provide a broader network of
emotional ties. Simultaneously, as emotional support from a broad community of family and friends has disappeared, marriage has been reduced
to providing that one subjective element:

> Basically the wife used to be the producer of goods (bread,
> cheese, clothing), the performer of essential services (edu-
> cating the young, ironing shirts, nursing the old and ill); the
> husband was the provider of food or money, the defender —
> and ruler — of his wife and children. But factories, trans-
> portation, schools, hospitals, and modern merchandising
> changed all that. Man and woman no longer need marriage in
> order to survive, and marriage has ceased to be basically
> practical and productive, but has become instead a special kind
> of friendship. When it fails to provide us with companion-
> ship, sex, and the satisfaction of our individual emotional
> needs, we are deeply dissatisfied — no matter how many
> goods and services the spouse provides.[78]

Edward Schillebeeckx agrees:

I would go so far as to say that there is only one function left
to marriage and the family — that of being marriage and
being family. All that remains to the family and to marriage is
this personal and subjective aspect, this intimate, inner life,
since all the other functional aspects of marriage and family
life have been assumed by the various specialised depart-
ments of modern society.[79]

That is the ultimate challenge we face. Not, perhaps, since Adam and
Eve have couples found themselves so alone and so dependent on one
other person for emotional support. We are asking more of each other
than ever before. Can human beings, with the grace of God, meet this
test? What should we be saying and doing about marriage as we move
on to the third millennium of the Christian story?

CHAPTER NINE

Laws, Covenants, and Contracts

*C*an marriage be separated from the legal controls that have defined it since the Middle Ages? Churches are moving away from the language of "contract" to the language of "covenant" but still accept the state's right to license marriage. Governmental control no longer serves a valid purpose but, on the contrary, distorts the Christian vision of marriage.

CIVIL LAW

Robert Bolt's play "A Man for All Seasons" dramatizes the story of Thomas More and his controversy with Henry VIII. As the play begins, Henry has declared himself "Supreme Head of the Church in England." More is unable to accept the title — but he also has no desire for martyrdom. Therefore More has managed to use the letter of the law to protect himself against arrest and trial. There is also in the play a man called Richard Rich who is interested in More's daughter, Alice, and in using More's influence to his own advantage. Early in the play, Rich has been asking for More's help and has been refused and gone away angry. William Roper, a servant of More's, says, "Arrest him," and More asks, "For what?"

ALICE: He's dangerous!

ROPER: For libel; he's a spy.

ALICE: He is! Arrest him!

MARGARET: Father, that man's bad.

MORE: There is no law against that.

ROPER: There is! God's law!

MORE: Then God can arrest him.

ROPER: Sophistication upon sophistication!

MORE: No, sheer simplicity. The law, Roper, the law. I know what's legal not what's right. And I'll stick to what's legal.

ROPER: Then you set man's law above God's!

MORE: No, far below; but let *me* draw your attention to a fact —
I'm *not* God. The currents and eddies of right and wrong, which you
find such plain sailing, I can't navigate. I'm no voyager. But in the
thickets of the law, oh, there I'm a forester. I doubt if there's a man
alive who could follow me there, thank God . . .

ALICE: While you talk, he's gone!

MORE: And go he should, if he was the Devil himself, until he
broke the law!

ROPER: So now you'd give the Devil the benefit of law!

MORE: Yes. What would you do? Cut a great road through the
law to get after the Devil?

ROPER: I'd cut down every law in England to do that!

MORE: Oh? ...And when the last law was down, and the Devil
turned round on you — where would you hide, Roper, the laws all
being flat? . . . This country's planted thick with laws from coast to
coast — man's laws, not God's — and if you cut them down — and you're
just the man to do it — d'you really think you could stand upright in
the winds that would blow then? . . . Yes, I'd give the Devil benefit of
law, for my own safety's sake.[1]

Law has a vital role to play in the structuring of human society, and
none of us would be secure without it. There are, nevertheless, at least
two ways of approaching the subject, though More's way is the one on
which Western society has been built for almost a thousand years.

We have already seen how medieval Western society chose between
Germanic folklaw and the codified law of Rome. Harold Berman,
tracing the twelfth-century revolution in which the Roman way of using
law gained ascendancy, suggests that our acceptance of that revolution
has begun to break down. Ursula Le Guin describes one of the many
causes of that breakdown:

After all, almost all the rules, laws, codes, and commandments
we have — all our ethics — were made by men. Until just a
generation or two ago, this was entirely and literally true.
Women had no voice, no vote. We let the men make all the
choices . . . Where man-made ethics differ most radically
from female morality, from what women think and feel to be
right and wrong, is precisely in this area where we need a new
morality: the area in which men and women differ: the area
of sexuality, of conception, pregnancy, childbirth, and the

responsibility for children. I must admit that to me personally most of the rules men have made on these matters seem, if not simply irrelevant, disastrous . . . I suppose a morality that arises from and includes the feminine will have to be invented as we go along. Rigidity and codification are exactly what we want to get away from after all . . .[2]

People crave objectivity because to be subjective is to be embodied, to be a body, to be vulnerable, violable. Men especially aren't used to that; they're trained not to offer but to attack. It's often easier for women to trust one another, to try to speak our own experience in our own language . . .[3]

A thousand years of dependence on carefully codified law for our "own safety's sake" may make most of us, male or female, nervous at the prospect of some other arrangement, but Le Guin's reference to being "embodied" and "vulnerable" must remind Christians of a very basic aspect of their faith. If God in Christ could become "embodied" and "vulnerable," perhaps God's people could take the same risk. The loss of authority of the existing legal system may leave us, in any event, with little choice.

The widespread questioning of authority is nowhere more obvious than in matters of sexual relationships. That the proportion of those applying for a marriage license from a common address increased from 3 percent to 20 percent in England between 1966 and 1986 is just one statistic of many that might be offered in evidence.[4] More broadly, we could make lists of the areas that government once attempted to regulate — from Sunday closing laws to laws against profanity — where laws may still be on the books but could no longer be enforced without exposing the enforcer to ridicule. All law, finally, depends on a community consensus in support of the law if it is to be effective. Environmental laws and anti-smoking laws are passed now and enforced because there is such a consensus in favor of them. The prohibition amendment, lacking such a consensus, weakened the whole fabric of society. Today, whatever consensus remains in favor of laws regulating sexual behavior seems to be disappearing rapidly.

Do we need such laws? That we need some laws for our own protection is obvious. Laws against child pornography and sexual harassment are needed to protect some individuals against those who have not internalized the necessary boundaries for social behavior. But do we still need government laws regulating marriage, and does the church need to be governed by such laws? Does the church itself need laws controlling the circumstances of marriage?

The problem with civil laws in this area is not only that such laws are ever more frequently ignored by couples who see no need for them, but that the church's identification of its sacraments with those laws calls the church's faith into question also. Couples who live together without benefit of law or sacrament will frequently argue that church marriage is a matter of laws while their relationship is a matter of love; a legal marriage arrangement seems irrelevant to them — or worse. It is also true, in a society where one third to one half of all marriages end in divorce, that a great many young people have never seen a good marriage. They have watched while their parents have gone through the legal agonies of divorce and they have learned to think of "marriage" as a legal entanglement having little to do with the love they themselves have begun to experience.

Ruth Silbermann, a Roman Catholic who describes marriage as "the savage sacrament" quotes one woman as saying:

> "The young people are saying 'no' to the legalisms that do not make a marriage or guarantee fidelity of any kind. Now they are simply living together, or they obtain a civil license. Maybe later they will consider having their union blessed in the Church."

Comments Silbermann, "Maybe they won't."[5]

If they come to the church and find that, in addition to the church's regulations, they can only be married if they have a marriage license registered with the state, that only confirms their suspicion that marriage has to do with the attempt to control human lives with law. It may be unfortunate that the concepts of law and love have become so widely separated in our society, but that is the situation — and we cannot pass laws to change it.

Suppose, on the other hand, the church were to declare its independence. Suppose we were to take seriously the concept of "separation of church and state" and deal with marriage wholly in terms of human love and God's love: what might we lose and what might we gain?

The most obvious difference would be that the church would no longer serve as the certifying agent for contracts arranging people's financial and legal affairs. A marriage license is, at one level, a simple device for arranging the disposition of property: if one partner dies, the other inherits; if both die, the children inherit. A marriage license tells the state who's who and who gets what. A marriage license can also determine who is responsible for bringing up children and paying the bills, something the state does need to know. But the courts in recent years have established ways of determining the same matters for un-married couples out of sheer necessity. Similar rights and obligations have begun to be extended to same-sex couples as well, sometimes by law and sometimes by judicial or administrative action. Of course it is convenient to have such matters settled along with the wedding license, but the courts will settle them anyway if necessary. Those who would prefer not to leave their affairs to a posthumous court decision can easily arrange their affairs in their own way with the help of a lawyer. Even simpler, there are computer programs that will print out the necessary papers for less than the cost of a moderately good restaurant dinner. The fact is that a large number of people are getting along quite well without a license from either church or state. To insist that a church wedding requires some sort of permission from the state is to claim that we still live in the Holy Roman Empire.

Americans are brought up to believe that they, unlike the English and certain other Europeans, have separated church and state. The fact is, however, that Americans still live with the lingering remnants of an established church, whether they are Baptist, Anglican, Lutheran, or Roman Catholic. Baptists have been the most determinedly separatist of the major churches, yet even they seem never to have questioned the state's authority over marriage. Luther spoke dismissively of marriage as "a civil matter" and showed some willingness to perform marriages as he pleased, yet his followers have continued to perform marriage cere-monies while allowing the state to decide for them who can be married and who cannot. Anglicans and Roman Catholics are quite used to working with the state in various parts of the world, so their compli-ance may be in keeping with their tradition. But it does seem surprising that any church would willingly allow the state to decide through the tax code who will have an incentive to marry and who will not.

Why, for example, should a retired couple have to consider the tax consequences of their decision whether or not to marry? And if it is true, as statistics indicate, that significant numbers of retired people choose to live together without benefit of marriage because of the tax laws, why have the churches made no significant protest? In third-century Rome, the pope performed secret marriages for slaves who were forbidden to marry by the law of the state. Why, then, should the church today not likewise marry without license those who are faithful and who love each other and who would like God's blessing on their relationship even if the state puts obstacles in the way?

We are undoubtedly inhibited to a degree in this area by unexamined assumptions. Until 1979, the clergy of the Episcopal Church began the wedding service by exhorting those who knew any reason why the couple should not be married to come forward, "For be ye well assured," they read from the Prayer Book, "that if any persons are joined together otherwise than as God's word doth allow, their marriage is not lawful." How many ever stopped to consider the assumed identity in those words of church and state, an identity that had, in fact, been ended in 1776 and even before that had existed only in some of the colonies?

In a similar way, a Protestant theologian at the beginning of the twentieth century could write:

> [T]he state and the church agree in the conception that marriage is for life, and that it cannot be dissolved at will by either of the married parties. . . The state and the church agree in the judgment that at the present time divorces are unjustifiably numerous . . . [and] threatening to undermine the foundations of the social and civil fabric.[6]

We might not be so sure that "the state and the church agree" anymore, but the same assumption is still made that the frequency of divorce threatens the social fabric — though that frequency has multiplied many times over and the state is still functioning well enough to send out the income tax forms on a regular basis.

Until this generation, we have tacitly assumed and accepted the medieval arrangement: All marriage is Christian marriage; the church and the state are one. It has been a long time since this was true, but somehow we haven't noticed.

Now, on the other hand, there is a generation that feels free to enter a sexual relationship without the warrant of either church or state. For centuries we have said they were one and the same, and we have been believed. Thus those with questions about Christian marriage must also question all marriage. We have told them that the two are the same, and they have believed us.

Indeed, the continuing connection between church and state at the altar rail muddies the water for both. If the state issues a license which the church signs (in England the church itself can issue the license for the state), then the church in some sense endorses the state's law of marriage — and divorce — and is inevitably drawn into the political process to make those laws acceptable. In England, for example, the church fought hard in 1969 to see that divorce was defined in terms of "marriage breakdown" rather than "consent." Thus the church could feel that its views on indissolubility had not been totally rejected. Helen Oppenheimer, an English theologian, could note with satisfaction that the English law . . . does not rest the permanence of marriage upon the mere will of the parties . . . Marriage remains in law as in Christian belief, "the union of one man with one woman, voluntarily entered into for life."[7]

But the state has the power to change that law and, as long as the church feels obligated to sign a civil license, it tacitly endorses whatever view of marriage is enshrined in it. Oppenheimer points out quite rightly that if divorce were allowed by mutual consent, then "marriage in English law has become essentially perishable. The trouble is that if this is believed widely enough it will at last become true."[8]

There was a time when Christian belief shaped the law; now, unless the separation is complete, law can shape belief. But that would seem to be a reason to make the separation clear, not to preserve it.

The larger question remains: Do we need a civil law of marriage at all? It is commonly objected that marriage is, after all, the building block of society and that the state has an interest in the stability of families and the welfare of children. No doubt it does, but can these matters really be regulated by law? The evidence of historical experience suggests that there is, in fact, very little relationship between the laws and the stability of families. Scotland, for example, has permitted divorce for adultery and desertion with remarriage for the innocent party since the sixteenth century while England forbade divorce under almost any circumstances until the mid-nineteenth century, yet the divorce rate in both countries was negligible until the twentieth century and then, without a change in law, rose rapidly on both sides of the border.[9]

No doubt the same government that discourages the elderly from getting married by means of the tax code could encourage young people to get married by the same means. Tax codes are used to shape society in any number of ways, from discouraging smoking to encouraging saving. Many governments have used the tax code to encourage or discourage childbearing, and a lower tax on couples who are legally married might bring crowds to the church door. But would the church be comfortable dealing with couples who came to be married simply because it was financially advantageous? Would marriages made under those circumstances be equally stable?

If stable homes for children are a proper goal of government, and if a way to determine financial responsibility is needed, the present laws seem ineffective in providing the former and quite capable of managing the latter. Children's parentage, after all, is not determined by possession of a marriage license but by information given at the time of birth or, if necessary, by genetic testing. The government can readily determine responsibility if necessary. Family stability, on the other hand, desirable though it surely is, is obviously not promoted by the present laws. The question of whether a child is harmed more by living with an unhappy and conflicting pair of parents or by living in a less stressful environment without an adult male or female presence is still open. Neither situation is ideal. Until governments find a way to compel people to live together happily, there seem to be no other choices available. Law, at best, is a rather blunt instrument for guiding the emotional development of small children.

The civil law of marriage comes down to us from a distant past in which authorities thought it their duty to promote procreation and determine parentage. The church assumed final responsibility for the task in the chaos of the Middle Ages, largely because people of property were concerned to establish clear lines of inheritance, and the church, in its attempt to gain control of society, was happy to provide that service. The close identification of law and sacrament led the reformers to reject the church's legal role in marriage but accept the pastoral responsibility under state authority. Thus, for the better part of two thousand years, marriage has been as much or more a civil matter as one of religion, and a separation of state interests from church interests may now be hard to visualize. But Luther was half right: marriage is a civil matter in part, there are aspects of marriage which require legal arrangement; these are handled better by the state or through legal arrangements than by the church.

But, in fact, marriage need not normally be even a civil matter. Most marriages will probably require some legal documents to determine matters of property: will husband and wife share equally or not, will inheritance go to a surviving spouse unconditionally or in trust for children? Matters like that may require a lawyer but need not involve the government except as an enforcer of legal arrangements. Beyond that, except to satisfy a census-taker's curiosity, why should the government care who is living with whom and under what arrangements? Our society is, in fact, already one in which people live together as they please. Those who register their marriage with the government today are those who choose to do so or who are required to do so by the church.

Christian marriage, however, is something more. Luther, looking at marriage through the lens of arrangements made in the twelfth century, could not have been expected to see that marriage is not simply a civil matter; the church had framed it in such strongly legal terms that it was inevitable that it would be supported or rejected on those grounds. Our own perspective is distorted still by a relationship between law and faith shaped many centuries ago. Perhaps if the civil or legal issues are separated out we will be able to see more clearly the element that remains and the churches will then be free to come closer together in a common understanding of what marriage is. If, then, we are to make a serious effort to "reinvent" marriage, this is probably the place to begin: let the church deal with marriage in terms of faith, and let the state and the lawyers make whatever arrangements they wish to govern the economic and legal aspects of human relationships. Christian marriage has to do with something more than that, and we will explore what that is in subsequent chapters.

One further aspect of all this might be mentioned before moving on: the possibility that the controversy over what are sometimes called "domestic partnerships" might be, if not resolved, at least dealt with more clearly if the civil and legal aspects could be separated from the religious. In recent years, some civil authorities have begun to allow the registration of "domestic partnerships," thus allowing those involved certain legal benefits in relation to housing, inheritance, and other matters. The difficulty is that, so long as the state is in the business of licensing marriages, the state is put in the position of making moral judgments by licensing or not licensing certain relationships and the church is then drawn into the political arena to support or oppose such measures.

Here again, a separation of church and state might be helpful to all concerned. Certainly the civil authorities would have a simpler time of it if they limited their role to enforcing contracts freely entered into by competent persons. Different benefits for individuals or partnerships of any kind ought not to be a matter of government policy; ideally government should treat all individuals equally. Those who wish to create relationships with other human beings should be free to do so with the help of a lawyer or computer program. Maternity benefits and related matters can appropriately be left to negotiation between employers and employees.

What churches may then chose to do about blessing various relationships would be a matter for each church to decide on the basis of its own theology and through its own political process. Such decisions are already being debated and the churches are not finding the matter easy. It is not the purpose of this book to participate in that debate, but it is possible that a clearer understanding of how Christian marriage has developed, what its theological and biblical bases are, and what potential it holds may help to clarify that debate also.

CHURCH LAW

Most Christians are probably completely unaware of the existence of something called "canon law." Nor do they need to be aware unless they decide to get married. Then, especially if they have been divorced and if they belong to a church with codified regulations, they will find out. Whatever rules or laws churches have, they are most likely to affect lay people in matters of marriage. So, if we are going to face the full range of questions about marriage, canon law must be talked about as well as civil law. This is not, we must admit, the world's most interesting subject, so let's begin with a story.

In the year 1198, Pope Innocent III wrote a letter to the Bishop of Troyes in France. In the letter he said he had learned that the priests attached to the cathedral in Troyes had changed the way in which the cathedral revenues were divided. It seems that there were grapevines in the area which, by tradition, belonged to the individual priests and were passed on to their successors in office. But now the priests of the cathedral had decided that, when a priest died, the revenue from the grapevines would not go to his successor but would be divided equally among them all. The pope attacked this provision on the grounds that those who make a law for others should obey it themselves.

A generation later, when Gregory IX (1227-41) was updating Gratian's summary of the laws of the church, he included the portion of Innocent's letter that dealt with the grapevines.[10] Why would you include a bit of a letter like that in a compilation of laws to govern the whole church? Why not just make a new law governing the rights of cathedral chapters or the sources of clergy income? But laws of that sort can go quickly out of date, while examples of past wisdom may still provide useful guidance. Perhaps the case is similar to one in which a company today agrees with the union to hire new workers at a lower wage than those with seniority. There may be no civil or church laws to prevent it, but Pope Innocent's letter suggests that such an agreement is unfair.

What we have here, in other words, is a very different approach to the subject of law. This is not an attempt to fix precise speed limits on highways or exact penalties for specific crimes. It may have more in common with Germanic folklaw or with the subjective approach to law recommended by Ursula Le Guin. Isn't it, in fact, this approach which marriage counselors take already? It would be contrary to all their training to provide their clients with rules; but they have studied and handled cases that will help them provide guidance in each new situation. A common complaint about the institution of marriage is that it has to do with law rather than love. Might clergy find themselves better able to carry out their ministry if equipped with case studies rather than canons?

The various churches today have widely different approaches to that subject. Some churches have no laws at all on the subject of marriage and never did. Some of these churches take that stand because they see the Bible as the sole and sufficient guide to church life, and from the Bible they may be able to draw clear and definite guidance prohibiting, for example, divorce. Such churches might well differ very little at a practical level, in the experience of those coming to them for ministry, from those with books of laws. Other churches may have no laws because they believe that the pastor should be guided by the Bible in a more general way or by the law of love.

Still other churches do have laws governing their conduct in relation to marriage. The Roman Catholic church has a thick book of laws and many of them relate specifically to marriage and offer answers to many questions. Canon 1090, for example, provides that those who murder their spouses in order to marry someone else may not celebrate the proposed marriage in the Roman Catholic church. The Episcopal church, though its rules are not as complete as that, also has several pages of laws about marriage, some requiring a period of instruction in preparation for marriage and others describing the procedures to follow if one of the candidates for marriage has been divorced. The Presbyterian *Book of Common Order,* on the other hand, has less than two pages of rules and discusses only the content of the pre-marital instruction and the structure of the marriage service.

If the church we belong to does have such laws, however, we may find it easier to use them wisely than to change them. Such matters change slowly; it is too easy to interpret the elimination of a law as a license for of all kinds of shocking behavior. Politicians seem to have learned that "family values" is a subject best avoided. Most of us are eager to have laws requiring other people to live up to our standards, but other people can create quite a fuss when we try to impose them. Churches in recent years have become deeply divided over sexual issues and the attempt to legislate human behavior. So change will be slow, but church laws ought not to be narrowly drawn up or, in any event, narrowly administered; there should be room for some variety of interpretation so that we can not only provide guidance but learn as we do so.

Laws, after all, are not all of one kind. A Roman Catholic expert, Ladislas Orsy, points out that the canon law of his church contains at least seven different kinds of material, ranging from dogmatic statements to theological opinions and even "affirmations borrowed from the empirical sciences." When the canons say that the laity "should greatly value schools," that is really an exhortation, not a law. According to Orsy, Canon 1055, on marriage, contains a dogmatic statement, a theological opinion, a statement on the history of dogma, and a statement of belief — but no legal statement as such.[11] There are also, of course, clear legal statements, but even these are somewhat different from what secular lawyers deal with in drawing up contracts and defending a client. The Episcopal church, for example, has a canon that says, "All members within this church shall celebrate and keep the Lord's Day . . . by regular participation in the public worship of the church. . . ." But what would happen to the membership roles of the Episcopal church if the clergy were to list as members only those who have obeyed that law from the time they were baptized?

The point is that there may have been a time when church laws had enforceable status but today, except for those that govern clergy training and placement and matters of internal church life, the "laws" of the church are really guidelines and aspirations. We are not generally talking about laws to be enforced with penalties. A standard guide to the new Roman Catholic Code of Canon Law says:

> The entire maze of canonical penalties has been considerably simplified in the new law. The canonical penalties now remaining are excommunication, interdict from the sacraments, and suspension. Such penalties as infamy and local interdict have been dropped.[12]

Christians no longer burn each other at the stake either. On the whole, this is a good thing, but the old yearning for control still flares up from time to time, and the churches will probably be reluctant to let go of even the minimal guidelines some of them still have. But law has its limits: "Whatever other merits it may have, a statute is not the best instrument for directing the spiritual life of a community."[13]

Orsy puts it more bluntly:

> Legalism is a sickness in the system; it places greater value on the observance of formalities than on the granting of true justice. When it is rampant, it erodes the strength of laws from the inside, and it brings them into bad repute on the outside.[14]

And that is the problem many people have with the institution of marriage. Rightly or wrongly, they have come to think of church and state as more concerned with "the observance of formalities" than with human beings in love. That appearance and reputation are all too easily developed; they may even be accurate. Those who are given laws for guidance will often find it much easier to apply the law than to listen to the person. But ministry begins with people.

So, in relation to Christian marriage, the primary concern should be spiritual formation — about which more will be said later. If we must have laws, our concern should be not how to apply them, but how to use them for ministry.

> The aim of church law is to preserve, to direct, and to edu-cate. It does not therefore consist primarily of a series of commands and prohibitions to which penalties are attached, though it contains some of this. Much of it is rather normative and exhortatory and when penalties are necessary its favorite instrument is admonition.[15]

The Roman Catholic church has been learning that also since Vatican II, and the guide to the new Code says very much the same thing:

> A growing discovery in the post-Vatican II Church has been the pastoral potential to be found in the Church's law. Church law is broader than a set of canons or detailed prescriptions. It reflects the fundamental communion of the Church and is dir-ected toward fostering the mission of all the people of God.[16]

Eric Kemp sums this point up as follows:

> More than most systems, the law of the Church must rest upon moral authority rather than coercion and those who admin-ister it must have large minds.[17]

Moral authority: But, finally, what other authority would the church want? Those who said of Jesus that "He speaks with authority,"[18] did not mean that he had coercive power; just the opposite. He had auth-ority because he had renounced the temptation of power. Our making of laws, civil and ecclesiastical, often reflects our loss of authority and our attempt to accomplish through power what we have failed to accomplish through moral authority.

Canon law cannot be coercive; today, people will simply turn away from clergy or churches that use it in that way. It can be educational: Those churches that have laws or regulations concerning marriage do center attention increasingly on the educational role. It can also be re-visioned as something more flexible and more human: An inheritance of wisdom from which to draw guidance, rather than a law to be enforced.

It is interesting, then, to turn back to the tradition of Germanic folklaw to understand another way of looking at the ordering of human life in community. Americans and Europeans, it should be noted, are also becoming aware of similar patterns in the African, Near Eastern, and Asian traditions. Harold Berman believes that the Roman legal tradition has come to a dead end in our day and that we need to recover a more flexible pattern of community life, one with

> a sense of the wholeness of life, of the interrelatedness of law with all other aspects of life, a sense that legal institutions and legal processes as well as legal norms and legal decisions are all integrated into the harmony of the universe. Law, like art and myth and religion, and like language itself, was for the peoples of Europe, in the early stages of their history, not primarily a matter of making and applying rules in order to determine guilt and fix judgement, not an instrument to separate people from one another on the basis of a set of principles, but rather a matter of holding people together, a matter of reconciliation.

He advocates a society like those of other times and places in which "the traditional, collective, and intuitive sides of life were emphasized, and the intellectual, analytical, and legal sides were fused with and subordinated to them."[19]

It might well seem to us that a society organized in that way has no law. This is because the legal processes have not been separated out from the whole fabric of life, but instead have been completely interwoven with the religious, political, economic, family, and other social institutions and processes.[20] Their society seems lawless to us because the laws have been so completely integrated and internalized. Our society seems lawless because the external structure of law seems irrelevant to so many.

When we complain as so many do today, that our own society or church seems to have become disordered and lawless, we commonly react by calling for a reestablishment of law and order. To imagine living without a clear structure of law on which to build can seem frightening; like Thomas More, we might ask, "d'you really think you could stand upright in the winds that would blow then?" But fierce winds are blowing already and the existing legal structure provides all too little security. The difficulty may be deeper than a matter of the right laws and a will to enforce them. It may be that we are observing a society in which basic values and understandings have not been integrated into the whole pattern of life. It may be more a matter of vision than of law.

Marriage, as the most ancient and universal human institution, may be a good place in which to begin to reshape and reorganize our lives. But "folklaw" cannot be drawn up in committee or enacted by a convention, and most of us know no other way to proceed. There are not likely to be short-term solutions and any suggestions made in the following chapters can only be of the most preliminary sort. We will need to begin to reeducate ourselves, learn to listen more carefully both to individuals and to the Spirit at work in the world, and re-vision the marriage process in ways more responsive to human beings and their Creator. If this seems vague and lacking in specific detail, it should; precise legal formulations are a crisis measure and, even then, not often able to minister to human need.

CONTRACT AND COVENANT

Contract

Many years ago a man came to see me about his marriage. He and his wife were on the verge of divorce and he was clear whose fault it was: Not his. He told me that his wife was a terrible housekeeper. Recently one of his socks had fallen onto the bedroom floor. He had left it there deliberately to see how long it would be before she picked it up, and it had remained there a week.

I suggested that he might have tried picking it up himself and saved himself a week of irritation, but no, that was *her* job. He was very clear about whose job it was and, no matter how angry it made him, he saw no reason to change.

This is a good illustration of the "contract" idea of marriage. Roles are defined and assigned and each party is expected to do their job. It's a good arrangement for those with a certain approach to life — provided that their spouse is equally satisfied with that approach. For many people still, this is what marriage is all about. Typically, the husband goes out to work and earns money; the wife stays home to cook, clean house, and raise children. There was a time when such a pattern was taken for granted; as the statistics in the last chapter indicate, it is typical no longer.

The contract idea was, as we have seen, a central principle in the standard theological description of marriage. It remains a word very much in use when Christians and non-Christians alike talk about marriage. But "contract" is an idea inherited from societies in which marriage was, indeed, a contract. From the time the parents or clans first began attempting to arrange a marriage, a contract was involved. The bride's security had to be arranged through dowry or in some other way, family and clan interests had to be protected, bride and groom had to assume responsibilities that they needed to understand clearly. For that last area, there might well have been a standard pattern: the husband will do this, the wife will do that. In a world in which almost everyone was a farmer, those roles would have been easily defined and readily understood, but a contract provided clarity and left no room for complaint afterwards. A contract, like other types of law, supplied a certain security.

In the Middle Ages contract constituted the essence of a marriage. The chief concern of feudal society was to establish titles and inheritance and the contract of marriage served that end. Two different patterns of contract had been inherited from the Roman and German traditions and the church adapted these to the needs of the time. Then, in a move that has left its mark on Christian marriage ever since, the church defined the marital contract as constituting the sacrament of marriage, giving it divine authority and giving the church control over this critical social institution. Thus the Sacred Congregation of the Holy Office of the Roman Catholic Church stated in 1817:

> Marriage is a sacrament because the contract itself is a sacrament. To say it differently, the contract pertains to the substance of the sacrament, and is part of the definition of it. This is a dogma of the Catholic faith.[21]

It was because he also accepted the idea of marriage as contract that Martin Luther rejected marriage as a sacrament and transferred it, in theory at least, to the realm of civil government. In the following century, the theory of contract gained a new importance with the writings of John Locke and, still later, with Rousseau, who, as the authority of the new nation-states began to be questioned, provided the theory of the "social contract" as a way to understand the purpose of government. Americans enshrined these theories at the center of their national identity in the Declaration of Independence, which held it to be self-evident

> that all men are created equal, That they are endowed by their Creator with certain unalienable rights. . . That to uphold these rights, governments are instituted. . .

And this theory of human relationships, so dramatically affirmed, then played a significant part in the rise of modern feminism and its questioning of the marriage relationship. The theory of contract seemed at first to be a basis from which to question the fairness of the contracts between men and women. It was not the theory of marriage as contract that was questioned but the terms of the contract. Thus in 1825 William Thompson, a man much influenced by the Owenite movement, used the idea of a just contract as a weapon against the contemporary form of marriage:

> Each man yokes a woman to his establishment, and calls it a contract. . . Audacious falsehood! Contract! Where are any of the attributes of contracts, of equal and just contracts, to be found in this transaction? . . . Have women been consulted as to the terms of this pretended contract? . . . Men enacted, that is to say, *willed* the terms, let women like them or not; man to be the owner, master, and ruler of every thing, even to the minutest action, and most trifling article of property brought into the common stock by the woman; woman to be the moveable property, and ever obedient servant, to the bidding of man.[22]

In other words, if marriage is seen as a contract, the terms until recent times were not those of a proper contract agreed between two equal partners. It was men who defined the terms, and those terms, not surprisingly, were very much to their advantage.

It is important to try to understand exactly what was involved in the contracts of the past in order to understand why so many people now have strong reservations about formal marriage by whatever name. Consider, for example, the story of Caroline Sheridan Norton (1808-77), who was a successful author in her own right but the victim of a disastrous marriage. Whose fault the violent scenes and arguments were is irrelevant. In 1836, after eight years of marriage, her husband, George Norton, accused her of adultery with the Prime Minister. Although she was judged innocent, she was denied access to their three children, and her husband took legal action to obtain the proceeds of her writings. She summed up her position — and that of all women in that society — in these terms:

> A married woman in England has *no legal existence:* her being is absorbed in that of her husband. Years of separation or desertion cannot alter this position. Unless divorced by special enactment in the House of Lords, the legal fiction holds her to be *"one"* with her husband, even though she may never see or hear of him. She has no possessions, unless by special settlement; her property is his property. . . .
>
> An English wife has no legal right even to her clothes or ornaments; her husband may take them and sell them if he pleases, even though they be the gifts of relatives or friends, or bought before marriage . . .
>
> An English wife cannot legally claim her own earnings. Whether

wages for manual labour, or payment for intellectual exertion, whether she weed potatoes, or keep a school, her salary is *the husband's;* and he could compel a second payment, and treat the first as void, if paid to the wife without his sanction.

An English wife may not leave her husband's house. Not only can he sue her for "restitution of conjugal rights," but he has a right to enter the house of any friend or relation with whom she may take refuge, and who may "harbour her," — as it is termed, — and carry her away by force, with or without the aid of the police.

. . . As *her husband,* he has a right to all that is hers: as *his wife,* she has no right to anything that is his. . . . [23]

Ruth Silbermann adds modern sequels, describing the result of an attitude formed by the idea of marriage as indissoluble contract:

One woman, who hid her bruises under long sleeves and behind dark glasses, was lectured on the beneficial results of sincere prayer and reminded that it was a mortal sin to say no.

Another, the wife of a philandering husband and mother of his six children, was told by her confessor, with a reminder of the Pauline dictum that the husband is the head of the wife, and that wives should be submissive to their husbands, that she had "made her bed and now must rest in it." Believing and dutiful, she suffered her panic and her rage. She "worked at love" for three more years, and then, lacking the support of her church in the person of her confessor in terminating her marriage, terminated her life and her child's. [24]

Michael Novak asks: "How many marriages have a merely legal union? And are such marriages, whatever canon law might say, profoundly inhuman and immoral?" [25]

It is against such a background that all too many see marriage. They have a reason for their reluctance to get involved. Today the language of contract in marriage seems to be on its way out. The Roman Catholic church still retains the term in some of its canons, but since Vatican II it has preferred the term *covenant.* The Episcopal church has dropped the word from its canons. The Presbyterian Church *Directory for Worship* sums up an emerging ecumenical consensus as follows:

Marriage is a civil contract between a man and a woman. For

> Christians marriage is a covenant through which a man and a woman are called to live out together before God their lives of discipleship. In a service of Christian marriage a lifelong commitment is made by a woman and a man to each other, publicly witnessed and acknowledged by the community of faith.[26]

So marriage is defined today, just as Martin Luther defined it almost five hundred years ago, as a "civil contract" first of all. We have suggested it need not even be that, that the contract elements can be isolated and dealt with, if desired, by a legal paper with no intervention of civil authority. All this makes it sound as if we can dismiss the idea of contract as having no real importance for Christians. But that may be a mistake also. Marriage as contract, as defining fundamental concerns like procreation and inheritance, may belong to an earlier stage in human history, but there may be people today who are at that stage and need, if only for a while, the support a contract can give.

Those who work in the area of counseling often speak of the value of making a contract: "Let's agree that we will meet at these times and work on these issues." The advice is often given to couples: "Why not make a contract with each other that for the next few weeks you'll both try to look at the way you handle this subject?" To segregate one part of a relationship and work on it in a defined way can be of value. A contract — limited in time and purpose — can play a useful role. But we hope to be able to grow out of it. In the same way, an athlete may analyze a particular action frame by frame and repeat it systematically until it becomes natural and easy. Then, when the skill has been acquired, the analysis can be forgotten. So a contract, limited in time and purpose, can also be a means of growth in a marriage relationship.

Contracts also, as Locke and Rousseau understood, can be a defense against tyranny, a way to establish justice. The medieval marriage contract could be seen as a defense *of* tyranny, but the primary reason why the church found contract language congenial was to establish equality. The free consent of partners was at the heart of the contract theory. Granted that the consent was often between parents rather than partners, granted that the contract in that time and place removed the woman's freedom and established the man's authority; the fact remains that that was not the theory of it. Theories can be a long way from facts, but they also tend to be rediscovered and to re-assert themselves. Contracts have to do with justice, and that fact, asserted by Locke, Rousseau, Thompson, and others did provide a standard by which marriage could at last be measured and found wanting.

Justice remains a concern in the marriage relationship. Some of the issues that arise in any marriage can be dealt with at that level. Is it fair? Is it right? But justice, in any relationship, is a basic and preliminary concern, not a final goal. Those who are oppressed will have justice as their first goal. In most human societies, it remains a goal. But still it is only a first step toward the possibility of a deeper relationship based on mercy, forgiveness, and love. Marriage relationships should be just, but they should be much more than that as well. To define marriage as contract, to specify obligations and roles and never grow beyond that, is to limit the potential marriage holds, to limit the challenge to grow.

Covenant

Because of the limitations inherent in the idea of contract, the church has turned to the language of covenant. This, at least, has the advantage of being biblical terminology. Few ideas are more central to the biblical tradition. But the biblical idea of covenant can be too easily given a modern definition not fully supported by Scripture. It is nice to think of marriage in terms of a deep, personal commitment, but the biblical word implies much more than that and we will need to decide whether we are willing to accept those implications or create our own definition. It is a human tendency, especially in our scientific century, to want clear and precise definitions. But to provide such clarity for the term *covenant* is to move back into the legal realm and return to the language — however improved — of contract. If *covenant* is to be our terminology, it needs to keep its biblical lack of precision, its role as metaphor and model rather than diagram.

In using covenant language it is especially important to remember that the central biblical use — the relationship between God and God's people — can be applied to marriage only with the greatest caution. A man and a woman are not comparable to God and God's people, nor is their relationship comparable on a one-for-one basis. The church, following the letter to the Ephesians too literally, has fallen into that trap before. The relationship between husband and wife *is* like that between Christ and his church — but not in terms of inequality. There are ways in which the metaphor has much to teach us, but that is not one of them.

In the first English Prayer Book of 1549, and all subsequent books into the twentieth century, the woman promised to "love, honour, and obey." The man made no promise of obedience, but when he gave the ring he said, "with my body I thee worship." Worship is the greater promise, the deeper commitment, and that is the relationship of the church to God in Christ. So the Book of Common Prayer has from the beginning reversed the expected terms of the metaphor in terms of gender. If we are to use covenant language, we must be equally willing to let either spouse "play God" and to let both see themselves in the role of God's people. Both also should be willing to see themselves in Christ's role of loving the church and dying for it. In a Christian marriage, these roles are not gender specific.

A second hazard involved with the use of covenant language is that it is all too easily converted to the language of contract. Indeed, the difference between contract and covenant in the Bible itself is not always clear and remains a matter of much debate.[27]

Here is one vital point at which good marriage theology can help us see into the very heart of what it means to be God's people, and vice versa. No Christian church has concerned itself so much with the idea of "covenant" as the Presbyterian, especially the Scottish Presbyterian. Yet even in Scottish law, covenant and contract are said to be equivalent terms, and the struggle for the soul of the Scottish church has been fought out on this field. A review of that struggle shows how time and again the two notions have become confused. Thus an early Scottish catechism described the covenant of grace as "a contract of marriage" between Christ and the believer and then proceeded to outline the "conditions of the contract."[28] But that makes grace conditional and inverts the biblical order in which we repent because we are forgiven.

That confusion continues to occur in the writing of both Roman Catholic and Protestant theologians. A Protestant author on the subject of marriage, for example, writes: "Marriage is essentially a covenant relationship for which mutuality and companionship are primary values."[29] Yes, mutuality and companionship may indeed be primary values in a marriage, but that is not the same as covenant. Covenants are not mutual. Covenants are unqualified.

A Presbyterian scholar has commented:

> The sin of the human heart in all ages — was to try to *turn God's covenant of grace into a contract.* . . . In the Bible, the form of covenant. . . is such that the *indicatives of grace are always prior to the imperatives* of law and human obligation. "I have loved you, I have redeemed you . . . therefore, keep my commandments" [becomes] "If you keep the law, God will love you. . . ."[30]

There are no "ifs" in a covenant. There can be no "ifs" in marriage either.

The final reservation to set in place about the language of covenant is that it measures marriage by something other than marriage. All metaphor does that, of course, and we need to be careful about comparisons for this reason. But the language of covenant tends to go beyond metaphor to say not "Marriage is *like* a covenant," but rather "Marriage *is* a covenant." This is a problem that we will look at in more detail in the next chapter, connected with the idea of sacrament. The difficulty is the language of category in which we try to learn something about one item by grouping it with others. Thus the statement, "Marriage is a covenant," means we can learn about it by comparing it with other covenants. But if our primary understanding of covenant comes from the covenant between God and God's people, this category is flawed at its heart. There are things we can learn about marriage by seeing how God is related to the people of Israel and the church, but they are not the same, and we can draw the wrong lessons entirely unless we remember that fact.

As for the values of covenant language, it offers a terminology that can be used to speak of a one-sided and total commitment, a personal relationship in which both partners give themselves fully and unreservedly to the other for love alone, expecting nothing in return. So long as we ask no more of it than that — though that is quite a lot — we can use it to good advantage. "Covenant," in short, is a better word than "contract" for getting at the essence of marriage, but it is not itself that essence.

CHAPTER TEN

What Is Marriage?
What Is Not?

T he church has called marriage a "sacrament" but, in the past, "sacrament" has been defined legalistically in the Catholic tradition and rejected by the Protestant tradition. Today a more personal and experiential understanding of marriage is gaining favor. The church has also said marriage is "indissoluble" — but has found ways to make exceptions. The difficulty is, again, in a legalistic understanding of marriage that sees indissolubility as a given rather than a goal.

A wonderful thing is happening today in the church: love is beginning to make a difference. It may have taken four hundred — nearly five hundred — years, but the church is beginning to move beyond the ancient arguments that divided it for so long.

One of the most significant points of division in the church since the Reformation has concerned the central acts of Christian worship: are they sacraments or not? Traditionally, Roman Catholics have said yes; Protestants have said no. Anglicans have tried not to get involved but have tended to take the Catholic side: The Book of Common Prayer did say unequivocally that there are two sacraments "generally necessary for salvation."

Of course, when people choose up sides for a fight, the first thing they need to do is be very clear as to the reason for which they are fighting. Sixteenth-century Christians made sure they were very clearly divided on the subject of the sacraments. They all still used the term, but the issue was: what is a sacrament, and what does a sacrament do? The Roman church made its views clear in the sixteenth century at the Council of Trent: "If any one shall say that the sacraments of the New Law do not contain the grace which they signify. . . , let him be anathema."[1] So there! The church of Rome condemned that opinion because it thought that was exactly what Protestants were saying. The Protestant churches responded in turn by moving further and further away from the idea of sacraments as means of grace or even from the use of the term *sacrament.* Instead they spoke of "ordinances" and "commemorations" and "institutions"; these were important, of course, but certainly not in the way Roman Catholics said they were. For four hundred years, the two sides dug in their heels, or wandered further apart, or built higher walls. Choose your metaphor.

But suddenly, in our day, the walls have started to crumble. The crumbling has not been sudden, like the crumbling of the Berlin Wall that came down in a matter of days; that wall, after all, had been in place less than forty years. The Reformation walls have been in place more than ten times as long and have run not simply through one city or one country but through the whole Christian world. Those walls were not built in a day and will not come down in a day. But Protestants are beginning to talk about the sacramental aspect of Christian life with new interest, and Roman Catholics are beginning to suggest that the sixteenth-century formulas may not be eternally adequate after all. There is hope at last.

It would be nice if we could talk about marriage without having to get into all this. Sacramental theology is an enormous subject and currently in a great state of flux and change. Can we try in a few pages to pick a sensible path through ancient and modern mine fields? In the hope that no one will invoke the saying about "fools rushing in . . ." (though my friends, by applauding my "courage" in taking on this subject have implied as much), I think we should give it a try.

MARRIAGE AS SACRAMENT

Instead of trying to find neat and narrow definitions as the theologians of the twelfth and sixteenth centuries did, let us try to open the subject up as broadly as possible. Let us go back to the first Christian theologians who, for all their fears about sex and marriage, dealt with the idea of sacrament with a wonderfully wide lens on their theological cameras. St. Augustine, for example, although he may have thought celibacy a better way, not only insisted steadily that marriage was good but also said that the joining of the first man and woman had "a certain sacramentality" about it.[2]

When Jesus was asked about marriage, he referred back to God's purpose in creation. To understand the nature of the marital union, we need likewise to begin at the beginning. Augustine suggested that a sacramental quality was present from the first, long before the church or clergy came on the scene. When the first two human beings joined in sexual embrace, it had something of the nature of a sacrament about it. That implies that any significant sexual relationship, Christian or non-Christian, still today must have a sacramental quality — at least as St. Augustine used the term.

Augustine, of course, did not use the term sacrament in the medieval sense. He was the first theologian to make extensive use of the word, and he meant first of all that a sacrament was a sign of something holy. Such signs were by no means limited to the life of the Christian church; they were found in the Old Testament as well. Circumcision, for example, was a sacrament, and so was the Passover. When Moses lifted up the serpent in the wilderness, Augustine said that was "a great Sacrament."[3]

In brief summary, Augustine used the word *sacrament* to describe material things that reveal spiritual things.[4] On the whole, material things distract us from God; a computer might conceivably fill us with wonder at the Creator who provided silicon for our use, but it is far more likely to preoccupy our minds with spread sheets and data bases. Bread and wine, however, when held up as symbols, can draw our attention to the invisible realities without which life would be little more than silicon. But sacraments do more than remind us of God, according to Augustine; God is present in them and acts in us through them. Christ himself is made known to us in the bread and wine; the one who is baptized is sealed forever as God's own.[5]

So why does Augustine call marriage a sacrament? What does marriage show us about God? How is God present there? When Augustine said there is something sacramental about marriage, he did so in a sentence about the lasting quality of marriage. He was saying that marriage can only be dissolved by death. God's relationship with us is even more enduring than death, but, even so, marriage can be a sign of the lasting relationship between God and God's people. Augustine also speaks, as the Bible does, of God creating Eve so that Adam would not be alone. God's primary purpose in creating two human beings was to remedy loneliness. Marriage can show us unity and love and friendship, and so remind us of — and embody — God's love for humankind. This is not, we need to remember, medieval theology, nor is Augustine that kind of systematic theologian. Augustine did not even ask many of the questions the medieval theologians answered. Augustine's thought has no system of seven sacraments with outward signs and inward grace. Augustine's theology is much more open: he is pointing to a quality in certain areas of human life and experience which might be called "sacramental." To call them that is not to define them but to notice something about them. That quality may differ in various ways in the places where it is present, and it is possible that it might be seen elsewhere.

One modern scholar has suggested that we will come closest to Augustine's ideas if we approach the eucharist, for example, as an art-form — becoming involved in it and changed by it, as it resonates with different parts of our imagination and experience, and calls out the surprises, which are our experiences of grace, of insight and growth that we had not thought possible.[6]

Perhaps we can expand on that idea and suggest that the medieval theologians provided an explanation of the art-form they called "sacrament" — as we might explain music, theater, literature — in terms of categories and techniques rather than in terms of the joy experienced and the insights gained. Understanding the construction of a Bach fugue or the instrumentation of a Beethoven symphony may help us to understand the pleasure they give, but they are not the thing itself, and finally it is the thing itself which has an impact on our life. It is the concert, the drama, the sacrament itself which affects us.

The medieval explanation may still have a certain value, but it fails to answer the kinds of questions people ask now. For better or worse, our focus today seems to be on the experience more than on categorical analysis. So it is that Christians in our day are seeking a new language with which to discuss the deepest experiences of the Christian faith. That language, in turn, may help us to understand how God acts in the marriages of Christians. It is also significant that Christians of many different backgrounds seem to be looking for the same kind of language and learning to speak together.

As far back as the beginning of the twentieth century, P.T. Forsyth, a well-known English Congregationalist, was using words not unlike those of St. Augustine concerning the sacramental quality of marriage:

> [I]t is to be hoped that we shall never come to mere civil marriage, as if it only concerned society. . . . the more one ponders the solemn implications and slow effects of marriage, moral and spiritual, the more one feels that it has something sacramental in its nature. It may be less than a church sacrament, but it is a moral; it is certainly more than a contract. . . . If not a sacrament, it is a means of grace, it sweetens or hardens according as it is used. At any rate the ethical and social view of marriage is quite inadequate . . .[7]

Other Protestant theologians were slow to take up Forsyth's suggestion, but Donald Baillie, a Scottish Presbyterian, suggested in the 1950s that the modern concept of the "personal" might provide the best approach to understanding:

No man is living his true life if he is not living as a real person, in personal communication with other persons, and above all in that basic personal relationship with God which we call religion.[8]

This approach is echoed in the work of an American Roman Catholic theologian, Donald Gelpi, who wrote in 1993 of a personalist approach to the sacraments. He suggests we can appropriate the insight from the existentialist philosophers "that in the sacraments we encounter in a personally transforming way the God revealed in Jesus and in his sanctifying Breath."[9]

The English Methodist Trevor Rowe also speaks of sacraments in personal terms: "The sign displays, not only cosmic redemption on the grand scale, it makes effective that redemption in a particular human being."[10]

The American Roman Catholic Joseph Martos, has written that the theology of the sacraments settled on by the church of Rome at Trent "was rather limited, and that the Catholic church today is growing beyond those limitations." He suggests that "sacramentality . . . ought not to be restricted to the seven ecclesiastical sacraments" and that a number of new ways of thinking about the sacraments can be helpful.[11]

This feeling that the previous categories of Roman Catholic thought are too limited is not far from what an American Protestant theologian, James Nelson, has said about the traditional Protestant approach, that it is too limited and needs to be reexamined. He discusses that more open approach in terms specifically of marriage, and criticizes

> the overly sharp distinction between nature and grace, between marriage as an order of creation and marriage as a sacrament or order of redemption. Protestantism early insisted upon the former, holding marriage to be a worldly and not a sacramental institution. It has no redemptive significance. No one is saved through it. God has established it and its validity does not depend on the church's rites or on the couple's faith. . . . This view of marriage, however, tends to establish a sharp disjunction between nature and grace, a dualism of lower and higher orders that undercuts a fully incarnationalist theology wherein we might see that the whole creation and its embodied, fleshly relationships are potential media of God's healing and life-giving salvation.[12]

That phrase "overly sharp distinction" is a critical warning. The divisions between the churches are often a matter of insisting on statements more complete and more definite than others are prepared to make. A willingness to settle for common ground more often would enable us to move forward together more often.

What, then, can we say about marriage in the area of sacramental theology that will be true to our understanding of Scripture and Christian experience and helpful to a broad range of Christians? I would suggest that the first thing to say is that the word *sacrament* itself might well be considered optional. That word is coming back into wider use and has a certain value, but it also brings with it a long history of misunderstanding. Too often we have found ourselves doing arithmetic — are there two sacraments or three or seven or more? — when we should have been doing theology. We have been talking about the medium instead of the message. Perhaps we will do better to begin by thinking about marriage itself, and then, if we still have time and energy, we can look for an appropriate category to put it in, rather than to begin with a label or category and so prejudge the issues.

Human beings have a need to sort things out and put them in categories. It's the main work of some branches of science and helpful up to a point. If I've never seen an oak or a terrier, it can be helpful to be told that one is a tree and the other a dog. But if I've never seen broccoli and am told it's a vegetable, I may go looking for something like a carrot or tomato and never find broccoli at all. (In fact, is a tomato a vegetable or fruit? I've never been sure!) So, too, to be told that marriage is a sacrament leaves us looking for ways in which it may be like baptism or the eucharist and not looking for those things that are unique and distinctive about marriage itself.

Begin then with marriage itself: a man and a woman coming together out of a strange and wonderful mixture of sexual attraction, personal compatability, and mere happenstance. Notice also that the human race has since the beginning of history felt a need to surround that coming together with some ceremony and some continuing commitment. St. Augustine suggests that there is "something sacramental" about it, that there is an element of "mystery" — to use the older word — that there is an element beyond the human catching our attention. Sexuality by itself has a power and mystery about it; the human race has always felt a need to connect sexual expression with religious expression. Even the element of what we called "happenstance" makes us feel that a power beyond ourselves is at work. Popular songs very often express it in their own way: "Some enchanted evening, you may see a stranger . . . and somehow you know . . ." There are, of course, scientific dating services that will attempt to make the proper matches on a rational basis, but I suspect that even if a couple did come together in that way, they might still congratulate themselves on the good fortune, the providence, that took them to that particular dating service at just the right time. A couple may ponder their relationship, the rightness of the way it feels, the way they feel about themselves in each other's company and say, "This is bigger than both of us." The marriage process begins with that sense of mystery which we can, if we want, call "sacrament" — a sign of the mystery of God's presence.

That mystery, in turn, tends to be expressed in a personal way. All the traditional sacraments are centered on the personal, however impersonally sacramental theology has been expressed. Baptism has to do with the beginning of human life and the creation of new relationships. Eucharist has to do with the nurturing of human life and the building of relationships. Marriage, supremely, has to do with the creation of new life (quite apart from procreation a man and a woman give each other new life whether children come of it or not) and the building of relationships. If we like, we can call that "sacrament" also — a sign of the presence of a personal power working to create and nurture and build relationships in human life and beyond human life.

And then there is the physical. In a word, there is sex. And sex has to do with bodies coming together. I point out this fairly obvious fact because — I don't expect to be believed but I will provide references and footnotes — it has not always been noticed.

Karl Rahner, for example, one of the great Roman Catholic theologians of our day, has recognized also that there is a need for "a new point of departure" in contemporary discussion of the sacraments. He suggests that that point may be found in a common recognition by Protestants and Roman Catholics that the fundamental element in the sacraments is the word.

> All medieval and modern speculation concerned with rescuing a sacramental hylomorphism of matter and form, of element and word, in the case of these two sacraments [penance and marriage] amounts to nothing more than futile hairsplitting. There are, according to Catholic teaching, two sacraments which are effected in word only, and therefore the fundamental essence of the sacrament must really consist in word.[13]

Protestants, of course, have, historically, given God's word a central place in their thought and practice while Roman Catholics centered attention on the sacramental system. Rahner's emphasis on the word might be seen, then, as a great step toward Christian unity. Augustine also pointed to the word as a central element in the idea of sacrament.

But if the essential idea of a sacrament is that it is a material sign of the holy, how adequate is "word" as the essence of it? More to the point, how can we possibly talk about marriage as a sacrament with any of the traditional meaning of a material sign and then say that the essence of the sacrament is word? Can a word be a physical sign? If any of the traditional sacraments has a physical aspect, surely it is marriage. Rahner is historically correct: the medieval theologians did say that the essence of marriage was an exchange of promises, a verbal contract. They also said that consummation ratified the contract but, to preserve the tradition that Mary was a perpetual virgin though married, they insisted that consummation was not the essence. Surely we are entitled to ask whether the idea of "word" as essence takes seriously what marriage is all about. Like someone searching for broccoli in the carrot patch, if we look for marriage in the area of verbal exchange, we are unlikely to find the real thing.

Marriage is physical; sex is involved. Christians have been squeamish about that from the beginning, but Christianity is, if anything, a faith that takes material things seriously. God in Christ took flesh and blood, hung bleeding on a cross, and challenged his disciples to touch and feel his resurrected body. Likewise, therefore, in marriage the physical element is real and central. Charles Williams is the modern Christian teacher who expresses this best:

> In that intercourse which is usually referred to as the consummation of marriage the presence of Love, that is, of Christ, is sacramentally imparted by each to the other. If this act is not capable of being a sacrament, then it is difficult to see in what way marriage itself is more sacramental than any other occupation; and its inclusion in that group of rites which have the Eucharist as their crown is undeserved. [14]

If, then, we want to make continuing use of the idea of sacrament as central to our life of faith, we may do best to begin with marriage, since marriage, touching more human lives than even baptism and eucharist, is able to bring us to a deep awareness of the power of love — personal, thoroughly physical, yet transcending the physical — to change our lives for good.

So let me suggest that we turn the tables on the theologians and define the sacraments in terms of marriage. This is not altogether a new idea; we already noticed one medieval theologian who said that marriage was the first sacrament because it was given by God in Eden. Jeremy Taylor, likewise, said, "The first blessing God gave to man was society: and that society was a marriage." So list marriage as the primary sacrament: it is God's first gift, it is the most physical, it is most deeply involved in inter-personal relationships, it, most often of the various aspects of human life, confronts us with the profound mystery of human existence. Whatever is to be called a sacrament should be like that.

But we were not looking for categories to fit marriage into; we were looking for the thing itself. These elements, discovered in looking at marriage in terms of the category "sacrament," may provide a starting point in that exploration.

Having found my own way to open up the category "sacrament," it is important to recognize that others have done something similar in different ways. This is not a book about the sacraments nor is it possible to do justice to so complex a subject, but it may be useful to recognize briefly some other important points that are have been made recently.

First is the idea that the primary sacrament is the church or Christ himself. Karl Rahner, for example, has said that: "the Church is the primal and fundamental sacrament"[15] and Bernard Haring calls Christ "the great Sacrament."[16] However suggestive, even valid, it may be to call marriage the primary sacrament, there is enormous value in recognizing that whatever we call a sacrament (even if we prefer to use other terms for it) is an aspect of the life of the church and of Christ in the church. This recognition undercuts many of the disagreements over the sacraments. What does it matter, for example, whether we want to speak of two sacraments or seven, if we can see them all as secondary to the life of the church itself? It is the church which is the first sign and means of God's continuing presence among us. It is in the church (but not only in the church) that God is at work to transform human lives. Sacraments are a tool for that work, a means to an end; they have meaning and value only in that larger framework. To define marriage as sacramental is to assert, then, that God in Christ is at work in human lives; to speak of Christian marriage is to speak of that work as it takes place within the life of the Christian community.

Secondly, it is being said that baptism is the foundational sacrament, that every sacramental act draws us back to the "paschal mystery" of death and resurrection.[17] Baptism sets us in the church and first defines our relationship to each other and to God. Christian marriage has traditionally been defined by baptism. The fact that the persons being married are baptized is what first distinguishes Christian marriage from any marriage. Marriage is a particular calling for some of those who are baptized (which we will say more about later).

Finally, we are reminded that the idea of sacrament flows in the first place from an understanding of the world itself. Helen Oppenheimer writes that "the universe is sacramental through and through."[18] If it is true, as Walter Kasper suggests, that the idea of sacrament came to flower in the Middle Ages because that age was unable to hold onto the "sacral nature of reality," it remains true that a sacramental system enables us to hold on to the reality of the sacred in and through the material. Contemporary physics may be helping us to see the inadequacy of a world view that neatly divides all reality into "physical" or "spiritual" and may help us to arrive at a deeper understanding of God's presence than sacramental theology allows. Meanwhile, there is value in an approach that reminds us of the reality of God's presence in the physical world of creation. All marriage, like all life, has a sacramental quality.

"ONE FLESH," INDISSOLUBILITY, AND DIVORCE

"One flesh"

We will ask the question again: What is marriage? The answer "It is a sacrament" has a certain value but it is not an adequate answer. A carrot may be a vegetable, but the word "vegetable" is not a description of a carrot. It is only the name of a group of life-forms in which a carrot fits. The category tells us something but not everything; finally a carrot is a carrot, something unique, and must be known, if it is to be known at all, for the qualities it alone possesses. To use a different analogy: We can be told that Tokyo, Stockholm, and Kinshasa are all cities, that they are alike in having streets, people, offices, and homes. But if we therefore decide that travel is pointless — "If you've seen one city, you've seen them all" — we would, in fact, have seen nothing. So, too, marriage must be known for the distinctive qualities it alone possesses. Of these, perhaps the most prominent is lastingness.

The Bible and the theologians hold the same quality up in different ways. We are told that in marriage two people become "one flesh," that Christian marriage is "indissoluble." There is most obviously some sort of a unit formed when Ann and Alfred marry whether they are Christian or not. But few societies assume that that unit is indissoluble. Most societies make provision for the failure of that unit to remain united and allow divorce. Divorce was available under the law of Moses, but Jesus, when asked about divorce, replied in effect that the Mosaic law was a concession to human weakness and did not reflect God's purpose in creation.

So we are thrown back once again to the beginning and a single short verse in the Book of Genesis, chapter 2, verse 24: "Therefore a man leaves his father and his mother and clings to his wife, and they become one flesh." When we looked at Genesis before, we had slightly different questions to answer. Here are three words: " become one flesh." They stand at the center of Christian teaching. Each word requires careful study.

Question one: What is meant by *one* flesh? In the most literal terms, a man and a woman do not become one flesh; they remain two separate people. So the language used here must be intended to point to a deeper truth, perhaps a unity so deep that even the flesh itself seems joined.

Question two: What is meant by *flesh?* Hebrew, as we said before, has no word for the separate human body, only a word for the flesh all humanity has in common. So all humanity is already one flesh, and a man and a woman cannot be any different in that respect after their marriage than before. Perhaps we hear this verse as saying, "they become one *body*," but that is not the meaning. There is obviously an implication of deep unity, but a simple, literal reading says either too much or too little.

We should notice that St. Paul uses this terminology to discuss an extra-marital sexual relationship and reads "one flesh"as meaning "one body"): "Do you not know that whoever is united to a prostitute becomes one body with her? For it is said, 'The two shall be one flesh.'"[19]

But surely there is no idea of indissolubility here even so. Sexual relations of any sort are to be taken with very great seriousness. A potentially sacramental unity misused is blasphemous; it is to "take the members of Christ and make them members of a prostitute."[20] But it does not create a sacramental bond: love, friendship, faithfulness, God's presence, all the qualities that make for sacramentality are missing. A simple, literal reading, to repeat, says either too much or too little.

Question three: What is meant by *become?* When we say that Abraham Lincoln "became" president of the United States, we are talking about the outcome of a lengthy process, not something that happened immediately. When we say a man and a woman get married and "become" one flesh, do we necessarily mean that it happens in a moment, at the altar or during the first act of sexual intercourse — or over a longer span of time as they come to understand and respond to each other with the effortless grace of skilled dancers? One rabbinic tradition believes that the phrase "they become one flesh" refers to the child born of the marriage who, in one human body, contains the genes of both parents. But that, also, is not an immediate development; it takes at least nine months. And that would seem to indicate that we should hear the verb "become" as opening up for us a passage of time *during which* a joining together gradually becomes reality.

This is not a playing with words but an attempt to give the words their full meaning, to take them with very great seriousness. They would not have survived so long if they were not capable of such serious study. The implication of these words as we study them in these questions and answers is that we are being asked to look forward to the outcome of a process through which a man and a woman come to share each other's life so fully that the separateness of their bodies' flesh is no longer so noticeable or significant as the unity of their deepest being.

We should also remember that beyond what Jesus said about "one flesh" there is the critically important passage in Ephesians 5.* That passage tells us that we are talking about Christ and the church. Of course, Christ and the church are even less literally "one flesh" than husband and wife. Very clearly, we are using words to point to something beyond words. And may there not also be an aspect of that Christ-church relationship which is incomplete, still becoming? Ultimately Christ and the church will be perfectly one but they are not yet. There is, however, a profound sense in which the value and even the nature of something is known by its potential rather than its immature form. A child has value as a child, but even more as a potential adult. The whole abortion controversy turns on that same point, and few on either side would think of an embryo as mere extraneous tissue: it has enormous potential, and decisions made for or against an abortion need always to bear that in mind. The church as we know it is very far from the glorious bride of Christ it is destined to be, but we cannot merely dismiss it as a hopeless jumble of failed humanity. It is in some sense already what it is called to be and is loved and valued for that partly-glimpsed potential.**

We come here to a view of marriage that is very different from the one traditionally taught by the church. We begin to think of marriage in terms of a process rather than an event, a promise rather than a given, a vision rather than a status. Marriage is a calling, a vocation. Every calling or vocation leads through a period of preparation to a time when the one called is licensed to practice, but even then a vocation requires continued growth if the potential is to be fulfilled. No doctor can rest content with what was learned in medical school nor any priest with what was learned in seminary. For that matter, no baptized Christian

---

*See chapter four, pp. 85-88.

**Perhaps we should also remember how the words God spoke to Moses (Exodus 3.14) are sometimes translated "I will be who I will be." "The consensus of modern scholarship supports the Biblical text in associating the name Yahweh with the root *haya* [hayah], 'become.' *(Theological Dictionary of the Old Testament,* ed. G. Johannes Botterweck and Helmer Ruggren, William B. Eerdmans Publishing Company, Grand Rapids, Michigan, 1986.) Is there a sense in which God's own being is also a becoming?

acquires all the gifts of grace and understanding of them and skill in using them at the moment of baptism, even if they are baptized as adults. So Donald Gelpi has written of marriage as being, like baptism, a "sacrament of on-going conversion" and says that marriage "poses then a practical moral challenge that precludes understanding its sacramentality as a metaphysical given."[21]

In a similar way, to focus more narrowly on the idea of marriage as indissoluble, Mackin calls it a "condition-to-be-attained"[22] and Schillebeeckx calls it "a vocation, a commission to be realized despite and through a host of obstacles."[23] One of the difficulties with the medieval definition of marriage as something contracted by the mutual consent of the partners and ratified by the first act of sexual intercourse is that it pins the entire sacrament to two brief moments. Even to speak of the first act of sexual intercourse in marriage as "consummation" is, as Charles Williams pointed out, to rob words of their meaning:

> It is of course nothing of the sort; at best it is the channel by which a deeper marriage is instituted; the consummation, however it may be in this act signified, foretold, and hastened, is usually far away in the Divine Life.[24]

Theodore Mackin agrees:

> It is simply not believable that one act at its outset can complete the marriage's imaging of, or incorporation in, Christ's redemptive love for his people.[25]

A useful, if unexpected, analogy may be found in the way motor cars are built. There was a day when American manufacturers believed that a complete inventory of all the required parts should be on hand before beginning to build. In recent years they have adopted a new system, learned from Japanese manufacturers, called "just in time" supplying. Rather than build up big and expensive inventories, supplies are timed to arrive at the moment they are needed. Marriage, too, needs exactly that "just in time" supply of grace; it cannot be inventoried and handed over at the altar. Marriage is more than a moment; it is for that reason that the theologians have come more and more to rely on terms like "development" and "process."

Of course, this language has its hazards also. It has been criticized as preventing us from calling anyone married until they are dead.[26] Two responses can be made. In the first place, it may be true that "final and absolute immunity to dissolution is a goal not attainable in this life," but it does seem possible that over time a marriage should reach a point at which habitual commitment will make it all but indissoluble.[27] Many years of a stable relationship are unlikely to be jettisoned on a sudden impulse — or even in a gradual transformation of character. Secondly, the Western church might do well to consider the Eastern church's view that marriage is not made only "till death us do part," but for eternal life as well. Christian marriage is no mere earthly union of sexual bodies but an eternal bond that will continue in the risen bodies of the kingdom. As a union of two beings in love it provides a foretaste of eternity when we will be one in Christ and Christ will be "all in all."[28] To call no couple married until that Day may be a truer perspective and a wiser understanding.

At this point, however, two warnings may be in order. In the first place, this view of marriage can result in a notion that marriage comes in a "do-it-yourself" kit. When Mackin interprets Schillebeeckx as saying that "like indissolubility, the sacrament in a marriage is not there a priori and given. The spouses put it there by their decision and their work," marriage begins to sound like a problem to be solved or a chore to be carried out. But God is at work in a marriage, as in all of life, and the gift of God's love *is* a priori and given. Our work would be wasted without it. Of course we need to respond to the grace we are given, but a grim determination to make it work would be self-defeating. Responding to love may be a challenge, but it should not become a chore.

Secondly, a "process" approach to marriage might tend to diminish the seriousness of the commitment made. We may be tempted to treat marriage more lightly because it has not yet arrived at its full growth and realized its final potential. But perhaps the reverse is true. We are prone to value children above adults just because of their unfulfilled potential. ("Women and children first!" is the ancient cry to preserve potential life.) Likewise, an immature marriage might be handled with greater care just because the calling is so high and the vision so far from realized. All freedom can be abused, but that is no reason to reject it. A cage protects but it also constrains.

The medieval theology of marriage recognized its holiness and calling to permanence at the cost of freedom. In searching for language to correct that imbalance, we ought to make every effort not to concentrate so completely on freeing ourselves from the burden of legalism that we lose sight of the vision of lasting unity.

To understand marriage as vocation may enable the church to deal more easily with failed marriages, but that should not be seen as its primary value. Surely all marriages are enhanced by a perspective that sees each one as holding unfulfilled potential, that sees marriage as a gift to grow into, that understands that the fiftieth year of a marriage may hold more joy than the first.

Divorce, annulment, failure

How does an understanding of marriage as process and vision affect the traditional church teaching that marriage is indissoluble? Few issues have caused so much agony in the church in recent years as how to hold to that doctrine in a society where one-third to one-half the population goes through at least one divorce. Can those who have apparently disregarded the church's teaching remain communicant members in good standing? Can they remarry in the church? If they remarry outside the church, what is the status of that marriage?

Slowly and reluctantly, in the second half of the twentieth century, even those churches that have opposed divorce most strongly have come to recognize that failed marriages are a reality that cannot be ignored.

In a larger sense, of course, the church has always recognized a need to deal with failed marriages. St. Paul wrote to the Corinthians about it and felt no compunctions about directing that unbelieving spouses should be allowed to depart. We cannot tell whether those who did so were then counted as the "unmarried" for whom "if they are not practicing self-control . . . it is better to marry than to be aflame with passion."[29] Sometimes the church did interpret Paul's words that way and the Western church extended the so-called "Pauline privilege" to several other types of marriage as well.[30] Popes and penitential books allowed remarriage in circumstances ranging from impotence to the taking of monastic vows. Few of these circumstances fit easily into a high doctrine of marital unity in "one flesh." Theodore Mackin points back to the twelfth century and comments that when Pope Alexander III ruled that only sacramental marriages cannot be dissolved, he "finished undermining the position that marriage is of its nature indissoluble."[31]

Whatever is said in this book should not be allowed to ease the pain and failure of a failed marriage or the conflict between the Christian vision of marriage and the fact of such failure. Whether we prefer to speak of divorce, annulment, or simple failure, what has happened is inconsistent with the Christian doctrine of marriage and leaves the church torn between clinging to a valued ideal and ministering to those who need healing. Every major church today makes a wider provision for a ministry to those whose marriages have failed than it did in the past. Some churches feel more compelled to justify that wider provision for ministry than others, but the priority appears to be in the ministry rather than the justification. Jesus taught that the laws were made for human beings, not human beings for the law. Perhaps that is justification enough.

It is important, however, to understand the approach being taken by the Roman Catholic church both because that involves the largest number of Christians and because it seeks hardest to reconcile law and compassion. Gelpi suggests that a marriage can cease to have a sacramental quality, that the process of marriage can come to a halt and even cease to exist:

> If the sacramentality of Christian marriage flows from the transformation of marital love that Christian conversion effects, then the absence of conversion may desacramentalize married life as well. When spouses refuse to forgive one another with the love of atonement, when they relate to one another out of sinful self-reliance rather than from faith, when they selfishly withhold from one another parts of themselves or their personal possessions, when their lives together embody secular, class values rather than the vision of the kingdom, then their relationship to one another ceases to image forth the life of God.[32]

The Roman Catholic church has not officially moved that far, but it has in recent years adopted a policy that does seem to move in that direction while holding fast to the belief that marriage is a given and a married couple cannot be divorced. The church has always had a process called annulment. If it is discovered that a true marriage could never have taken place because essential elements were lacking, the marriage can be declared null and void. Thus, if one party was not of legal age, not mentally competent, or acting under compulsion, an annulment could be granted; free, competent consent was impossible and therefore no true marriage existed. Now the Roman church has added to the list of grounds for annulment the lack of "psychological readiness for marriage."

Theodore Mackin explains this by describing a typical couple, Ian and Margaret, who, as time goes by, find that their goals for their lives and marriage are driving them further and further apart. It's a familiar story. He has a career; she has small children. He feels a need to succeed in his work; she wants his company and support. These different needs are deeply ingrained in them, a part of their psychological makeup. A wise counselor might have anticipated that this issue would inevitably arise sooner or later and might have urged that they not be married. (Whether they would have heeded such advice is another question!) So, when Margaret applies for annulment of her marriage, it is granted on the ground that the full consent necessary to a marriage could never have been given. It is an attempt to deal with the reality of divorce while holding to the teaching of indissolubility. Is it a satisfactory solution? I would argue that it is not, that it continues to see marriage as a given and to analyze it in terms of what happened at the moment of marriage as if nothing else mattered. That was, perhaps, the way our ancestors understood life; it is not how people understand life today.

Let me tell you a story. Once upon a time, in a hypothetical world, there were two sets of identical twins, John and Bill, Mary and Sue, who grew up, met, fell in love, and married. John married Mary and Bill married Sue; I don't know how they told each other apart, but twins do somehow know. Since this is a hypothetical world, I will ask you to believe that their backgrounds were as identical as their genes and that the psychological readiness for marriage of both couples was identical. They received instruction, understood it as well as they were able, and set out to live happily ever after. For five years they led identical lives and their love developed in response to the stresses of early marriage. They might well have continued to grow identically except that the corporation for which they both worked then transferred John and Mary to Tokyo while leaving Bill and Sue in Peoria. Mary and John couldn't handle it. Mary was suddenly cut off from her family and friends and familiar surroundings at a time when she was already feeling unsupported. Now she needed John's support more than ever, but John was busy trying to find his way around in a new set of circumstances and trying to impress his company with his ability to do it. He had little energy left over to meet Mary's need for support; on the contrary, he wanted her to support him. Bill and Sue couldn't have handled it either, but they didn't have to. So tensions grew between John and Mary, and finally Mary flew home to Peoria, talked to a lawyer, and in due time was divorced from John. A few more years went by and John met Jill while Mary met Manfred. They went to their parish priests, went through the long and complicated procedures to obtain annulments, were granted them, remarried, and lived happily ever after.

Now, what was the difference between the two first marriages? There was no difference at the outset, but at a critical time the one marriage remained in a setting where the support of family, friends, neighbors, and parish was available. The other was removed from that context and, lacking support, their marriage failed. But clearly the issue was not the psychological readiness of one couple at the time of marriage; neither couple had that. The issue was grace or good luck — maybe both — five years down the road. There was nothing internal to the marriage that failed to distinguish it from the marriage that lasted; both were vulnerable, but only one was subjected to the external circumstances that could destroy it.

I tell this story not to criticize the methodology of the Roman Catholic church which is doing the best it can with the hand it's been dealt, but to illustrate the thesis that a marriage is not made in a moment at the altar; a marriage is formed over time and the formative factors are very often external to the marriage itself.

Ask a roomful of happily married couples how many were "psychologically prepared" for marriage and few if any would claim that they were. If we had the testing equipment to determine who was psychologically ready, how many marriages would take place? If grace is given in marriage, it needs to be given on a "timed-release" basis. Every couple has a continuing need of such grace.

The fact is, we do not know what makes a good marriage nor do we know what God's grace can accomplish in particular individuals. Every "successful" marriage is, in a real sense, a miracle of God's grace and every failed marriage reveals the potential for tragedy in us all.

Must we then say that the church has been wrong, that marriage is not indissoluble? It was, after all, not until the twelfth century that the notions of indissolubility and contract were brought together to form a new type of contract that could not be voided even by those who made it.[33] Further, the popes made many exceptions to the notion of indissolubility over the centuries. No, the need is not to teach that marriage is a voidable contract but to see that lastingness is a quality acquired over time. Marriage has to do with a human mirror of a divine relationship. It is meant to reflect God's faithfulness, and the inadequacy of the mirror tells us little about the object so dimly seen. Every marriage bond should therefore be treated as if it were in fact what it is not yet, but what it is called to be. Those who fall short can be allowed to separate, reluctantly and sorrowfully, without in any way denying the validity of the goal. No individual attains to perfection in this life and no human marriage fulfills its potential. But perfection remains our calling and the potential remains to be fulfilled. Indissolubility — or, more positively, lastingness — is the vision toward which we are called, and some marriages (a surprising number, in fact) do bear witness to the reality of that vision.

Human marriage is called to lastingness because it is intended to mirror the relationship between Christ and his church. We are to be faithful because God is faithful. But it should be noted that even the relationship between God and the people of God is not proof against the possibility of divorce. The prophets compared the relationship between God and Israel to a marriage relationship and Israel's faithlessness to adultery. Jeremiah goes further and says that God did divorce the northern kingdom (Israel) and that the southern kingdom (Judah) should be warned.*** God can divorce a faithless people; God's faithfulness does not annul human freedom. Here again, indissolubility is not absolute even when God is one of the partners; it is a goal, not a given.

The point is also made that we may presume too much when we proclaim at the end of a marriage service, "What God has joined together let no one put asunder," as if there were no doubt at all that that is what has now happened. Did Jesus really intend us to understand that whenever a couple exchange marriage vows, it is God's doing? Do human beings never make mistakes? Or does God, in this case, insist that we must live with the mistake for the rest of our lives? To be sure, even if it was not God but fallible human beings who made the marriage, it has a potential sacramentality about it. The doctrine of "one flesh" is surely as applicable here as the union St. Paul speaks of with a prostitute. But many theologians today would consider that a marriage made without an informed faith and a truly discerned vocation lacks sacramentality. God alone can join a couple in the sacrament.[34] I insist again, this is serious business; no separation is without pain. If no marriage is to be entered into "unadvisedly or lightly," that may be even more true of divorce. A bad marriage can probably be more easily redeemed than an unwise divorce.

One final point on this subject: The possibility of divorce is a threat to every marriage, but human freedom holds more potential than does artificial constraint. The words about marriage written by the Anglican Bishops at Lambeth in 1958 apply here as well. The greater freedom we have to order our marriages may involve risk, but it may be "also, and equally, a gate to a new depth and joy in personal relationships between husband and wife."[35]

Good marriages thrive because partners are committed to each other and God's grace is at work, not because the partners are compelled to be together by law. Love involves risk; all who risk in the venture of marriage will be hurt; some will not survive; but those who do will know a depth of joy that can come only out of testing and triumph.

This, then, is what marriage is. The love between two human beings, whoever they are, has the same vocation and the same potential. Every marriage reflects in some measure God's love for humankind. Where love is at work, God is at work. There is in every marriage a sacramental

---

***"She saw that for all the adulteries of that faithless one, Israel, I had sent her away with a decree of divorce; yet her false sister Judah did not fear, but she too went and played the whore" (Jeremiah 3.8).

quality, a mystery beyond our understanding through which we are able to come nearer the purpose of human life.

Marriage itself

We come back, then, to the question of what marriage is in itself and we find its meaning in mystery. There is something about marriage that remains always beyond our grasp or vision. Our vision is, perhaps, like that of the moon seen through broken clouds as we catch a glimpse of one aspect and another, but never the thing entire. And we find ourselves reduced to saying, "It is like this . . . and like this . . . and like this." The wonder of that mystery is that the likenesses given are so close to the nature of God. A marriage is meant to be like God in faithfulness, like the relationship between Christ and the church, like the unity of the triune God.

The Trinity may, in fact, give us a critically important image, for there at the heart of the Christian faith we find what we ought to find in a marriage: distinction of persons in ultimate unity. Nothing could be more distinctive than the person of Christ beside us, the Spirit within us, the Creator who is source and goal of all life — yet all that each is, the other is; where one is at work, God is at work. A good marriage is indeed like that, as, over time, each partner reflects the other more fully and is known and present in the other while remaining uniquely herself or himself. What marriage is and will be gives us an insight into the ultimate being of God.

And, finally, if all marriage has this potential, is there a distinctive quality about the marriage of Christians? Christopher Brooke is an historian, not a theologian, but in a book about medieval marriage, Brooke paused for a personal statement. For that reason, because it has the quality of a personal testimony, I end this section with his words:

> For many of us married folk God's blessing on our marriage is central to our faith, indistinguishable from the graces and blessings we receive in these other ways. If it has not received God's special blessing my faith is void; and for that reason to deny the word sacrament to marriage seems to me wrong, misleading, a play on words. . . . It is evident that one may achieve the quality of Christian marriage without the faith. And that to me is the point: it is precisely because my faith in God's blessing on human marriage is deeply united to my faith in God that I believe Christian marriage to be sacramental — God's grace can be showered on man in innumerable hidden ways; but faith in Christ and in Christian marriage can only be united in a Christian.[36]

CHAPTER ELEVEN

What Is Marriage For?

M arriage has been defined in the past in terms of purpose: Having children, propagating the species. In our time, these goals are secondary for most and irrelevant to many. Though the church has been reluctant to define marriage in terms of love, that definition may be not only what we need but a more adequate fulfillment of the biblical vision.

VIRGINITY, MARRIAGE, AND FREEDOM

Human beings can "invent" but not create; we can find things out and recombine existing elements, but we can never make something from nothing. So, when it comes to "reinventing" marriage, what we really mean is the recombining of existing elements or using them in new ways. We have looked at the elements of marriage as they have been combined and recombined over the centuries. We have seen some elements brought forward and others rejected. Simultaneous polygamy has faded from favor but consecutive polygamy has become common. Dowries have gone out of fashion but college tuitions cost even more. Civil ceremonies have been incorporated into church sacraments and sacraments have been rejected again in favor of civil ceremonies. Where do we go from here?

Perhaps out of sheer contrariness, let me begin a reconstruction by dusting off the element the early Christians knew as chastity or virginity. When the early Christians praised celibacy and relegated marriage to the status of second choice, what were they really saying? They lived in a different world than ours and spoke a different language. We have trouble hearing them accurately. We like to get a committee report in official language supported by a public opinion poll; they tended to make their points by shouting. Remember St. Basil saying the one who makes a fourth marriage is a pig? Remember Calvin saying that he had "pulled the lion's skin from these asses"? They had no polls or committee reports to give weight to their words so instead they were impolite. And that makes it hard for us to listen. But what the early Christians were really saying when they commended celibacy was, "The resurrection of Christ has changed our values so radically that we no longer depend on marriage and posterity to give our lives meaning. Christ gives our lives eternal value — so who needs children?"

St. Paul says almost exactly that in his first letter to the Corinthians:

> I think that, in view of the impending crisis, it is well for you to remain as you are. Are you bound to a wife? Do not seek to be free. Are you free from a wife? Do not seek a wife . . . The present form of this world is passing away. I want you to be free from anxieties.[1]

Of course, Paul sets his argument more in terms of the second coming than of the resurrection — if Christ comes again before we die, even resurrection is unimportant — but the point is the same: This world is not a place of lasting values; God's kingdom is. Therefore, since we know the reality of that kingdom, we are free of the compulsion to preserve a name for ourselves in this world by marriage and childbearing. We are free to develop relationships out of love rather than need.

Why did the people of Israel and Greece and Rome put such a value on marriage and children? Because deep in the human psyche is a need for eternal value and, without the resurrection, only children can "make a name for us"; only if we have children will anyone know that we have been here.

But what a fragile hope that is, and what a weight it puts on us and, for that matter, on our children. What if their values are different from mine? Does that make me a failure — or are they compelled to accept my values and my priorities, bend themselves to my shape to pay tribute to me for giving them life? Human beings are the supreme individualists of creation. A bluebird migrates from the same clearing in Connecticut to the same patch of jungle in Mexico that bluebirds have inhabited for a million years; to change is to die. Each groundhog makes the same kind of burrows other groundhogs have made for a million years; to change is to die. But human beings are free: A lawyer's daughter can become a sculptor; a teacher's son can become a nurse; the farmer's child can move to the city and sell insurance. This is not a rejection of our parents: It is a human need to explore and create and reinvent. To allow our children to be themselves sets them free and frees us also. But most of us have — inherited from our neolithic ancestors, perhaps — a nagging need to have children who will image us and preserve our name. We need others to whom to leave the photo albums even if they never look at them again. We forget too easily what the first Christians knew.

When the first Christians said, "Virginity is better," it was really another way of saying: "Christ is risen. My life has eternal value to God so there is no need to stamp my image on perishable flesh and blood. The physical compulsion of earlier ages is dead. Who needs marriage? Who needs children? We have been set free." "If the world is now perishing," Augustine wrote, "the married woman, for whom beareth she?"[2]

> Now this propagation of children which among the ancient saints was a most bounden duty for the purpose of begetting and preserving a people for God . . . now has no longer the same necessity. . . . We may acknowledge that the scripture which says "there is a time to embrace, and a time to refrain from embracing," is to be distributed in its clauses to the periods before Christ and since. The former was the time to embrace, the latter to refrain from embracing.[3]

Begin with the assertion of freedom. We are neither bluebirds nor groundhogs. We do not all need to marry and have children to be fulfilled. That does *not* mean that none of us should marry or have children, and most of the early Christians were clear about that as well; the groups who condemned marriage totally were always rejected as heretical. What it does mean is that *if* we marry and *if* we have children, we do it as a free act of love and not from any need or compulsion. We love out of love alone, not from mere animal urgency. That puts sex in its proper place — though the rest of the world (and often Christians as well) has yet to understand what that is.

Now, we probably won't want to speak of this as virginity — people won't hear us. We will probably want to talk in terms of freedom and vocation: Christian marriage is a calling, a response to a vision. If everyone were required to be married, it would not be a vocation. But if there are alternatives — if celibacy, for example, is also an honored vocation — then the calling of marriage can be freely chosen or not.

For us, sex is not the be-all and end-all of life, but an aspect of our lives that can be offered in love to the God who values us, who gave us life, and who promises that we will live forever in our own being, not merely in children and grandchildren. Married or unmarried, childless or not, we have a name that will endure because God has called us by name and will know us by name forever.

So the first thing we need to say in reinventing marriage is that marriage is not for everyone; children are not for everyone; each human being is unique and has a particular vocation. Each human being has a unique and irreplaceable value in the eyes of God. As God could say to

Moses "I AM WHO I AM," so we can say "I AM WHO I AM." I am valued not for my children or my marriage but for myself. That is the gift of freedom. With that gift in hand, I can begin to construct a new understanding of marriage.

PROCREATION

Gifts come in many disguises. When we open the strange-shaped package under the Christmas tree, we may be moved to ask several different questions: What is it? or What's it for? or Who made it? or How do you make one of these? All of these are useful and natural questions, but we will get quite different answers depending on which one we ask.

The question about marriage that interested the first Christian theologians was not what marriage is, but what it is for. That is an interesting and important question and one which practical people like ourselves should think about. Most people assume they know already, or, more likely, they are too preoccupied with the business of making a marriage even to ask what they are doing or why. Many people will stop to ask what marriage is all about only after they are involved in one, and maybe only after they decide they want out. But you are reading this book and have time to ask these questions. We should try to have good answers for ourselves and any others who might stop to ask. An unexamined marriage can be tragic.

The first question Christian theologians, being — like most of the human race — pragmatists, tended to ask was "What is marriage for?" St. Augustine makes numerous references to the fifth chapter of Ephesians which has a lot to say about what marriage is (or is "like") but he sees it only as information about what the church is like, and never about marriage in itself. And when he does talk about marriage, he is concerned to analyze only its purpose, not its essence. He enumerates three "goods" of marriage: Offspring, faithfulness, and the sacramental bond.[4] Cranmer also lists three purposes of marriage: procreation, a remedy against lust, and mutual fellowship. The first two are, for Augustine, two sides of one coin: Marriage serves as a remedy against lust by having procreation as its purpose,[5] but Cranmer is dubious about sacramentality and rounds out the necessary threesome in this way. Either way, from the beginnings of the church through the Reformation and down almost to our own time, the first thing the church has had to say about marriage is that procreation is its purpose.

The Middle Ages asked a different question: how is marriage made? Just as they asked about the eucharist—how and when is the sacrament made?—so they asked about marriage: what makes it come into being?

The answer that a marriage is made by consent and consummation has much to commend it. But they assumed, with marriage as with the eucharist, that an instant and permanent change can take place. Although they lived in a world of great change as we do, they thought of it as stable, or perhaps they tried to make it stable with a fixed and stable theology. We, however, believe the world to be part of a constantly evolving and changing universe, and are less satisfied with the rather static theology we inherited from the past.

We are also concerned, as they were, to know purposes and to understand the process by which change comes about, but we live in a very different world and see these questions in a very different light. As infant mortality rates have declined, for example, social conditions have changed, procreation has become a lower priority, and theology once again has changed in response to the new circumstances in which people live.

It has always been so. The view that procreation is the primary purpose of marriage was derived, as we have seen, primarily from secular sources. The New Testament itself says almost nothing about procreation. Jesus himself said nothing about it, nor does the great passage in the fifth chapter of Ephesians. A careful study of the early church theologians, moreover, reveals not so much an enthusiasm for procreation as a somewhat embarrassed acceptance of its necessity. The central importance of procreation was, after all, the nearly unanimous tradition of Jews and Gentiles alike and, besides, it seemed to them that it provided a justification for sexual intercourse, a rationale for an otherwise irrational act. Once established, that logic became deeply entrenched and modified only with the greatest difficulty. But it has been modified. The Reformation, in rejecting the monastic tradition, put a new emphasis on the unity of husband and wife. The 1983 revision of the Code of Canon Law of the Roman Catholic church marriage calls marriage a "partnership . . . ordered to the well-being of the spouses and to the procreation and upbringing of children."[6]

Social conditions have changed and theology is changing in response. Augustine's view that there were already enough people in the world to fulfill God's purpose now makes very good sense to most of us. Secular governments that once saw people as power now see increasing numbers as an economic detriment. The government of China, unhampered by a tradition of Christian theology, has taken Draconian measures to limit its population. Beyond that, the increased span of human life means that childbearing, for many couples, will only be possible for less than half the span of their marriage. Marriage in one's early thirties allows a maximum of ten years of childbearing but the possibility of forty or fifty years of married life beyond that. The proportion of those marrying after their childbearing years is also increasing. So procreation has been sliding down the scale of priorities, but no real effort has been made to fix its place in a reoriented theology of marriage. How can we continue to speak of procreation as the first of three "goods" of marriage when most marriages for most of their span will not be able to produce that good? Perhaps the time has come to respond not to social and economic pressures but to the clues that Scripture and tradition give us and begin to build a new way of looking at procreation.

Traditionally, Christians have interpreted the first chapters of Genesis as containing a command to procreate. In the light of an apparently universal assumption that procreation was an essential human function, the church grounded its theology in that presumed command. Had the social consensus been what it is now, however, the church might have read Genesis with more care and seen other aspects of it.

The church might have noticed, for example, that God is said to have created a second human being because the first had no appropriate companion. So the creation of male and female was for companionship, not procreation. The story of Adam and Eve mentions procreation directly only after the Fall and then in terms of the woman's punishment. But the man's punishment is to till the ground, and no one has ever suggested that all men must therefore be farmers.

It is true that the other creation story, in chapter one of Genesis, speaks of being fruitful as soon as male and female are created, but the church has never interpreted that as a universal command or it could not have sanctioned and promoted celibacy. Indeed, even the Roman Catholic church does not teach that all marriage and every sexual act must be procreative. Rather, it has taught that there must be no "artificial" prevention of conception. Marital abstinence on the model of Joseph and Mary is acceptable; so is intercourse during a woman's infertile period; so is the marriage of those who are infertile or beyond the age of childbearing. Augustine states clearly that an infertile marriage is as sacramental and indissoluble as any other. Those of other religions might divorce an infertile wife and marry again, but Christians agreed that the sacramental bond could not be broken even so. Indeed, when the first good of marriage was no longer possible, it seemed to Augustine that a marriage might at last come into its own, "the purer by how much it is the more proved, the safer, by how much it is the calmer."[7] Many older couples today would say "Amen" to that.

Apart, then, from the question of the means of family planning, there seems to be a solid Christian consensus that mere procreation is not an indispensable aspect of every marriage. If Adam and Eve are taken to represent the human race, the human race as a whole may be under orders to replenish the earth, but not every man and woman is necessarily included. Those with a vocation to celibacy have always been considered free of such a command. If, then, we are able to speak of a vocation to celibacy and a vocation to marriage, should we not also be able to speak of a vocation to procreation?

We do not really know what the optimum population of the world may be or whether we may need to concern ourselves some day with populating other planets. Perhaps we could feed earth's present population adequately if resources were fairly shared, but in the present state of our knowledge, we cannot see a way to provide a good life — one with room for other species and a balanced ecosystem and a chance to be alone with one's thoughts — for a population much greater than we now have reached, and perhaps even that is too large.

We see also that a great many human beings in the societies we are now building are unwilling or unable to set aside the necessary time to provide the sort of care and nurture of children that will enable children to grow in grace and develop their full potential. The problem of children having children will not be solved by esoteric discussions of the theology of marriage, but those people, unfortunately, are not likely to come to the church for premarital counseling. Those who do come are very often men and women who are working hard to establish their chosen careers and for whom the decision to have a child is not easy. For many, it is a decision postponed until after thirty and, for many, the presence of a child may be an unwelcome burden. For many, the decision to have a child may seem, for various reasons, an impossibility. Ruth Silbermann tells one such story:

> One woman who wanted to marry but never did, said that her reason stemmed from a real terror of repeating the experience of her own mother who had given birth to an epileptic child, and another who was severely retarded. This woman would have been happy to adopt, and the man she hoped to marry was understanding and agreeable. But no priest was willing to witness such a marriage as sacramental, and they were chided for lack of faith and courage . . . . Such a waste of love is savage.[8]

In their ministry to such couples, then, it seems high time that the clergy and other counselors speak of childbearing as a vocation not given to all. That is not a negative position; it is a challenge to raise the vocation of parenting to a higher level. Why should we treat this most demanding of all human responsibilities as something that anyone can fulfill who has the normal sexual equipment? Loving and caring for children takes more than that; it requires love and patience and a willingness to sacrifice self. These are desirable characteristics in every human being, but they are not equally present in all. Already most people in the more developed countries are using the means available, and those in less developed societies are being urged to use them, to plan their parenthood. Protestant and Catholic theologies alike have often exalted parenthood as a supreme good; it is good, but there are other vocations as well. Teachers, medical professionals, clergy, and many others also, married or not married, parents themselves or not, help fulfill the command to replenish the earth as they help to create a society in which children are properly nurtured. Why should we assume that the fruitfulness of the whole human race must be literally and directly fulfilled in each of its members?

Let us say, then, that procreation is one value that may be found in marriage, a vocation given to some, a responsibility to be shared by all.

LOVE

"Joy and hope" were the opening words of the final declaration of the Second Vatican Council. *Gaudium et Spes,* as it is known to its friends, summarizes the church's understanding of its role in the world, and it speaks, of course, of marriage. "The intimate partnership of married life and love has been established by the Creator," said the bishops.[9] What could be less controversial than that? In fact, it generated a controversy that raged for years. Did the council mean to say that love was of the essence of marriage? "No," said Pope Paul VI; love is not a bad thing to find in a marriage, but it is not essential to it.[10]

Was Heloise right, then? Are love and marriage two separate kinds of relationship that not even the skills of twentieth-century science and psychiatry can bring together? The pope seemed to believe they are, and he was by no means alone in his opinion; eminent theologians and experts in marriage law agreed. So did an American psychiatrist, Don D. Jackson, who defined it, in the title of a book as one of "The Mirages of Marriage." Jackson and his co-author, William Lederer, enumerate the following "false assumptions":

(1) that people marry because they love each other
(2) that most married people love each other
(3) that love is necessary for a satisfactory marriage.[11]

So that takes care of that! But we need to think this through very carefully because, as *Gaudium et Spes* insists, love and marriage are not totally unrelated. But what is the relationship, and how does it function?

We can begin by gathering together the evidence that marriage and love are separate. The Book of Genesis (always the first place to look) makes no reference to either love or marriage in the story of Adam and Eve. Eve was brought to Adam as a companion and, after the Fall, they "knew" each other and raised Cain. Presumably their relationship would qualify as a common-law marriage, but whether they "loved" each other we are never told.

Love is not one of the "goods" of marriage cited by Augustine. Love is not one of the purposes of marriage cited by Cranmer's marriage service in the Book of Common Prayer. Augustine does speak of "fidelity" as the second "good" of marriage, but by that he means primarily the avoidance of adultery. "A member of Christ," he writes, "ought to be afraid of adultery . . . and ought to hope to receive from Christ the reward of that fidelity which he shows to his spouse."[12] Cranmer speaks more positively of "mutual help and comfort." Clearly the emphasis is not on love; how could it have been in an age when many marriages were arranged and the purpose of marriage was an economic partnership and procreation?

There are also substantial authorities who question whether love as we think of it could have existed in the High Middle Ages or even the seventeenth century. We suggested that there are reasons to question their findings, but love in the modern sense cannot be simply assumed to have existed in former ages. Love "as we think of it" is, however, an important qualification; Mackin suggests that only in recent times have people seen marriage as we see it:

> Since the Enlightenment, but more commonly since the Roman-
> tic era of the nineteenth century, Western men and women
> have come to experience marriage as a one-with-one quest for
> happiness within the marital union itself. Only since then have
> they come to see marriage the social phenomenon — not the
> bond of contracted persons nor the family concordat — as in
> essence a love relationship reciprocal, personal and embodied
> in sexuality. For the first time in the West sexuality was empha-
> sized as the bodily exchange of interpersonal love.[13]

Perhaps it is with that emphasis on the "bodily exchange" that we begin to find ourselves in trouble, since the physical aspect of the sexual relationship is so often and easily disassociated from any love whatever. We are aware that sex can be sold without love, but we may not stop to think how easily they can be disconnected in our ordinary experience. It is this point that Lederer and Jackson make in saying that it is a "mirage" to believe we need love for marriage. Courtship, they maintain, norm-ally involves a substantial loss of judgment.

It is a false assumption that people marry for love. *They like to think of themselves as being in love;* but by and large the emotion they interpret as love is in reality some other emotion — often a strong sex drive, fear, or a hunger for approval.[14]

And this is exactly what Augustine and the other early theologians were afraid of where sex is involved: A loss of rational control leading to irrational actions:

They may realize that the man is unable as yet to earn a living; or that the woman is incompetent to manage a home; or that each has radically different tastes and values from the other. These and many other obstacles to a workable marriage usually have no significance to a couple in the courtship stage. The courting individuals are obsessed by one desire only — to mate.[15]

So love should — if possible! — be distinguished from a mere sexual urge, however powerful. "Love," it is said, "makes the world go 'round"; but look at the shape the world is in! Apparently we possess something powerful, but have not yet learned how to work with it constructively.

What, then, do we mean by love? It is always useful to remember that the Greeks had at least four words for our one word. In the New Testament we find *erao* or *eros* as sensual desire, *phileo* as friendship, *agapao* or *agape* as fondness.* To find all this wrapped in a single human package is rare, but *eros* alone is not normally sufficient as the basis of a satisfying, long-term relationship. Strong as it is in the short term, it has very little endurance. Some other elements need to be blended in to create a love that will last.

But the English language short-circuits that wisdom. We say "I love you" and we may really mean "I am sexually attracted to you," "I enjoy your company," "I adore you," or "I find my life fulfilled as I offer it to you," but we have only that one word available to express it. So all these different feelings are expressed by a single word, and none of them, it may be, will provide a sound basis for a lasting marriage.

In the hope of clarifying things, Lederer and Jackson offer a rather turgid definition of love by another psychiatrist, Henry Sullivan:

When the satisfaction or the security of another person becomes as significant as one's own satisfaction or security, then the state of love exists.[16]

---

*A fourth type of love, *stergo,* which included relationships ranging from ruler and ruled to master and dog, occurs in the New Testament only in compound words.

Turgid and not likely to be much help to people in the erotic state described above, it is, nonetheless, an analysis well worth pondering. On the positive side, it describes a relationship: This condition called "love" involves another human being. Furthermore, this significant other is one I am at least as anxious to care for as myself. A deep and lasting love would certainly be likely to include those qualities; certainly this is a safer definition than, for example, "a deep emotional involvement" or "an erotic attachment." But is it enough to satisfy us as a full and comprehensive description?

Could we not, to begin with, imagine other relationships than that of husband and wife which would very nearly fit this same description? Might not a parent be as concerned for the security and satisfaction of an infant as for self? Might not a daughter have such concern for an elderly mother, and might not siblings who have lived together for many years be so concerned for one another? And what would distinguish this kind of love from the fear I might have of a madman holding me hostage and likely to lash out in violence unless his satisfaction and security were given not equal but first priority?

Can we really provide a satisfactory definition of love with so little emotional content? Of course emotions are dangerous, but so is love. Love without emotion is easier to analyze, easier to control, easier to distinguish from mere erotic desire, but is it really love — the kind of love that draws a man and a woman together, leads them to the altar, enables them to love a family into being, and leaves them smiling contentedly at each other fifty years afterwards? Would a concern that the other be equally as safe and satisfied as oneself survive three problem pregnancies in a row, a job so insecure that the tension affects both spouses day and night for many months or years, a constantly nagging in-law, blighted ambitions, inadequate housing, crippling illness, radically different sexual appetites?

Lederer and Jackson dismiss as unattainable the great thirteenth chapter of St. Paul's Epistle to the Corinthians — "love bears all things . . . love never fails": "It is our opinion that it would be too difficult for spouses to practice this kind of relationship described by St. Paul — unless both were saints."[17]

Yes, but St. Paul was addressing saints. When he wrote the same people a second letter he addressed it to "the church of God in Corinth, together with all the saints throughout Achaia."[18] Finally, a satisfactory definition of marital love will need to include a Source of love capable of carrying human beings beyond their own capacities. Don't most people in love feel themselves to be moved by a power beyond themselves?

Granted, an overwhelming erotic urge *may* be mistaken for an inrush of divine love, but the fact that human beings may be mistaken is not an adequate reason for ruling out the nonrational element in our makeup. Divine power and human emotion are part of the normal human experience of love. We may indeed be mistaken about them, but the problem is not solved by eliminating them from the equation. Reason has also been misused in human history, but we do not on that account give up the use of reason.

We have seen how suspicious Saint Augustine and his contemporaries were of the nonrational component in sexual matters, how they longed for a hypothetical Eden where the ears and sexual organs moved in response to reason and where people could be sexual without losing their dignity. Their world was one in which the leading pagan philosophers taught the supremacy of reason, and they agreed. We live in a world in which the sensual has been restored to favor — perhaps because our rational skills have produced a world of computerized impersonality and atomic terror, perhaps because our affluence has given us opportunity to take our emotions more fully into account. If our theology is simply a reflection of our world as their theology was of their world, then we are at least equally likely to be right. We do need to be cautioned by their example to be careful that what we take for the light of the gospel is not the reflection of some passing and transitory meteor. But if we attempt to respond to a love that seems to involve our whole selves, body as well as mind, emotions as well as reason, and that believes God is at work in all — would that be completely untrue to Christian tradition and experience, or our own? Our instinct is to say it would not.

Having said all that, we should also affirm a very basic and valid point in Lederer and Jackson's analysis. Love *can* be a mirage; we can fool ourselves badly about love. And we can ask and expect more from love than a good marriage really needs. Wild passion is not necessary; it may be more destructive than constructive. A warm and caring relationship that endures may be a stronger, more lasting love than the one that sweeps us off our feet — and leaves us flat on our back.

Language being what it is, we need the word "love" to do justice to the marriage relationship, but we need to be warned about creating false impressions. Love is not fifty years of rapture; there is "worse" as well as "better," gray skies as well as blue. Being human, we need the dark days to help us value the bright ones. A marriage may be deepened and strengthened more by what it endures than by what it enjoys.

But it is easy to be carried away by contemporary expectations of marital bliss. Those who edited the current American version of the Book of Common Prayer, for example, seem to have been carried away when they replaced Cranmer's statement of the purposes of marriage (or the last previous revision of it) with the solemn assurance that "joy" is the first purpose of marriage:

> The union of husband and wife in heart, body, and mind is intended by God for their mutual joy; for the help and comfort given one another in prosperity and adversity; and, when it is God's will, for the procreation of children and their nurture in the knowledge and love of the Lord.[19]

Set "joy" as the chief purpose of marriage and you create grounds for a good many dissatisfied customers and divorces. How many mornings can we really expect to wake up joyful? We would be on far safer ground to offer Cranmer's "mutual help and comfort" and be surprised by joy when it comes. Lederer and Jackson's description of the requirements of a solid marriage may also not be very exciting, but perhaps we would do better to get our excitement from surfing or sky-diving:

> The happy, workable, productive marriage does not require love as defined in this book, or even the practice of the Golden Rule. To maintain continuously a union based on love is not feasible for most people. Nor is it possible to live in a permanent state of romance. Normal people should not be frustrated or disappointed if they are not in a constant state of love. If they experience the joy of love (or imagine they do) for ten per cent of the time they are married, attempt to treat each other with as much courtesy as they do distinguished strangers, and attempt to make the marriage a workable affair — one where there are some practical advantages and satisfactions for each — the chances are that the marriage will endure longer and with more strength than the so-called love matches.[20]

I will continue to argue a bit with their use of the word love but they do have an important point. The pope's reluctance to make love central to the official definition of marriage is well founded. Many marriages are made without love, and many good marriages endure and prosper on the basis of qualities that might not be instantly recognized as love in the grand sense. As many marriages may grow into love as grow out of it, and the one, like the other, may happen quickly or over a long span of years. To hold up love as a measure of marriage is to provide a standard God alone may be able to use effectively.

Is love a "good" of marriage, a proper goal toward which to move? If God is love and if love involves relationship, there is no human arena in which it is more likely to be found. We are told that Jacob worked seven years to win the right to marry Rachel, "and they seemed to him but a few days because of the love he had for her."[21] On any one of those days, as he sweated in the fields and went to bed alone, he might have felt exhaustion or frustration more keenly than anything one might call love, but love sustained him nevertheless. That passage comes very close to the heart of what love and marriage are all about.

LOVE AND MARRIAGE

Theologians have often written that marriage is a "sacrament of nature," which is to say that it came into existence naturally; no one invented it. But perhaps the truth of that statement depends on your definition of marriage. True enough, most societies have institutionalized the relationship between men and women, but can we easily identify that institution as marriage, as an institution as closely connected to love as a carriage is to a horse? A look at the history of marriage seems to raise serious questions.

Where does that history begin? Again, the theologians have a standard answer: With Adam and Eve. But look at your Bible. Nowhere, as we noted earlier, does the Bible say either that Adam and Eve were married or that they loved each other. They had, indeed, a relationship, and they had a command from God to "be fruitful and multiply and replenish the earth." But "every creeping thing that creepeth upon the earth" had the same job description as that.

The fact is that in most societies, at most times, the institution of marriage has been centered on the procreation of children and the orderly transmission of property. Sometimes, by a convenient coincidence, the duty of procreating children and producing inheritors has fallen to the lot of a man and a woman who love each other. More often it has been a question of taking love where you could find it, and that has often been well outside the bounds of the institution of marriage.

A parable may be in order. There was once a man who lived beside a deep, fast river and who owned the land on both banks at the narrowest point for many miles. Long ago, someone, (no one remembered who, though there were various legends) had built a bridge and generations of the man's ancestors had maintained it. They sat beside the bridge and collected tolls to repay them for caring for the bridge and, since there was no other good crossing to be found, they became very rich. There *were* other, less satisfactory ways to cross the river. Some travellers swam across; in a dry season some were able to brave the currents and wade; some made the long journey toward the source of the river and crossed it where it was smaller; sometimes a strong man would come with an army and simply force his way across the bridge, ignoring the toll takers and sometimes killing them. To prevent such attacks, the bridge keepers narrowed the access roads and built walls to defend them. But the bridge, in spite of the narrowness and cost, remained the simplest, most obvious route across the river. Since the people on both sides of the river needed to exchange various goods and services, they continued to use the bridge.

As time went on and the population on both sides increased, the narrowness of the bridge led to a demand for alternative routes and additional bridges were built. They were longer than the first bridge and not always secure. Some of them collapsed and travellers were swept away. But with time, those who built new bridges learned from the old bridge and from their own experience, and the alternative bridges became better and more and more people were able to make the journey safely.

I will leave the parable unfinished because I do not happen to know whether God, the ancient bridge builder, intends at last to enable us to build one bridge for all, or whether there is some deep purpose in providing alternative routes. I wish we could all travel together, but I also notice that the various routes do tend to converge. The varieties of human marital custom (to abandon the parable completely) seem to be fewer as common patterns emerge and are accepted. Far fewer people practice polygamy; dowry and bride-price are becoming obsolete; however seldom realized the ideal of monogamous, life-long relationships based on mutual respect and love may be, it is, increasingly, the ideal among people of every culture and faith. For a Christian, it is hard not to see God's purpose in this. Charles Williams made a further claim, the same one made in the fifth chapter of Ephesians:

> If marriage is not Christ, it is either a morality or a natural phenomenon, expending all this illumination, all those graces, merely for the sake of reproducing the race. But if it is, then indeed He is the light that lighteneth every man that cometh into the world, then indeed our eyes have seen his salvation . . .[22]

That is a measure of the vocation we are called to explore and to which we are called to bear witness.

For all the difficulties with the use of the word *love* to define marriage, the logical conclusion is not that love and marriage should therefore be kept apart. On the contrary, though there are many kinds of love outside (and inside) marriage, love remains always the ultimate meaning of all marriage. Contrary to those who have said that love cannot be found in marriage, where else could you find the sort of love that can grow between a man and a woman who have committed themselves entirely to each other "for better or worse" for the whole of life? There is a richness and depth in married love that is not likely to be found in temporary liaisons, however emotional, or in the variety of friendships that enrich our lives, however sustaining they may be. Married love is capable of imaging the love of Christ for the church; that is the norm against which it is to be measured. If other love reaches such a measure, it is of grace rather than promise.

But grace is real; God is not limited. As the Welsh poet R.S. Thomas put it, "There is nothing too ample for you to overflow . . ."[23] Whatever claims may be made for marriage as the *normal* human way of approaching the meaning of love, God is too various for exclusive claims to be made even there. Nor is the imaging of God's love limited to explicitly *Christian* marriage; Judaism has often been clearer about the goodness of marriage than Christianity; there are people of no faith at all whose marriages are means of grace for themselves and others. Charles Williams wrote:

> There are souls to whom religion is not much more than a mere formal duty, if that, who are yet capable of heroic achievements in love, of temptation and crucifixion in marriage if not in the Church. Vigil and fast, devotion and self-surrender are aimed in the end at one sole End, and holiness may be reached by the obvious ways as well as by the more secret. The years of marriage may have removed almost all memory of the high genesis of marriage, and the altar may be "to an unknown God," for the name of his deity is forgotten. . . . "He is received perfectly and entire under either species" . . . the work of salvation is not hindered by the adoption of the other method . . .[24]

These qualifications are not intended to narrow the claims made for Christian marriage but to recall the limitless nature of the love to be found there. A glass of water can hardly empty the city reservoir, but that is no reason to stop drinking or to throw away the best glasses I have as useless. Furthermore, since marriage is a vocation and it is God who calls, all marriage should lead not only to a deeper knowledge of love but to a deeper relationship with the Source of love.

Such knowledge begins with creation. The struggle we saw in the work of the first Christian theologians was a struggle, ultimately, over whether or not to affirm God's creation. Are flesh and matter good or evil? The battle still goes on. Those who would reject creation as evil have never been allowed to define what Christians ought to believe, but it has always been a struggle and the church has seemed reluctant to say too much good about the physical world. As Charles Williams put it:

> [W]hen the official representatives of the Church have talked about such things as sexual love (to take one example), they may have said the right things, but they have said very few of them and they have generally said them in the wrong style . . . There has been a wide feeling that the more like an indeterminate soul the body can be made the better.[25]

Williams said this in an article about D.H. Lawrence, author of books like *Lady Chatterley's Lover* which were banned in their own day for their shocking honesty about sex. "The Christians of Lawrence's day," Williams wrote, "did not care for the exploration of the body; he reacted against them with a natural but undesirable violence."[26] Williams described Lawrence as a heretic, but, he said, "he was concerned with a Christian orthodoxy — the orthodoxy of the blood of Man."[27] Lawrence was able to shock because the church had so largely forgotten what incarnation involves. We have not done well at keeping soul and body together, at affirming the goodness and unity of creation.

No wonder, then, that we have trouble uniting love and marriage. But perhaps our own problem is not that our world has placed so much emphasis on the body and the sensual aspects of love as that it has trivialized them, and it has trivialized them because we have allowed them to be cut loose from anything that would give them ultimate meaning. The label we use for this failure is "Puritanism," but that is unfair to the Puritans. In fact, as we have seen, it has been a pervasive tendency in the Christian church from the beginning.

The unity of love and marriage, then, begins with the unity of flesh and spirit and a full appreciation of the goodness of the sexual aspect of married love. No recent author has made more of that aspect of love than Charles Williams who wrote a short book called *Outlines of Romantic Theology* and developed some of his ideas in writing about Dante and Beatrice and in a series of novels and plays. One blunt sentence sums up his approach: "The kingdom came down from heaven and was incarnate; since then and perhaps (because of it) before then, it is beheld through and in a carnality of joy."[28]

Paul Ramsey said something very similar: "Sensuous sexual love is an important part of that world of which it is said that, when Christ came, he came to his own."[29]

Is it, perhaps, because the audacity of the incarnation still stunned those who called themselves Christians, that it has taken the church so long to come to terms with it? But Ramsey insists, and rightly so, that we can hardly be incarnational Christians and isolate any part of ourselves as somehow a mere instrument for the use of a separable and higher soul. Every part of myself is *me* and communicates myself to others:

> Human sexual passion and coitus is quite definitely a matter of *ourselves,* of our souls *de profundis.* It is no more sex organs that desire intercourse with sex organs than it is my vocal chords that speak or this hand that is writing. *I* speak with my vocal chords, *I* write with this hand, to *you*.[30]

The high claim Williams and Ramsey make for Christian marriage centers on this holding together of the wholeness of human experience. It is time to look very specifically at ways in which such an understanding might be enfleshed in the local Christian community.

CHAPTER TWELVE

Reinventing Marriage

*B*etrothal has been an important stage of the marriage process in most societies. It has disappeared in the Western world — although the increasingly common pattern of living together before marriage seems to be a way of meeting the same needs. This chapter proposes that the church re-create a betrothal period as a preparation for marriage and provide appropriate ceremonies and instruction.

WHERE WE ARE NOW

Mark Twain once said that a folk song is a song nobody ever wrote. The customs and traditions of marriage are like that also. No one knows who first said a Christian prayer at a wedding or what the prayer was like. No one knows why the bride and bridegroom in an Eastern wedding are crowned or who the first bride was to wear a white dress. No one knows who first played the march from *Lohengrin* at a wedding — or how long it will take to outlive that mistake. No one can really explain either why almost every young couple for over a hundred years has felt the need for a formal wedding, or why so many no longer feel that need.

It is unlikely that either particular customs like the bridal procession or cultural patterns like the frequency of formal marriage will be changed by any book ever written. The objective here is much simpler: To suggest alternative patterns that may commend themselves to some and, perhaps more important, to raise questions that may inspire still others to experiment with a variety of alternative ways of understanding and solemnizing Christian marriage. Better ways will come from a process of questioning and experimentation. It seems likely that, when they do, the patterns that last will be like the cathedral at Chartres which was built by everyone and no one.

Kenneth Stevenson, who has probably written more about the liturgies of marriage than anyone else in recent years, observes that some things are not likely to change no matter what we do:

No amount of didactic teaching or self-conscious rubrics (or for that matter Church law) is going to dislodge the old Western understanding of marriage, however pagan its roots, however inappropriate for what we believe to be a truly biblical and contemporary view of the sacrament of matrimony. . . . [We] know that many brides are walking into church on the arm of their fathers, and they are going to perceive the marriage either in the way that this implies, or quite differently, but they will still adhere to the old custom because they like it. Here, if ever, is incongruity not easily dislodged . . .[1]

It is, indeed, incongruous, that a young woman who has found a career in a law firm or as a biochemist and manages her own affairs with great success should be escorted down a church aisle by her father and handed over to another man who then walks her triumphantly out of church, as if she were a dependent being transferred from one authority to another, and as if nothing had changed since the twelfth century. Obviously this ceremony does reflect some other deeply felt realities, such as the significance of father-daughter relationships, that continue to speak even after the meaning that created the ceremony has vanished. That does not mean that the ceremony can survive forever when its roots are gone. In fact, there are weddings today in which this ceremony is modified toward something that more accurately expresses the reality of the occasion. Perhaps in a generation or two new customs will have replaced the present tradition and no one will remember how it happened.

Our focus, however, is not on liturgy — important though that is — but on the whole process by which a man and a woman move from the single status to that of the married. The sociologists speak of a "liminal period," a time when thresholds (the literal meaning of *limina*) are crossed, a time of transition, and of the ways in which a society accommodates the disruption of its life when this kind of change takes place. Birth and death, puberty and marriage, parenthood and occupational change are among the "liminal" events that mark our lives and that we, in turn, mark with ceremonies and celebrations. Of these, marriage may be the most significant, the one for which we prepare most carefully, and the one which we celebrate most extravagantly. Usually many months and much agony are appropriately spent in the planning, for never, except in marriage, do we make a commitment of ourselves to another human being for the rest of our lives.*

It is hardly surprising, then, that most cultures have developed carefully orchestrated methods for solemnizing this transition. It is only

---

*Clergy in some traditions make a lifelong commitment, but even they can retire.

surprising to realize that contemporary Western society seems to be on the verge of losing whatever vestigial systems have survived for supporting those involved through this critical time of change.

Arnold van Gennep, who first described this period and christened it with his book, *The Rites of Passage,* said that these transitions

> do not occur without disturbing the life of society and the individual, and it is the function of rites of passage to reduce their harmful effects. That such changes are regarded as real and important is demonstrated by the recurrence of rites, in important ceremonies among widely differing peoples . . .[2]

> For every one of these events (birth, puberty, marriage, etc.) there are ceremonies whose essential purpose is to enable the individual to pass from one defined position to another which is equally well defined.[3]

There was a time when this was true of European society as well. Families negotiated an advantageous marriage and marked the completion of that negotiation with betrothal celebrations so boisterous that clergy were sometimes forbidden to attend. Years might then pass during which male and female were prepared by families and colleagues for their change in status. Finally, a wedding celebration was held and a new family unit was established in society. Why did this whole process disappear with hardly a trace? In part, it may have been just because the character of the betrothal celebration was less receptive to church participation; it part it may have been because of the church's concern to define a sacramental moment; in part it may have been the aristocracy's anxiety that the church provide a legitimizing endorsement for its concern about inheritance. Whatever the particular factors, the result was a total theological and ceremonial concentration on the final exchange of marital consent which left the betrothal stage a fading echo of what had once been critical.

In older cultures, Van Gennep found a very different pattern of behavior:

> A betrothal forms a liminal period between adolescence and marriage, but the passage from adolescence to betrothal itself involves a special series of rites of separation, a transition, and an incorporation into the betrothal condition; and the passage from the transitional period, which is betrothal, to marriage itself, is made through a series of rites of separation from the former, followed by rites consisting of transition, and rites consisting of incorporation into marriage.[4]

But neither theology nor ceremonial can eliminate the human need for liminal ritual. We remember how John Cotgreve and Alice Gidlowe stood in a meadow in Cheshire one evening in 1549 and exchanged betrothal promises in the presence of friends. We may remember the moment when we ourselves gave or accepted an engagement ring. We remember being invited to bridal showers and stag parties. So we continue to make rituals — as we should — but the engagement rituals we make are now completely secular in nature. Neither church nor state is interested at all in these events. Church and state, it would seem, have been concerned with the witnessing of documents, with certifying status, rather than with a continuing involvement in human lives.

For some years now, many churches have strongly emphasized marriage preparation of some kind. The Roman Catholic church has established a well-known pre-Cana program that is ordinarily required before marriage. One probably typical East coast diocese ordinarily requires that marriage preparation begin a year in advance and that "three formational sessions with a priest/deacon and at least eight hours of instruction in a marriage preparation program" be included. The eight-hour requirement can be met by attending an Engaged Encounter weekend or a pre-Cana Conference.[5] The Anglican Diocese of Kootenay in Western Canada provides four three-hour programs twice a year for couples planning to be married. There are talks by priests and married lay people, by doctors and counselors and lawyers, there are audio-visual presentations and small group discussions on everything from finances to sexuality. Other similar programs have been organized in many places and many ways. To say that these weekends and conferences are of widely different quality and effectiveness is to say only that they are led by human beings. Other churches, for lack of ability to organize such conferences or because the pastor prefers a more personal approach, are likely to depend largely on individual meetings, conferences with the clergy and, sometimes, with trained pastoral counselors. The same criticism undoubtedly applies to this approach: Pastors and counselors are human beings and some will do a better job than others. The value of individual counseling may be offset by the potential advantages of group involvement and the wider variety of approaches possible in the weekend and conference method. A combination of the two approaches may have the most to offer.

But all these methods are ultimately an approach by way of instruction, the head trying to reach the heart. And the head is not always closely connected to the heart in the premarital period. As for the postmarriage time, that seems generally to be almost completely ignored. Nonetheless, it is significant that the church has felt a need to deal in some way with the liminal time between singleness and marriage and has produced a response.

More powerfully by far, people themselves have created a liminal process, unshaped, inchoate, largely unritualized, which has become widely accepted. Once again, as in earlier centuries, we are seeing men and women enter into a period of premarital sexual relationships which still, for most people, leads eventually to a formal marriage ceremony. John Gillis notes the radical change from the 1950s, when only 1 percent of the men and women coming to be married had lived together first, to the early 1980s, when it had risen to 21 percent. For those marrying a second time it had risen to 67 percent. Gillis comments:

> The new cohabitation had many of the features of the old betrothal. It was an extended rite of transition — a liminal period — which was brought to a ritual conclusion when the couple decided it was time to incorporate themselves into the adult world of mothers and fathers.[6]

The difference is that John and Alice in the sixteenth century could make promises based on the familiar words of the liturgy** while we, perhaps because the church has insisted so long that premarital sexual relationships are sinful, cannot easily imagine invoking God's blessing on this new and deeply significant phase of human development.

Speaking very personally, I would prefer a world in which the first act of intercourse took place within marriage.*** I believe it is a great gift to "know" only one other, to be able to give oneself wholly to only one, to image in human life God's eternal commitment to us: "You only have I known of all the families of the earth . . ."[7]

I am also unconvinced by the theory that people can learn by living together what being married is like and how suited they are to each other. There is, in fact, evidence to suggest that the contrary is the case. A study reported by *The New York Times* in 1988 showed that those who had lived together before marriage were more likely, not less, to experience marital failure.[8] Why that should be is, of course, another question. Does it reflect higher expectations of marriage or a lower level of commitment? Whatever the reason, there is no evidence that premarital cohabitation helps prepare a couple for marriage.

**Although in 1549 the brand new Book of Common Prayer was still unfamiliar, John and Alice would have known by heart the words of the Sarum Missal, an ancient incantation that relied on poetry rather than printing to fix itself in the popular mind: "to haue and to holde, from this day forward, for better for wurs, for rycher for porer, in syckenes and in helthe, to be bonoure and buxum, in bede and at borde . . ." Cranmer, perhaps at his wife's suggestion, omitted the "bonoure and buxum (agreeable and compliant) in bed and at borde," but it is that sort of alliteration that makes memorable the conjugal commitment.

***But see the comments below about "preceremonial" as distinct from "premarital" sex.

Living together (normally) involves no commitment; it's easy to walk away. Marriage is not like that. Marriage does involve commitment and although it is not impossible to walk away from a marriage, it is usually harder to do. So whatever I say hereafter about living together apart from marriage is by way of starting from where people are rather than by way of sketching out an ideal world. But the church fails in its calling if it does not begin where people are.

We have tried to begin with the facts as nearly as we can establish them. The age of puberty is continuing to fall, and the average age of marriage continues to rise. The age of social maturity and stability has increased as educational demands have grown in a technological age. Some accommodation to these facts is obviously necessary for many people. To insist that sexual relationships must be confined to marriage may be to insist, as the medieval church attempted to do, that marriage should take place at an age as close to the age of puberty as possible. But the fact that people are sexually mature enough for intercourse is very different from being emotionally and socially mature enough to form lasting commitments. The landscape is strewn with the wreckage of the marriages of those who have tried. It may be a reflection of some inherent wisdom that so many young people wait so long to get married and find their own ways to deal meantime with needs they are unable to quiet.

The church seems never to have sacralized the betrothal period, but this period was at one time recognized and accepted sufficiently that those entering it privately in the presence of friends felt comfortable in doing so with liturgical words. The church also was sufficiently aware of what went on in the betrothal period to provide in the marriage liturgy a prayer for the legitimation of a child that might have been produced.****[9] Is it possible that an informal or formal sacralizing of such relationships would contribute to their stability and lead them more naturally to the altar for completion and ratification? Questions like this do at least need to be asked. The church needs also to meditate more deeply on what is meant by speaking of marriage as a "sacrament of nature" and to ponder the difference described by Edward Schillebeeckx between marriage as a "secular reality" and as a "saving mystery." How much "ownership" can the church expect of a "secular reality" and a sacrament older than the church itself? I will suggest some of my own answers to these questions, but it is vital that other answers also be

---

****A discreet rubric adds that "should the parish priest judge that his public legitimation might give rise to scandal, the rite can be conducted privately apart from the Mass." Note also that in some societies the whole point of the betrothal period was to see whether the woman became pregnant; if she did, the betrothal was considered successful and the marriage was arranged to celebrate that success.

suggested. The growing separation between the answers the church has traditionally given and the answers being proposed by society is not helpful to either.

REINVENTING BETROTHAL: THE PREMARITAL NOVITIATE

On April 20, 1993, the crown prince of Japan arrived at the door of a large house in a select suburb of Tokyo carrying with him two large fish and five bolts of silk. When the woman inside opened the door and accepted the gift, she had become officially betrothed to the crown prince. They had, in fact, been formally engaged in the modern way for some time, but now they had taken the first step in the traditional Japanese process leading to marriage. A similar story in the Book of Genesis tells how Rebekah became betrothed to Isaac when Abraham's servant put a ring in her nose and bracelets on her arms and gave Rebekah and her father silver and gold and fine clothes.[10]

Almost every human society has had some equivalent of betrothal, and normally it has centered on the arrangement of the financial terms of the marriage contract. Jack Goody in his major study of marriage practices in non-European societies has shown that the dowry, usually the most important part of the financial agreement, was ordinarily designed to provide economic security to the bride.[11] She and her children needed to be secure against the possibility of her husband's death, and she herself needed to be secure against the possibility of divorce. Her brothers might inherit their father's property, but she was provided for in the dowry. Often, as in Rebekah's case, the dowry was portable; jewelry was an ideal form of endowment in a society without bank accounts or social security. Often, in medieval society, the wedding ring was given at betrothal as a symbol of the larger dowry. The dowry might be given to the bride by her family or to her family by the groom's family (as "bride-price"), depending on custom, but usually it passed into the bride's possession and gave her the security she needed in a world where few aspects of life were secure. In societies that need to be primarily concerned with the economic aspects of marriage, that is inevitable — but that is no longer the issue. We can also see, looking back, the value of a transition time in which two families and two individuals could come to know each other in greater depth. All this was the effort being made by people in older societies to find security in an insecure world through a careful, step-by-step process. Perhaps that is exactly what young couples today are seeking in a world hardly more secure, though perhaps the insecurity is different in nature.

In our society, increasingly secularized and distant from the church, there is a growing need for the church to hold up the essential meaning of its faith. One response the church has made to that need suggests a pattern that may be applicable to marriage preparation as well. Searching its memory, the church has revived a system long forgotten but once at the center of the church's formational process. The forty days of Lent were first set aside as a time of preparation for baptism. At a later stage, the church often spent three years preparing candidates for what may have been the only significant decision they would ever make. Two-thirds of the citizens of the Roman empire were slaves and therefore had no career choices to concern them. The other third as well often inherited their role in life, whether it was farming, military life, or commerce. Marriage choices also were often made by others. Indeed, before the Christian era, few people had a choice of religion; that, too, came with the territory. Your tribal, ethnic, or national identity included your religion as well. But in the vast new cosmopolitan turmoil of the Roman empire, suddenly there were religious decisions that even slaves were free to make. The church ensured that they made them with careful preparation and understanding.

Contemporary life faces us with many decisions, a multitude of life-styles from which to choose. Many of them can be made casually and later changed again. Mid-career crises are a familiar syndrome. Churches and faiths can be freely changed as well — and are. The reinvention of a baptismal preparation program for adults is necessary in such a world to deal with adults who are coming to faith for the first time and preparing for the gift of baptism. There are many more, of course, who return to the faith in middle years and who may go through some sort of recatechizing process, but the traditional catechumenate will be appropriate for the still small numbers who come to faith for the first time as adults.

In entering marriage, on the other hand, the majority of those being prepared are being prepared for the first time for what (except for professing their faith) may well be the most significant decision they will ever make. Even if they are coming to marriage for the second time, the odds are that they will be approaching it for the first time as a truly mature decision. For all of these, a premarriage "catechumenate" seems appropriate and could make a significant difference.

The word "catechumenate" does not fall trippingly from modern tongues, and the need for a better title is urgent. Even so, in a growing number of congregations of various denominations, a process for the incorporation of adult converts has been set at the center of the community's life. No doubt there will be few people still who are converted and baptized as adults, but those few, publicly accepted as catechumens (candidates for baptism), deliberately nurtured by *lay* members of the church, and publicly baptized at the Great Vigil of Easter, can help restore to the whole congregation an awareness of its essential identity. We are the church of God, "a chosen race, a royal priesthood, a holy nation, God's own people, . . . called . . . out of darkness into his marvelous light."[12]

We are by nature a baptized people, an evangelizing and witnessing body. The existence in our midst of a select group (even one individual) making that transition in a conscious, deliberate way reminds us all of who we are.

We are also a body defined by marriage. The marital relationship becomes in the Bible the supreme metaphor for the relationship between God and the church; it is to a wedding feast in the kingdom that we are called in baptism; the sexual relationship, not yet preempted by test tubes and petri dishes, remains the immediate source of all human life. We may dismiss marriage as a mere "civil affair" or unnecessary legalism, but marriage keeps coming back to the church door nevertheless, and those who fall in love continue to become aware of the holiness in life in a new way. The church needs to deal with marriage better for its own sake and for the sake of the world. The interval before marriage is an excellent time to begin.

The opportunity presents itself in one of several ways. Perhaps a couple phones the church office, or a new couple in church on Sunday morning asks to speak to the pastor as they leave. It may be that one of those aspiring to marriage grew up in the parish. A generation ago that would have been typical. Today that is less typical. The couple approaching the church may be older, perhaps in their early thirties; one or both may have been previously married; it is likely that they are already living together. They are in love and prepared to commit themselves to each other in a formal way. They have not been to church regularly in some time, but they feel a need to make public their love and ask God's blessing on it. The church has some knowledge of love and commitment. How does it respond?

All too often the church's first response is to present the couple with a form to fill out. Church secretaries do what they are good at. Surmounting that hurdle, the couple may find themselves involved before long in a counseling process of some sort. Clergy also do what they are good at. Ideally the counseling is presented not as a required procedure (legalism again) but as an offer of support and guidance in their preparation for marriage. But what the church does best is not forms or even counseling; what the church does best is to ritualize occasions and build community. The marriage service itself will bring out that best.

But why wait? What if, after the pastor first meets with the couple and has ascertained a basic maturity and stability, a readiness for marriage, a "marriage catechumenate" were set in place?

We have already suggested that this is a clumsy term. The tradition of the Eastern church suggests *novitiate* as an alternative. The Russian Orthodox at one time treated the vocations of marriage and celibacy as parallel and complementary. Candidates for both went through a novitiate including, for the newly married, a monastic retreat to prepare for their "nuptial priesthood," while for the monastic candidate the church spoke of their betrothal and marriage in the rite of entrance to the monastic order.[13] Nuns in some orders in the Western church are still presented with a wedding ring to symbolize their marriage to Christ. "Novitiate" may be a somewhat more familiar term than catechumenate (and somewhat more pronounceable) — at least we all know what a "novice" is — but better ideas would be welcome.

What is a "premarital novitiate"? It is a way for the church to help shape the phase van Gennep describes as "liminal" by providing "a series of rites of separation from the (single state) followed by rites consisting of transition, and rites consisting of incorporation into marriage."

Some of those "rites" are already in place: The "pre-Cana conference" or its equivalent already exists. What is lacking is parish liturgy and ritual to mark the transition and to provide what the baptismal catechumenate offers the candidate for baptism, which is witness and incorporation.

One further preliminary question may need to be answered: How does the pastor determine readiness for marriage? Some clergy may be prepared to function as ordained equivalents of a Justice of the Peace and perform a marriage for everyone with a wedding license in hand. Most clergy have favorite stories of those they turned down: The couple in blue jeans hoping for a service "in about half an hour," the interracial couple who said they would not have children "because her parents don't want mixed-race grandchildren," and so on. There are times when a mature, competent consent is clearly lacking.

Some churches raise the most serious questions when one or both partners have been previously married and divorced. The Roman Catholic church requires a judgment that the first marriage was null and void. The Episcopal church requires approval from the bishop of the diocese. There is an absurdity here that ought to be recognized: the man or woman who has made solemn promises and tried to keep them is made to face an extra hurdle, perhaps even turned away, while the man or woman who has slept with innumerable others without ever being married is not. The early church rejected a heresy called gnosticism which cared only for spiritual things and rejected the body as unimportant. When the church rates one promise above innumerable acts of the flesh, it would seem the same heresy is still with us. A divorce is a significant past event that needs to be weighed, but so is a pattern of promiscuity; so also might be patterns of aggressive behavior or an employment record indicating instability. In brief, "readiness for marriage" involves a number of factors not easily assessed. Pastors will do the best they can out of their training, skills, and experience. The responsibility for the decision to marry, however, rests finally with the couple.

The temptation also exists to turn away couples who have not been members of the congregation or who have not been attending church services. Clergy have many other responsibilities than conducting weddings and have a natural dislike for being "used." If we are right in seeing marriage as a process, it is hard to see how we can accommodate the people seeking marriage "in half an hour." But when people are willing to enter into a significant process, it is hard to reject the leading that has brought them to the church's door. A "liminal event" may involve more than one threshold. Helen Oppenheimer comments:

> The Church is not "going through the motions" of an unbelieved rite, making people mouth what they do not mean. It is doing for them what they have asked, allowing them to take each other as husband and wife "in the presence of God and in the face of this congregation". . . . If people still want to do this solemn act in church, however inarticulate they may be about what it means to them, it smacks of meanness and possessiveness for Christians to try to ration God's blessing. It must be faced that often people's motivation will not only appear but will be decidedly inadequate. So maybe was the motivation of the prodigal son. He came home only when he wanted something he could not get elsewhere; yet his Father came to meet him.[14]

The beginning of a novitiate

So the telephone rings, the appointment is made, and the pastor is ready to take the couple on to the next stage. That stage needs to occur on Sunday morning in the gathered community. It should not be lengthy or elaborate. At the time of the announcements, the pastor would say something like this:

> I am happy to be able to announce this morning that John Smith and Mary Jones are engaged and planning to be married next

June here in our church. As they prepare for marriage, they
will need your support and prayers. I will ask them to come
forward now to express their commitment to each other and
receive the expression of your support.

So John and Mary come forward to the front of the church. Perhaps
it's their first Sunday in this church, but all the more reason for the
congregation to know who they are. Of course they will be nervous,
but they can think of it as a direct preparation for their wedding, which
will no longer be the first time they have come down the aisle and stood
there to make promises. The congregation is also asked to stand and the
pastor says to each of the couple in turn something like this:

John/Mary, you have announced your engagement to Mary/
John; will you use this time before your marriage to seek in
every way to grow in knowledge of yourself, of Mary/John,
and of the Creator who made you and who has called you to
a deeper knowledge of God's love?

First one, then the other responds "I will." Then the congregation is
asked, "Will you who witness these promises do all in your power to
support Mary and John in this time of preparation and growth?" To which
the congregation responds, "We will." A prayer is then said for God's
blessing and guidance of the couple in this time of preparation.

If this seems reminiscent of an opening phase of the marriage service
in the Book of Common Prayer, it is intended to, because that segment
is said to be a remnant of the medieval betrothal with its promise for
the future. The promise is the "I will" which involves the future, not the
"I do" of the movie marriage which involves only the moment.

This brief ceremony accomplishes two things. It sets the betrothal
period in the context of God's care and of Christian faith; it says to the
couple that this is a time for something more than constructing invitation
lists and choosing canapes. It is a time that can be used to make a lifetime
commitment better. And, secondly, it involves the Christian community.
If the couple comes to the coffee hour, they will not be as likely as other
newcomers to find it hard to discover people to talk to or to have something to talk about. They will be approached with congratulations; they
will learn that someone else lives near them or knows their home town or
works for the same company. In short, the networking that builds a community will be off to a fast start. They will feel welcomed and supported.

Now, of course, not every couple will fit this program. There will be
the woman who grew up in the parish, went off to college, took a job

on the other coast, and is coming home only for the wedding. It may be that she and her fiance can go through a novitiate where they live rather than where they will be married. There will be others who will move away as soon as the wedding is over. This is, after all, a liminal time in which new patterns are being created. But as couples postpone marriage into their late twenties and early thirties, as divorced individuals become engaged for a second time, a higher proportion have roots in the community where they are being married and will stay there afterwards. This was not true a generation ago, but the hearsay evidence indicates that it is widely true today. It enables a continuing ministry in a way that was not as possible in recent generations.

One more opportunity presents itself at the beginning if the couple are already living together. In this situation, the pastor can take the opportunity to talk about the significance of the marital commitment. They would not be in the pastor's office if they didn't have some ideas about it themselves. There is a basis for some good discussion and for a point or two to be made. Paul Ramsey, paraphrasing Reinhold Niebuhr, observes that "the human capacity for responsible faithfulness makes marriage possible; the human inclination toward unfaithfulness makes marriage necessary."[15]

We could take that one step further and say, "The strength of our love for each other makes living together possible; the weakness of our love for each other makes marriage necessary." When we are in love, we want to do our best for the one we love but may well doubt that our best is good enough. God's strength supplied both directly in our love for each other and indirectly through the church and prayer and worship enables us to offer a better self to the other. Much more could be said in this area, but one further suggestion can be made at this early stage. The couple might be asked to take home this prayer and say it together that same day in a place that feels right, where one or the other (or both) is living, in the bedroom, dining room, or entrance:

> Lord God, we thank you for the gift of love which you have given us. Be with us now and help us love each other always. Guide us as we prepare to commit ourselves to each other and to you in marriage so we may grow in love and faithfulness and understanding of your will. Go with us in everything we do. We ask this through Jesus Christ our Lord. Amen.

When two people approach the church, God is at work in their lives. The pastor's role is to help them recognize and articulate that presence, at the earliest possible stage of the journey as well as at the ceremonial climax.

There is a further hope for this process: That those who enter it with the church's cooperation and support will tell their friends and pass on a copy of the promises and prayers. Let the engaged be witnesses and missionaries themselves. Is it too much to hope that there will be some who are not ready to talk to the church in a formal way but who are interested in making a deeper commitment to each other and in asking God's blessing on their relationship? No priest is needed; they can do what John Cotgreve and Alice Gidlowe did with their friends. The point is to make connections: our love and God's love; God's commitment to us and our commitment to each other; our support for each other and the support our friends can give us. And the point is not so much to draw people into the church as to draw them closer to God. If that eventually draws them into the church, well and good, but God is at work in people's lives outside the church, and perhaps we could follow that example.

The novitiate process

Existing marriage preparation programs often attempt to use married couples as role models and witnesses. The problem is that although these couples are placed in the role of mentor, there is no provision for a continuing relationship; indeed, the mentoring couples often come from another parish than that of the engaged couple. The baptismal catechumenate (where it is done well) provides lay sponsors from the same parish who meet with the candidate on a regular basis to share their faith. Their skills as a teacher are not so important as their ability to articulate what their faith has meant to them in the specific circumstances of their own lives and to be present as role models for the new Christian. The candidates' circumstances undoubtedly will be somewhat different, but what matters is not a one-for-one model to follow; what matters is the reality of a faith that has made a difference in a real life.

A marriage novitiate likewise depends on role models as much as specific teaching. The teaching, the counseling, the communication skills, and so on are very important, but witnesses are needed also. Every parish can find a few couples who worship together and who would be willing to invite an engaged couple to come for dinner at some time during their novitiate. I deliberately place almost no other qualifications because even a bad model can be useful. Most engaged couples will have had very limited exposure to marital role models. Their own parents may have been a negative model and be divorced. Their own contemporaries have little more experience than they do. And, in any case, the novitiate couple will have had almost no opportunity to look at another married couple together and evaluate what that marriage may say to them.

The agenda is simple. Over the time of the betrothal, the novitiate couple is invited for dinner into several homes. An older couple may well be included, but at least one couple should be fairly recently married (less than five years, if possible) and at least one couple should have children at home (unless the novitiate couple is beyond childbearing age or, for carefully considered and valid reasons, feel no vocation to childbearing). Where there are children, the guests should arrive before the children have gone to bed. They should have an honest look at a real family. There should be no program except food and conversation.

The fact that one couple is engaged and is there for that reason is sufficient to guide what happens. The host couple will inevitably ask them about themselves. Where did you meet? How long have you been engaged? When are you getting married? The host couple may well be moved to reminisce about how they met and became engaged. There will be a sharing of stories. Perhaps the host couple will say something about the church and its place in their lives. That is sufficient.

At one or more points during their novitiate, the engaged couple should have opportunity to reflect on these evenings. They will do that naturally between themselves, but there will be additional value in reflecting on it with the pastor or a program leader. Did you see or hear anything that made you think? That you could learn from? That you might imitate, or would do differently, or avoid? Good or bad, it's an opportunity to learn. It should not, however, become simply a critique of how two other people live: "Can you imagine having wallpaper like that?" Tastes differ, but let that kind of reaction be turned into self-analysis: Why do I have that reaction? Do you (the partner) have that reaction? What does that say about us? Reflection is helpful, but probably not so important as simple exposure to another marriage.

There are several additional benefits. In the first place, the host couple will have the opportunity to think about their own marriage and retell their story. To retell one's own story is to reaffirm it and be renewed. It is not only the guests who will benefit. In the second place, the guests have now become well acquainted with one other couple in the parish — and several during the time of their engagement. As a result, they have someone else to talk to at the coffee hour, another familiar face to smile at when they enter the church, a greater feeling of belonging to a community.

The completion of a novitiate

A novitiate ends, of course, with the taking of final vows. The significance of these is usually over-rated. I am referring now to any final vows, whether of marriage, ordination, monasticism, the doctor's taking of the Hippocratic oath, the hooding of Ph.D.s, the swearing in of a president. All these come as the triumphant conclusion of a process and have a certain significance, but the more important decision was the decision to embark on the process. To enter seminary or medical school, to announce a candidacy for office, to commit oneself to the long apprenticeship that leads to a degree and an academic career — that is the real turning point. When we select one of the many options life holds, that is when life changes. To become engaged in the first place is to make the fundamental commitment that turns life in a new direction.

In an ideal world (as in the early medieval world, which was *not* ideal), the betrothal ceremony would be seen as more important than the marriage. From that time on, your life is joined with that of another. If the initial consent between a man and a woman leads (as it often has in the past and often does today) to sexual intercourse, to living together, that is, as Paul Ramsey points out, *not* "premarital sex." It is the church's tradition that consent and consummation make a marriage — not a ceremony in the church.[16] The church does not make a marriage, it simply asks God's blessing on it. The so-called "wedding celebration" is then exactly that: A celebration of the marriage and the blessing of the marriage.

In an ideal world (which we glimpse only in a darkened mirror), the betrothal would be celebrated as the launching of a new and exciting venture. Not all engagements are completed in marriage (thank goodness!), but to enter one is a life-changing decision. The wedding would be the certification that all seems to be in order to make the venture life-long. The wedding, reduced then to manageable proportions, might be held in the church on Sunday morning with the community that has offered and will continue to give its support. This, you will tell me, is unrealistic. Yes, but I told you I was offering an ideal world, not the real one. I note only that the real world has changed before and will change again. What matters is a vision of what that change might look like.

But let me also be realistic. The betrothal novitiate does need a conclusion in the church. Many couples will ride off into the sunset and not be seen again; they will be moving elsewhere or not be that deeply committed. Perhaps they will be back when a baby is born or at Christmas and Easter. People are at various points in their pilgrimage, and the church's role is to move at God's pace with them, not criticize or second guess that pace. But for some, at least, the marriage will be followed by a honeymoon and then a return to the community. That is the time to complete the novitiate with ritual in the church.

On the first convenient Sunday after their return to the community (or arrival in a new community), the new couple will again be singled out in the announcements and asked to come forward to be "incorporated." I hope there will be even a few chuckles about "John and Mary, Inc." The pastor might say something like this:

> Mary and John have completed their novitiate and we have celebrated their marriage. I ask you now to stand and join with me as we incorporate their married life into the larger life of the body and bride of Christ, the Christian Church.

> Mary and John, do you now commit yourselves to building up your married life as members of the Body of Christ, and to seek God's forgiveness, renewal, and grace toward that end?"

> They reply together: "We do."

The congregation is then asked:

> Will you who witness this commitment support Mary and John in their calling, and will you continue to support each other in your separate callings both married and single in the unity of the Body of Christ?

> They respond: "We will."

The pastor then prays in these or similar words:

> Almighty God, through your Holy Spirit you have given us various gifts to praise you in your church; help us so to offer these gifts here on earth that we may bring them with joy to the final wedding feast of unity and gladness in your eternal kingdom, through Christ our Lord. Amen.

This should not, of course, be the end of the matter. Perhaps they will now live happily ever after and perhaps not, but the church has done and will continue to do what the church is supposed to do which is to ritualize and support. The church has also succeeded in turning a marriage moment into a marriage process and put the wedding celebration itself in some better perspective. If all has gone well in the novitiate process, the couple now have at least the beginnings of the kind of support group that most people had by nature until very recent times. The extended family and the rural community in which most people lived helped to absorb the bad times and to enrich the good. There were always others who knew and who cared. The "knowing and caring" could, of course, be negative and intrusive; a freely chosen community may be less intrusive and more truly caring. A parish has the potential to be that kind of community. This process may help it to happen.

Theologians have argued, and still argue, as to whether it is the priest or the couple who are the "ministers of the sacrament." It may be at least as important to recognize that, if Christ and the church are "the primal sacrament," there is a sense in which it is the church which makes any marriage a Christian marriage. The sacrament of community needs to be mediated by the community. That may be the practical truth in the theology that says that a marriage made outside the church becomes a Christian marriage with no further ceremony when the spouses are baptized. The sacrament of baptism makes the marriage sacramental. Incorporation into the church makes the difference. What we have attempted to do is give ceremonial expression to that theological insight.

When a church provides a blessing of civil marriage, the same truth is being expressed. If the partners in a civil ceremony are baptized, their marriage is a Christian marriage although lacking important ingredients. When a blessing of the marriage takes place subsequently an important element is added, but, all too often, at a small and private ceremony. A public incorporation of the couple at the main service on Sunday morning would make explicit what is implicit in every marriage of baptized persons: That baptism involves community, a shared life within the body of Christ.

Nourishing growth in the novitiate

The head and the heart, as we said earlier, are not closely connected in the days before a wedding, but when else will a man and a woman come willingly to spend so much time listening to whatever wisdom the church may have to pass on? God is able, fortunately, to work in human lives in ways beyond our understanding. Neither understanding nor even faith is a prerequisite. First God struck Paul off his horse and then God began to work through the church to nurture him in faith and knowledge. Those who come to ask help in preparing for their wedding will know perfectly well what it means to be struck first by love, and they are beginning to learn how faithfulness and understanding grow in response to love's initiative.

Premarital meetings, then, are not the ideal time for lectures, but it may be possible nevertheless to use the time available to help the engaged couple see that the power controlling their lives is God, and that what they are learning about God through their love for each other is an insight into the heart of the Christian faith. So faith as a response to love is no longer dry doctrine but the very stuff of their experience.

Charles Williams has said all this better than anyone else. He points out first that the church has "lost any really active tradition of marriage itself as a way of the soul." It may have been "practised in a million homes, but it can hardly be said to have been diagrammatized or taught by the authorities. Monogamy and meekness have been taught instead."[17]

Marriage can become a "way of the soul" if those who are married can be made aware that their daily experience is an experience of God's love at work in their lives. So Williams brings it down to the understanding of love to be gained from ordinary meals and even a bad breakfast.

> In ordinary married life the meals they share are (in common with all other parts of that experience) sacramental. It is not merely a pleasing emotion that stirs in their hearts when they breakfast or dine with each other. . . Here, as in the Eucharist itself, whatever the emotion, the imagination is capable of belief and assertion; and the lover, at the most unfortunate breakfast, may be allowed to smile a little to himself at the contrast between his feelings and his creed. . . . Morality is to him (as perhaps it should be to all of us in its widest application) a matter of courtesy, and sullenness over such a breakfast may be a worse sin than adultery.[18]

Unfortunately, the opportunity to connect Christian faith with human experience is often lost in premarital instruction. One very good new marriage preparation program, for example, proposes four meetings that deal with, in order, "Our Dreams . . . Our Relationships . . . Our Values . . . (and) Sex." The couple's workbook provides twelve sections ranging from finances to sexuality and four sections on planning the wedding service. Chapter eight, in ten pages out of 120, deals with faith. Faith is explored in terms of "discovering your spirituality." "Questions to explore" include "Why am I getting married in the church?," "Do I know what you (the partner) think about God? Jesus?," and "Do I think God has a place in our marriage? What is it?" Such discussion starters do provide a few opportunities to relate the Christian faith to the experience of love and marriage, but no direct connections are suggested.[19]

The usual approach on these occasions seems to be, "Since you are getting married in church you should know something about the other person's faith and your own and you should try to find common ground on which to build your marriage." There is nothing wrong with that, but it seems to start from the wrong end, approaching church teaching as a given rather than something to be discovered from an immediate and powerful experience. Why not begin from the known rather than the unknown? What is known is interpersonal love expressed especially in physical ways. If faith can be learned from that, a "theology of romantic love" might well provide an opening for an opportunity to grow in faith, perhaps even a true conversion experience.

But let us begin again at the beginning. This time, however, the beginning is not the first chapters of Genesis; the beginning is the love of Mary and John for each other. Love comes into a human life always in personal form. A child experiences parental love, becomes aware of friendship in childhood, responds in the teenage years to the first inklings of the possibility of interpersonal love (confusingly mixed with sexual urges), and then at last encounters a depth of love previously unknown in a single human being.

Love, finally, is always personal, but somehow a great many people today seem to think of God as impersonal. Perhaps we have overreacted to the much-maligned image of God as a white-bearded old man on a cloud, but that image is better in many ways than the "Ultimate Force" or "Ground of Being." I cannot love the "Ground of Being," but I might love a white-bearded old man. The marriage novitiate offers an opportunity to explore the various meanings and levels of love and to come to a new understanding of the love of a personal God. Those who have encountered the power of a personal love are also able to understand more fully who God is.

Mary and John know love in a person; more specifically, they know it in a physical person and express it in a physical way. Would it surprise them to be drawn into a discussion of "the carnality of joy"? We have come a long way from Origen's notion that it would be inappropriate for the Holy Spirit to be present at the marriage bed to Williams' belief that marriage is "a way of the soul," but an engaged couple today will surely understand Williams better than Origen.

Here we face a dilemma: We are dealing with something words cannot contain and we have only words as a tool. The engaged couple know well enough that words are inadequate. The pastor who asks them to articulate their love for each other is asking the impossible. But a discussion that limits itself to the rational and verbal aspects of love has attempted to "draw out Leviathan with a fishhook"[20] or "count the stars."[21] A marriage novitiate must find ways to help the couple discover that the inexpressible physical love they have begun to know is given them not only for its own sake (though it is), but also as a way of experiencing the love of God the Creator. When St. Augustine spoke about "sacraments of nature" and understood that a sacrament had to do with the element of mystery in life, he was not far from a realization of the power of marriage to disclose the mystery of love. Augustine,however, never took that step; it would be a shame if we failed to do so as well.

Of the Greek words for love, only two, *phileo* and *agapeo*, appear in the New Testament. *Eros* is not there, and many Christians have been relieved by its absence. Erotic love may be a part of human experience but it has not appeared to have much relationship with divine love. The Greeks knew better. *Eros,* in Greek thought, went beyond human physical exchanges to open up a deeper knowledge of rightousness and wisdom. For Plato, eros became a striving for righteousness and the way to attain immortality. Aristotle developed the concept further, and Plotinus in the third century used it to express the "mystical aspiration toward spiritual union with the transcendent . . .".[22] Perhaps a short course in Greek and Christian mysticism is too much to ask of an engaged couple, but if ever an ordinary couple are to understand what Plotinus and Julian of Norwich and Catherine of Siena and John of the Cross and others were getting at, this is the time. If the effort is not made, we have only ourselves to blame when people think of the church as dull and unrelated to real life. In real life, an engaged couple often seems to know more about mystical transcendence than does the church.

Mysticism includes adoration and contemplative prayer. How many engaged couples realize they are being put to school for that? Charles Williams again makes the direct connection. Why does the church connect the Fourth Commandment with Sunday observance? That, says Williams, is

> where the lover is bidden see that for the seventh part of his time he rests from all kinds of labour and keeps it holy to the Lord. This consecration of the week-end, or at least the greater part of it, to repose and contemplation of the beloved, is thus seen to be — not a mere amusing bit for young lovers — but a duty imposed upon all her married children by the Catholic Church.[23]

Have those who are engaged moved beyond the nervous need to talk, which is typical of the newly met, so that they have begun being able to enjoy each other without words? Do they find that they enjoy simply looking at each other without a need to speak? It is unlikely they will be in the pastor's office otherwise. But if they have reached that point, then they have begun to see what a deeper relationship with God might be like when it also moves beyond the rote prayers of childhood to a joy in the Presence that needs no language. That is an opportunity for growth that should not be overlooked.

There are, of course, many more areas of love to be explored. That is one reason why marriage needs a lifetime of commitment. The sacramentality of marriage, however we use words to express God's loving concern to give us physical evidence of the divine presence, makes sense in this context. Fidelity can be seen not merely as the avoidance of adultery, but as a willingness to share resources fully and satisfy each other in the spending of time together (creating "golf widows" is not much different from adultery). The role of the church as the "Body of Christ" is also an aspect of our need for physical, tangible, and varied expressions of love. The suggested ritualizing of this role may help raise the congregation's consciousness of this facet of its ministry.

This does not mean that sessions on finances, communications skills, and so on are not appropriate matters to deal with in the marriage novitiate. Secular agencies could handle some of this as well or better, but they are not likely to, and if what we have been saying about the unity of the created world is true, the church can communicate that by providing instruction in these areas. A variety of approaches, including group sessions and individual, a variety of skills from theological to psychological, a variety of experiences from that of the recently married to that of the divorced and happily remarried, can only enhance the time of preparation.

Technique alone can never guarantee success. Good marriages are always a miracle of grace. But there is always more grace available than human hearts can contain.

In conclusion

Charles Williams speaks of Dante's experience when first he encountered Beatrice in the streets of Florence and she said, "Good morning." Dante said of this meeting that

> he was so highly moved that he was, for the moment, in a state of complete good-will, complete caritas towards everyone. If anyone had at that moment done him an injury, he would necessarily have forgiven him. He has not only fallen in love; he is, strictly, "in love."[24]

All the prayers and sacraments of the church are intended to bring us to that same state of grace. That is the point at which our vision of marriage and God's call to us come together and are one.

A Story

*E*verything said so far has to do with human lives, but lives, finally, are stories, not theories. This is how the story might be told today or tomorrow.

John Cosgrove, a computer programmer, met Alice Gallo while creating a new program for the law firm of Washington, Maslov, and Chang where Alice was a junior partner. When they saw each other in a nearby deli at lunchtime, they fell into conversation. One thing led to another, and two months later they decided to get engaged. John, who was thirty-two, had ended a disastrous marriage five years earlier and was more than a little nervous about trying again. Alice was twenty-eight and not nervous at all. But she accepted John's suggestion that it might be best if they lived together for a while to see whether they really were the perfect match they felt themselves to be. Neither one had an apartment large enough for two, so they found a new apartment, redecorated it, and decided to have a party.

At this point, Alice remembered something a friend had told her about a promise she and her husband had made when they became engaged. Her friend gave her a copy of it and told Alice about their experience in using it. She showed it to John and it led to one of their first serious disagreements.

"The problem is," John said, "it really raises the stakes. I thought we were going to go slow and easy and not get in further than either one is comfortable with. And I'm not comfortable with this."

"The problem is," said Alice, "I trust you further than you trust yourself and I thought we were going to work on that."

They were walking home from the neighborhood deli late one afternoon, and John walked about a block and a half trying out various ways of responding without raising tensions any further. Finally, while they were waiting on the corner for a light to change, he said, "I guess I don't see how throwing a bigger challenge at me is going to make me more comfortable. Somebody just learning to dive doesn't start on the twelve-foot board."

"I don't see it that way," Alice said. "But, look, the last thing I want is for us to be arguing. I guess I just wanted to say how much I care and how serious this is for me. I was looking at it as saying, 'Yeah, I don't know if we can do this, so let's get all the help we can.' Look, Love, if you see it as a demand or a commitment, I'll back off."

The light changed, and, as they started across the street, somehow they got off the subject. When John thought about it again a few days later he realized he had begun to see it the way Alice did: It had begun to look more like John asking God than God requiring John. So he said, "Let's do it. I'm for building, and maybe this is a way to do it." So they worked the idea into their plan for the party.

The party was held on a hot July afternoon, and they were glad the apartment had a little balcony so they could leave the door open and let some air in; their apartment had not been designed to accommodate parties for forty. They had tried, of course, to keep numbers down, but that was the best they could do. By five o'clock on Saturday afternoon everyone was there and John banged on a glass to get their attention.

"Welcome!" he said. "We're really glad you could come. This is a big day for Alice and me and we're glad you could share it. We want to start this off right and we want you to shut up for a while and listen. Alice is the one who's used to talking, so listen to her."

"OK," said Alice; "here's what we're going to do. Ginny is going to read something and Bill is going to say a prayer, and then John and I are going to make a promise to each other and we want you to make a promise to us. So Ginny goes first. Ginny, where are you?"

Ginny, the friend who had given Alice the idea in the first place, had gotten wedged into a back corner and it took her a while to get out, where she could be seen. She had a piece of paper with some verses from Genesis copied out. John and Alice liked the idea of a Bible reading — they were sure it would get their friends' attention as something different — but they didn't have any ideas of their own, so they said, "Why don't you just read what you read at your party?" So Ginny read: "Now the Lord God had planted a garden in the East, in Eden; and there he put the human he had formed. . . ."

She skipped the part about the different rivers that watered the garden and the bit about the tree, and read again from verse 16 to verse 24, ending with: "For this reason a man will leave his father and mother and be united to his wife, and they will become one flesh."

Alice said, "Thanks, Ginny; Bill, are you ready?" And Bill (somebody had told them Bill "did something in his church on Sunday") elbowed his way in toward the center, pulled a crumpled piece of paper out of his pocket, and read:

> Lord God, you made the first man and woman to be together and support each other; bless Alice and John in their companionship and let your love for them spread to all of us. Amen.

"OK," Alice said, "thanks, Bill. Now we're going to make our promises and we want you all to get into this. All you have to do is say, 'We will' — and mean it. John, have you got the paper?"

John had the paper, so he and Alice stood together at the center of the room and read as follows:

John: "Alice . . ."

Alice: "John . . ."

John: "I love you . . ."

Alice: "I love you . . ."

Alice and John together: ". . . and I commit myself to you, body, mind, and soul. I ask God's help in keeping this promise."

Then, turning to their friends, they continued: "And we ask your help. Will you support us as we build our lives together?"

There was a chorus of "We wills" with a few "A-mens" and "Right ons" thrown in. From the balcony came a shout of "Go to it!" And the party went on from there. The last stragglers were pushed out the door shortly before midnight, and Alice and John, deciding to clean up in the morning, collapsed in each other's arms with a feeling that this time was different.

*   *   *   *

They really hadn't talked about a wedding service up to this point. There was still a sort of feeling of testing and trying out about their relationship, but that was slowly changing as they settled into the apartment and got used to having each other around. They were also busy at work and still trying to get the apartment the way they wanted it, and they still wanted to do all the other things they had always done — weekends at the beach, lots of evenings with friends, and a few concerts when they could fit them in. It wasn't a lifestyle that left a lot of time for pondering deep questions. So it was months before either of them brought up the subject of a wedding. But two days before Christmas, John asked if Alice had thought about going to church and Alice said she would like to. She thought it would make their first Christmas together more like what Christmas ought to be. "Besides," she said, "we might want to begin looking for a church to get married in."

So they went to church with a double agenda that Christmas, but somehow it still didn't go any further than that. They visited his family and her family, and even though parents on both sides wanted to know their plans, they knew better than to ask, so the subject didn't come up. In fact, it was Easter before they really thought about it again. This time, too, the vague idea that to do the holiday properly they ought to go to church was what got them started. They didn't want to get in a rut, so they decided to try a different church this time. Later the same day it was raining, and they were watching a rather boring video when Alice said, "What did you think?" "About what?" said John; "I still can't read your mind!" "About a church to get married in," said Alice; "I thought we were scouting one out." "Right," said John; "I forgot. But I kind of liked the one at Christmas better." "So you can, too, read my mind; my reaction exactly. Now what? Want to make a phone call?"

But John wasn't big on phone calls to unknown clergy and suggested they might just go some Sunday and talk to the pastor at the door. Which they did a few weeks later and, as a result, found themselves in the pastor's office after work on a Wednesday afternoon in May, feeling remarkably insecure for the self-confident people they were in the other areas of their lives.

When they talked it over that night over a take-out Chinese dinner, they found they both had the same reaction. "What got me," said John, "was that he really seemed to get excited about our house-warming and that little ceremony we did." "Right," said Alice, who was not having much luck relating the noodles to her mouth with the chopsticks; "I guess most people don't bother. I guess we wouldn't have either if Ginny hadn't told me about her experience. But what do you think about this idea of his that we stand up on Sunday morning and make some more promises? Are we getting in too deep?" John had given up the chopsticks earlier for an old-fashioned fork and had already pretty well finished. "What I think," he said, "is that this pastor really seemed involved, and it might be good to go along with it. I mean, he told us that we can take our time deciding and he doesn't want us to do something we're not comfortable with. But, heck, I like committing myself to you. I'd do it on television if I had the chance."

"John?"

"Uh-huh?"

"Would you either finish these noodles for me or let me borrow your fork?"

"How about both?"

"What do you mean?"

"I mean, first I finish your noodles; then I give you the fork."

"I should give them to you in your face. How did I get involved with a guy with no manners?"

"You must have a hunger for mystical experiences."

"So you were listening. I thought you were getting restless about that point."

"Not restless; hungry. But doesn't that sort of lower your idea of God, connecting God up with sex that way?"

"Not for me; I thought it made a lot of sense. I mean, how could a guy who eats too much and won't share a fork make me so happy unless God was helping out?"

"For me, you were always explanation enough. I just figured you were really great and that was all that mattered. But if you don't mind sharing the credits, I guess it does give me a way of thinking about God I never had before."

Three weeks later, they sat down front on Sunday morning so as not to have too far to walk and stepped forward on cue and made another commitment. And the congregation was asked to support them and said it would. And someone who wanted to get his home computer on a network talked to John at the coffee hour and several elderly ladies congratulated Alice, and a couple who had been married in the church two years earlier told them about a couple of ways they had saved money on their reception, and they wound up being late for a lunch date with friends at their own apartment.

After that, there were other meetings, at least one every month. There was a series of evening conferences with speakers and small group meetings and audio visuals; there were several evening invitations for dinner with couples in the parish; and there were several meetings with the pastor.

They didn't start going to church every week. They were still away lots of weekends and sometimes it was too hard to get up after a late Saturday night out. But once in a while they did go and they always seemed to be welcomed and remembered. And they had met again with the pastor and felt as if they understood each other pretty well.

*   *   *   *

It was a Sunday afternoon in September. They had been to church that morning and come home and changed to old clothes and crossed the street to sit in the sun in the neighborhood park. Alice had been reading a magazine when she looked up and said, "Did communion feel any different today?" John, puzzled as usual by what he was beginning to think of as Alice's non sequiturs, asked: "Why, should it?" "Well, I was thinking about what the pastor was telling us last time about God using material things. It was the connection with making love that got to me this morning. I mean, that's something: God used a human body to say 'I love you' and God gives us each other's bodies to let us know we're loved and then you connect that to the bread and wine with you right there next to me and I didn't know whether I could handle it."

"I thought about it last night," John said, "I can't quite put it in words, but . . ." He thought about it a bit, started to say something, thought some more and finally just said, "I don't know. I was thinking of a line I must have picked up in a college lit course and I don't remember where it's from. Something like, 'The heart has its reasons . . .'"

Alice laughed, "You have to be kidding. Like, maybe it was in the sermon this morning?"

"Well, maybe it was; I still think I remember it from college. But the point the pastor was making is that you can't always use words. And I like that. Words are more your thing than mine anyway. But we don't need words, do we?"

"Sometimes we don't. I guess maybe the best times are when we don't. But still, when I went to Church School it always seemed like everything was words —and not words I understood a lot of the time. God using a body, Christ's body, your body . . . Well, it just really hit me this morning and I needed to say it."

John moved closer on the bench, put his arm around her, and gave her a kiss that made someone walking by with their dog embarrassed. Which is saying a lot these days.

*   *   *   *

Somehow it was the evening with the Robertsons that John and Alice decided had made the biggest impact, even though they really couldn't pin down why. It wasn't anything that was said so much as a whole approach to sharing that they hadn't seen before. When dinner was over and they got up from the table, Alice said, "Can't we help you with the cleanup?" expecting to be turned down politely, but Phil said, "Sure," and John found himself loading the dishwasher and Alice found herself putting things in the Robertson's refrigerator, and the four of them tripped over each other quite a few times in the small space. They wound up drinking coffee around the bar in the kitchen until well after midnight. As they drove home, John said, "You know, I feel as if I've known them all my life." And Alice said, "There was something about the way they let us help with the dishes. I think that was the difference. There was no sense of trying to impress us or anything like that. My mother never wanted anyone else to help, not even Dad. It was as if she had to prove how good she was at things. But Phil and Audrey weren't trying to prove anything. I really liked that. Maybe what it was . . ." John had stopped for a light and Alice stopped, too, and just thought for a minute or two. "It was as if they had a unity strong enough to invite others into it; as if they weren't afraid of anything."

By a minor miracle there was an empty space almost directly outside their apartment house. As John backed the car into it he said, "I don't think I'm there yet; I still want you all for myself. But it must be a nice place to be."

He got out of the car, and as he was locking the door he said, almost to himself, "And I think that was something I did wrong in my first marriage. I had to be right, had to win all the time." He came around the car and gave Alice a hug. "But this time I *am* right," he said.

*   *   *   *

The other evening that made them really think was the conference on finances and legal issues. A lawyer spoke and suggested that for many people there was really no need to worry about a wedding license. "You are responding to a gift of God," he said; "you don't need the state's permission or anybody's permission to do that."* He went on to explain that they could make their own legal arrangements, and he gave them a printed pamphlet that listed the various areas they ought to think about, from property they owned to who would inherit it. He explained how, in the Middle Ages, families had arranged all this well in advance of the wedding and said they ought to do the same. "Did you ever notice the way they have the wedding announcements right next to the business pages?" he asked them. "That's because it really is a business deal for a lot of people, a merging of assets. But for Christians getting married, it isn't whether I own it or you own it, since it all belongs to God anyway. The point is to get it settled so we can concentrate on the stuff that really matters. So my advice is to take care of all the legal and financial stuff right now and stop worrying about it, and then your wedding will be about love instead of contracts." He said a little about the difference between contracts and covenants (which they had already heard from a previous speaker), but this time Alice and John were listening because it had to do with specific things they needed to do.

At the end of his talk, the lawyer told them he had a computer program that would provide them with all the forms they might need and which he would sell at the end of the evening to anyone interested. Alice and John bought one and spent the next couple of evenings choosing the forms they needed, putting in the required information, and printing them out. When they got the papers witnessed by friends the following weekend, they both felt they had taken another major step toward their own union but, more important, toward freeing themselves up to concentrate on planning the wedding. "It's funny, isn't it," John remarked over supper one evening; "every time we make another commitment, I feel more free, not less."

---

*PLEASE REMEMBER: This is a story set in an unspecified future time in an ideal world. DO NOT take the fictional lawyer's advice without consulting a real lawyer of your own where you live!

*   *   *   *

There was still more than enough planning to do. The pastor had suggested they read through a booklet with the marriage service in it and a list of suggestions and alternatives. They spent more time in Bible study over the next few weeks than they had ever spent before in their lives, and narrowed their choices down to five passages. Finally they got down to three by thinking in terms of friends and relatives they wanted to have as readers. Somehow they thought Fred's deep voice would sound great reading Genesis (they thought it would tie things together to have the same passage as at the house warming), while Catherine had a slow, peaceful manner that would go well with the passage from Simone Weil about lovers who want "to love each other so much that they enter into each other and only make one being."[1] So that was settled. The pastor would read the gospel story about the wedding at Cana. They liked the fact that it talked about a party and about Jesus providing more wine than anyone could drink — like creating more love than you can take in, was the way it hit them.

The other big issue, as it turned out, was something neither of them had ever thought about before: How to start the service. Neither of them had ever seen a wedding that didn't begin with the bride coming down the aisle on her father's arm, but Alice's parents were divorced and she hadn't seen that much of her father in recent years. When the pastor raised a question about it, they realized immediately that they would be more comfortable with a different approach. What they finally agreed made the best sense was for the pastor to come down the aisle first, then the bridesmaids and ushers in pairs, and finally for them to come in together. "After all," the pastor said, "you came together a long time ago. What you are doing is bringing the unity that God gave you and that you already committed yourselves to — bringing it back to the church to be blessed. And you should do that together. It makes sense."

So they did. The wedding was late in January, almost two years after they had met and almost a year and a half after their betrothal. And it happened at noon on Sunday. They thought seriously about making it part of the regular Sunday service since they now knew so many of the members of that congregation, but they decided they were traditionalists in a lot of ways; and they did want to have their families there, and they did want to be able to make it their service. The pastor had made some good points about the danger of privatizing marriage, but they argued back that they'd be happy to invite the congregation to sleep late and come to their service instead of the other way around. The pastor grinned and asked if they could take up a collection, but they said the church would save money on flowers that day so not to worry.

So that was what happened. The pastor told them later that the ten o'clock service that morning had felt like the Sunday after Christmas all over again with the church half empty and all those extra flowers. The service at noon was definitely their service — but far from a private affair. Not that they remembered much of it afterwards very clearly. They remembered Catherine beginning to lose it half way through her reading and going very slowly until she got back in control. They remembered the pastor forgetting to announce a hymn until the organist waved frantically. They remembered how the pastor's homily started; it got their attention right away:

> I need to say up front that the skills you have aren't going to help you much in your marriage. I don't think you can computerize marriage, and I know legal expertise can't solve marital problems. But that's all right. Marriage is not a profession, and it's not a matter of skills or techniques. Marriage is a vocation, a calling, and only the One who calls us knows exactly where we're going and how to get there.

But they had to rerun it on their video player weeks later to hear the rest of it, about the distance between the garden of Eden and the marriage at Cana and the twenty-first century and the Banquet at the end of time. They played it back several times and liked it more each time.

They also remembered standing just outside the door of the church on a gorgeously bright clear day — though a little chilly — and talking to what seemed like an endless line of people they hardly knew. Even the reception in a small restaurant that wasn't usually open until Sunday evening was a blur, and they were glad John's brother had videotaped a lot of it and they could look at it again afterwards and see what had really happened.

*   *   *   *

Two weeks later, feeling much more tanned than anyone else in the church after ten days in Mexico, they stood in front of the church one more time. They exchanged commitments now with the congregation as well as each other. And then John surprised himself by asking if he could make an announcement too. By now they were used to the fact that in this church it wasn't just the pastor who made announcements, but anyone who wanted to get people's attention for something that mattered to them.

"In some ways this feels like the end of a process," he said, "but Alice and I really see it as the beginning. We want to thank all of you for your support and ask you to keep it up; we still need it. But we've found love here in you as well as in each other, and we hope to share that with you for a long time to come." And then, with the assurance and style of veterans, they said together, "The peace of the Lord be always with you" and went down the aisle greeting the congregation and exchanging the peace. Some of them, in place of the usual response, said, "Peace and love" and even "We love you."

After the service, toward the end of the coffee hour, the pastor broke free to join the other members of the congregation who had been making a point of wishing them all manner of good things. "Well," the pastor said, "do you feel as if it's all over now and you can go back to being normal people?" "No," Alice said, "absolutely not. I feel as if we've been involved in a process that's made some big changes and I don't want it to stop. I hope it doesn't." "I don't think it's going to stop," John agreed, "One thing I know about computer systems is that there's always a way to do it better. I would hope human beings aren't any different. I know I've got some way to go still, but I think we've made a lot of progress with your help." "Not me," said the pastor, "the grace of God." "Two years ago," said Alice thoughtfully, "I wouldn't have known what you meant by that, but between you and John and this congregation, I think I'm beginning to understand."

Notes

Chapter One

1. Thomas, David M., *Christian Marriage: A Journey Together,* Michael Glazier, Wilmington, Delaware, 1983, 71.

2. Duby, Georges, *The Knight, the Lady, and the Priest: The Making of Modern Marriage in Medieval France,* Pantheon Books, New York, 1983, 28.

3. Augustine, *Against Julian,* II,7.

4. Gold, Michael, *Does God Belong in the Bedroom?,* The Jewish Publication Society, Philadelphia, 1992, 75.

5. Thomas, *Christian Marriage,* 88.

6. Augustine, *Confessions,* Book VII, chapter 12.

7. Temple, William, *Nature, Man, and God,* Macmillan, London, 1935, 478.

8. Miles, Margaret Ruth, *Augustine on the Body,* Scholars Press, Missoula, Montana, 1979, 87.

9. Brown, Peter, *The Body and Society: Men, Women, and Sexual Renunciation in Early Christianity,* Columbia University Press, New York, 1988, 231.

10. Ibid.

11. Augustine, *The City of God,* Book XIV, chapter 16.

12. Ibid., Book XIV, chapter 24.

13. Ibid.

14. Augustine, *On the Good of Marriage,* chapter 15.

15. Augustine, *Confessions,* Book X. chapter 31.47.

16. Augustine, *On Continence,* 1.

17. Ibid., Book X, chapter 33.

18. Brown, *The Body and Society,* 182.

19.   Ibid., 181.

20.   Ibid., 77, 353.

21.   Hunter, *op. cit.*, 55.

22.   Augustine, *Of Holy Virginity,* chapter 1.

23.   Ibid., chapters 19 and 21.

24.   Brown, *The Body and Society,* 168.

25.   Goody, Jack, *The oriental, the ancient, and the primitive: systems of marriage and the family in the pre-industrial societies of eurasia,* Cambridge University Press, Cambridge, 1990, 40.

26.   Augustine, *Of Holy Virginity,* chapter 1, 2 Corinthians 11.2.

27.   Brown, *The Body and Society,* 181.

28.   Ecclesiasticus 44.9.

29.   Brown, *The Body and Society,* 221.

30.   Goody, *The oriental, the ancient, and the primitive,* 107, 208.

31.   Ibid., 210

32.   Ibid., 273-74.

33.   Brown, *The Body and Society,* 260-61.

34.   Lacey, W.K., *The Family in Classical Greece,* Cornell University Press, Ithaca, New York, 168.

35.   Brooke, Christopher, *The Medieval Idea of Marriage,* Oxford University Press, Oxford, 1989, 55.

36.   Demosthenes, "Against Neaera," cited by Goody, *The oriental, the ancient, and the primitive,* 392

37.   Augustine, *Confessions,* Book VI, chapter 15.

38.   Augustine, *On Continence,* 23.

39.   Ibid.

40.   Clement, "The Miscellanies," 23:140, quoted in Hunter, David G., *Marriage in the Early Church,* Fortress Press, Minneapolis, 1993, 47.

41. Proverbs 31.10-31

42. Mackin, Theodore, *What is Marriage?*, Paulist Press, New York, 1982, 47.

43. Lacey, *The Family in Classical Greece,* 21.

44. Augustine, *Confessions,* Book IX, chapter 9.19.

45. Hunter, *Marriage in the Early Church,* 80.

46. Augustine, *Confessions,* Book XIII, chapter 22.

47. Genesis 24.58 and 67.

48. Genesis 29.20.

49. Brown, *The Body and Society,* 330.

50. Romans 8.21

51. Brown, *The Body and Society,* 171.

52. Miles, *Augustine on the Body,* 70.

53. Brown, *The Body and Society,* 426.

54. Galatians 3.28.

55. Brown, *The Body and Society,* 73-76.

56. Wegner, Judith Romney, *Chattel or Person? The Status of Women in the Mishnah,* Oxford University Press, New York, 1988, 5.

57. Lacey, *The Family in Classical Greece,* 189.

58. Ibid., 197.

59. Ibid., 199.

60. Lacey, *The Family in Classical Greece,* 113.

61. Hunter, *Marriage in the Early Church,* 8.

62. Brown, *The Body and Society,* 63.

63. Hunter, *Marriage in the Early Church,* 12.

64. Ibid., 15.

65. Hunter, *Marriage in the Early Church,* 17.

66.   Roth, Catherine P., *St. John Chrysostom: On Marriage and Family Life,* St. Vladimir's Seminary Press, 1986, 85-86.

67.   Augustine, *On the Good of Marriage,* 19.

68.   Lacey, *The Family in Classical Greece,* 180, 189.

69.   Brown, *The Body and Society,* 426-27.

70.   Ibid., 142.

Chapter Two

1.   Goody, *The oriental, the ancient, and the primitive,* 139.

2.   Fox, Robin Lane, *Pagans and Christians,* Alfred A. Knopf, Inc., New York, 1987, 100-101.

3.   Goody, *The oriental, the ancient, and the primitive,* 304.

4.   1 Kings 3.1.

5.   Thiel, Josef Franz, "The Institution of Marriage: An Anthropological Perspective," quoting L. Mair in *The Future of Marriage as an Institution,* Bockle, Franz (ed.), Herder and Herder, New York, 1970, 14.

6.   Ibid., 15.

7.   Ibid., 15

8.   Ibid., 17.

9.   Goody, *The oriental, the ancient, and the primitive,* 57.

10.   Ibid., 366, 468.

11.   Ibid., 81.

12.   Wegner, *Chattel or Person?,* 13.

13.   Ibid., 71.

14.   Ibid., 79.

15.   Goody, *The oriental, the ancient, and the primitive,* 406.

16.   Ibid., 415

17.   van Gennep, Arnold, *The Rites of Passage,* trans. Monika B. Vizedom and Gabrielle L. Caffee, London, Routledge and Kegan Paul, 1960, 135.

18.   Ibid., 18.

19.   Goody, *The oriental, the ancient, and the primitive,* 184.

20.   Lacey, *The Family in Classical Greece,* 111.

21.   Exodus 34.15-16.

22.   Wegner, *Chattel or Person?,* 42.

23.   Ibid., 78.

24.   Schillebeeckx, Edward, *Marriage: Human Reality and Saving Mystery,* Sheed and Ward, London, 1965, 235-36.

25.   Mackin, Theodore, *What is Marriage?,* Paulist Press, New York, 1989, 69.

26.   Ibid., 71.

27.   Ibid.

28.   Ibid., 72-73.

Chapter Three

1.   Wieseltier, Leon, "Leviticus," in *Congregation,* ed. David Rosenberg, Harcourt Brace Jovanovich, New York, 1987, 27.

2.   Deuteronomy 5.2-3.

3.   See chapter one above.

4.   *The Interpreter's Bible,* Abingdon Press, New York, 1952, Vol. I, 510. (The Exegesis was done by Cuthbert A. Simpson.)

5.   1 Timothy 2.12-13.

6.   Trible, Phyllis, *God and the Rhetoric of Sexuality,* Fortress Press, Philadelphia, 1978, 108. The whole discussion in pp. 72 to 143 is helpful.

7.   For example, Childs, Brevard, *Old Testament Theology in a Canonical Context,* Fortress Press, Philadelphia, 1985, 189-91.

8.   Genesis 1.28.

9.   Genesis 2.20.

10.   Quoted in Packard, Vance, *The Sexual Wilderness,* D. McKay Co., New York, 1968, 244.

11.   Leviticus 39.15-17.

12.   Brooke, *The Medieval Idea of Marriage,* Oxford University Press, Oxford, 1989, 251.

13.   Genesis 9 (with Noah); Genesis 15 and 17 (with Abraham); and Exodus 19 and 20 (with Moses).

14.   Genesis 21.27,32 (Abraham and Ahimilech); Genesis 26.28 (Isaac and Ahimilech); Genesis 31.44 (Jacob and Laban).

15.   Mackin, Theodore, *What is Marriage?,* 51.

16.   cf. footnote 15.

17.   1 Kings 20.34.

18.   1 Kings 20.34. RSV, NRSV, and NIV for example.

19.   Deuteronomy 4.8.

20.   Psalm 119.16.

21.   Leviticus 26.16-17, 29-32

22.   Hebrews 10.31.

23.   Genesis 26.30.

24.   Hosea 1.2-3.

25.   Hosea 3.1-3.

26.   There are, of course, various scholarly opinions as to the historical character of the second passage and even of both passages. F.I. Andersen and D.N. Freedman in *Hosea,* Anchor Bible Vol. 24, pp. 115 ff., would be among those who treat this passage as I have done.

27.   Hosea 11.1-4,8.

28.   Ezekiel 16.8-14.

29.   Ezekiel 16.15.

30.   Ezekiel 1.28.

31.   von Rad, Gerhard, *Old Testament Theology,* Vol. 1, Harper and Row, New York, 1962, 129. He cites Joshua 9.6ff, 1 Kings 20.34, and 1 Samuel 11.1ff. as examples.

32.   von Rad, *Old Testament Theology,* 130.

33.   Davidson, Robert, "Covenant ideology in ancient Israel," in *The World of Ancient Israel,* ed. R.E. Clements, Cambridge University Press, Cambridge, 1989, 324.

34.   Deuteronomy 26.17-18.

35.   Augustine, *The City of God,* Book XIV, Chapter 26.

36.   Augustine, *The City of God,* The Modern Library, New York, 1950, 475.

37.   Ibid.

38.   Schulman, Grace, "The Song of Songs," in *Congregation,* ed. David Rosenberg, Harcourt Brace Jovanovich, New York, 1987, 349.

39.   Schulman, "The Song of Songs," 349. Schulman improperly attributes this view to Marvin Pope who, in the passage she cites (his *Anchor Bible* commentary, pages 145-153), is making reference to T.J. Meek and others.

40.   Corney, Richard, private correspondence, December 1993.

41.   Meek, Theophile, "The Song of Songs," Introduction, in *The Interpreter's Bible,* Abingdon Press, New York, 1952, Vol. 5, 92.

42.   Song of Songs 1.13

43.   Schulman, "The Song of Songs," 349.

44.   Miles, Margaret Ruth, *Desire and Delight,* The Crossroad Publishing Company, New York, 1992, 71.

45.   Augustine, *Confessions,* XIII, 15.

46.   Miles, *Desire and Delight,* 76.

47.   Schulman, "The Song of Songs," 359.

Chapter Four

1.   John 2.11.

2.   Isaiah 25.6.

3.   Genesis 1.1; John 1.1.

4.   Matthew 9.15; Mark 2.19; Luke 5.34.

5.   Matthew 25.1ff.,Matthew 22.2ff,

6.   Revelation 21.3-4.

7.   Luke 16.18.

8.   Hoffman, Paul, "Jesus' Saying about Divorce and Its Interpretation in the New Testament Tradition," in *The Future of Marriage as Institution,* ed. Bockle, Franz, Herder and Herder, New York, 1970, 51.

9.   Matthew 5.31 (but Matthew 19.9 does not include this phrase).

10.   Mark 10.11.

11.   Mark 10.12.

12.   Matthew 19.10.

13.   Matthew 5.48.

14.   Hoffman, *Jesus' Saying about Divorce,* 64-65.

15.   Mark 10.6-9.

16.   2 Corinthians 3.5-6.

17.   Ephesians 5.22-23.

18.   Aristotle, "Politics," *Introduction to Aristotle,* ed. Richard McKeon, Random House, New York, 1947, Book One, chapter 3, 557.

19.   Ibid., Book One, chapter 12.

20.   Quoted in Lincoln, Andrew T., *Ephesians,* Word Books, Publisher, Dallas, 1990, 357.

21.   Ibid., pp. 357-58.

22.   1 Peter 2.15.

23.   Galatians 3.28.

24.   1 Peter 3.1-2,7.

25.   Ephesians 5.18-20.

26.   For example, the Revised Standard Version, the New Revised Standard Version, etc.

27.   Ephesians 5.23-24.

28.   Ephesians 5.25.

29.   Ephesians 5.25-27.

30.   Song of Songs 4.7.

31.   Sampley, J. Paul, *"And the Two Shall Become One Flesh": A Study of Traditions in Ephesians 5:21-33,* Cambridge University Press, Cambridge, 1971, 42.

32.   Leviticus 21.17-23.

33.   Sampley, *"And the Two Shall Become One Flesh,"* 48.

34.   Leviticus 19.2.

35.   Ibid., 42.

36.   Ephesians 5.31.

37.   Blackstone, William, *Commentaries on the Laws of England,* Vol. 1, (facsimile edition), University of Chicago Press,Chicago, 1979, 433.

38.   As Robinson points out (footnote 1 on page 11), the word *gewiya* comes close but is in any event seldom used. The word *nephesh* may also be used in this sense though it has a much broader range of meaning.

39.   cf. Robinson, John A.T., *The Body,* for a major study of this subject.

40.   Romans 12.5.

41.   2 Samuel 5.1. In the same way, in 2 Samuel 19.12-13, David sends a message to the elders of Israel and Amasa that they are ". . . my bone and my flesh."

42.   Ephesians 3.6.

43.   Ephesians 5.29-20.

44.   Ephesians 5.31-32.

45.   cf. Ephesians 1.9-10.

Chapter Five

1. 1 Corinthians 5.1-2.

2. 1 Corinthians, 6.15-20.

3. 1 Corinthians 7.2.

4. 1 Corinthians 7.5.

5. 1 Corinthians 7.10-11.

6. 1 Corinthians 7.12-16.

7. 1 Corinthians 7.25-28.

8. 1 Corinthians 7.39.

9. 1 Corinthians 7.26-31.

10. 1 Corinthians 7.28.

11. 1 Corinthians 7.9.

12. 1 Corinthians 7.32-35.

13. 1 Corinthians 7.7.

14. 1 Corinthians 7.28.

15. 1 Corinthians 6.15-16.

16. 1 Corinthians 7.4.

17. Colossians 3.18-19; 1 Peter 3.1-7.

18. Fox, *Pagans and Christians,* 347, 373.

19. Ibid., 361.

20. Mackin, *What is Marriage?,* 77.

21. Fox, *Pagans and Christians,* 351.

22. Matthew 19.10.

23. Hunter, *Marriage in the Early Church,* 7.

24. van der Wald, Nicholas, "Secular Law and the Eastern Church's Concept of Marriage," in *The Future of Marriage as an Institution,* 76.

25. Mackin, *What is Marriage?*, 69.

26. Galatians 3.28.

27. Fox, *Pagans and Christians,* 289-90.

28. Mackin, *What is Marriage?*, 78.

29. Schillebeeckx, *Marriage: Human Reality and Saving Mystery,* 244.

30. Stevenson, Kenneth, *To Join Together: The Rite of Marriage,* Pueblo Publishing Company, New York, 1987, 17-18.

31. "Epistle of Ignatius to Polycarp," Chapter 5, in *The Ante-Nicene Fathers,* Eerdmans, Grand Rapids, vol. I, 95.

32. Ibid., 248.

33. Stevenson, Kenneth, *Nuptial Blessing: A Study of Christian Marriage Rites,* Oxford University Press, New York, 1983, 13.

34. Hunter, *Marriage in the Early Church,* 57-63.

35. Idem., 38.

36. Stevenson, *Nuptial Blessing,* 16.

37. Idem., 15.

38. Hunter, *Marriage in the Early Church,* 27.

39. Stevenson, *To Join Together,* 21.

40. Chrysostom, St. John, *On Marriage and Family Life,* trans. Catherine P. Roth and David Anderson, St. Vladimir's Seminary Press, Crestwood, New York, 1986, 79.

41. Ibid., 74-76.

42. Brown, *The Body in Society,* 313.

43. Stevenson, *Nuptial Blessing,* 26.

44. Duby, *The Knight, the Lady, and the Priest,* 34.

45. John Chrysostom, *Homilies on Timothy, IX,* 1 Timothy 2.11-15. Chrysostom sees the crown as "a symbol of victory, betokening that they approach the marriage bed unconquered by pleasure."

46. Stevenson, *Nuptial Blessing,* 58.

47.   Ibid., 22.

48.   Stevenson, *To Join Together,* 79.

49.   Hunt, Edmund, *St. Leo the Great: Letters,* Fathers of the Church, Inc., New York, 1957, 249.

50.   Duby, *The Knight, the Lady, and the Priest,* 41.

51.   Hillman, Eugene, "The Development of Christian Marriage Structures," in *The Future of Marriage as an Institution,* 33.

52.   Orsy, Ladislas, *Marriage in Canon Law,* Michael Glazier, Wilmington, Delaware, 1986, 23.

53.   van der Wald, Nicholas, "Secular Law," 81.

54.   Ibid., 81-82.

55.   Berman, Harold, *Law and Revolution, The Formation of the Western Legal Tradition,* Harvard University Press, Cambridge, Massachusetts, 1983, 229.

56.   Ibid., 168.

57.   Ibid., 226

Chapter Six

1.   Brooke, *The Medieval Idea of Marriage,* 260-62.

2.   Berman, *Law and Revolution,* 99.

3.   Duby, *The Knight, the Lady, and the Priest,* 63, 172, 180.

4.   Adams, Henry, *Mont-Saint-Michel and Chartres,* Doubleday Anchor Books, Garden City, New York, 1959 (originally published in 1913), 6-7.

5.   Ibid., 52.

6.   Duby, *The Knight, the Lady, and the Priest,* 64-65.

7.   Ibid., 81.

8.   Ibid., 106.

9.   Ibid., 218.

10.   Berman, *Law and Revolution,* 116.

11.   Ibid., 68.

12.   Ibid., 77.

13.   Brooke, *The Medieval Idea of Marriage,* 128.

14.   Orsy, *Marriage in Canon Law,* 27.

15.   Ibid., 27.

16.   Ibid., 24-25.

17.   Delhaye, Philipe, "The Development of the Medieval Church's Teaching on Marriage," in *The Future of Marriage as an Institution,* 86.

18.   Berman, *Law and Revolution,* 227.

19.   Ibid., 227.

20.   Thomas, *Christian Marriage,* 92.

21.   Adams, *Mont-Saint-Michel,* 67.

22.   Ibid., 69.

23.   Leeming, Bernard, *Principles of Sacramental Theology,* Longmans, Green and Co. Ltd., London, 1956, 358.

24.   Ibid., 561.

25.   Augustine, *Letters,* The Nicene and Post-Nicene Fathers, Eerdmans, Grand Rapids, 1979, 138.7.

26.   Leeming, *Principles of Sacramental Theology*, 563.

27.   Delhaye, "The Development of the Medieval Church's Teaching on Marriage," 85.

28.   Leeming, *Principles of Sacramental Theology*, 566.

29.   Ritzer, Korbinian, "Secular Law and the Western Church's Concept of Marriage," in *The Future of Marriage as an Institution,* 75.

30.   Schillebeeckx, *Marriage: Human Reality and Saving Mystery,* 332.

31.   Augustine, *On the Good of Marriage,* 32.

32.   Duby, *The Knight, the Lady, and the Priest,* 181.

33.   Ibid, 184.

34.   Leeming, *Principles of Sacramental Theology,* 409.

35.   Kooper, Erik, "Loving the Unequal Equal: Medieval Theologians and Marital Affection," in *The Olde Daunce,* ed. Edwards, Robert R. and Spector, Stephen, 47.

36.   Thomas, *Christian Marriage,* 92.

37.   Aquinas, *Summa Theologica,* Q.65, Art.2, Reply Obj.1.

38.   Ibid.

39.   Mackin, *What is Marriage?,* 186.

40.   Mackin, Theodore, *The Marital Sacrament,* Paulist Press, New York, 1989, 289.

41.   Mackin, *What is Marriage?,* 177.

42.   Kasper, Walter, *Theology of Christian Marriage,* Crossroad Publishing Company, New York, 32. Published in Germany in 1977.

43.   Spencer, Bonnell, *Ye Are the Body,* Holy Cross Press, West Park, New York, 1950, 178.

Chapter Seven

1.   Luther, Martin, "The Babylonian Captivity of the Church," cited in Leeming, *Principles of Sacramental Theology,* 385.

2.   *Luther's Works,* Pelikan and Lehman, Philadelphia, 1967, vol. 46, cited in Mackin, *What is Marriage?,* 196.

3.   Calvin, John, *Institutes of the Christian Religion,* Book II, Chapter 8, section 44, The Library of Christian Classics, Vol. XX, The Westminster Press, Philadelphia, 1960, 4.14.2.

4.   Luther, "On the Babylonian Captivity of the Church," 232-33.

5.   Calvin, *Institutes,* 4.19.34.

6.   Oberman, Heiko, *Luther: Man between God and the Devil,* Yale University Press, New Haven, 1982, 273.

7.   Ibid., 273-74.

8.   Calvin, *Institutes,* 4.19.36.

9. Oberman, *Luther,* 274.

10. Ibid., 272.

11. Ibid., 275.

12. Calvin, *Institutes,* 4.19.37.

13. *Luther's Works, Vol. 54, Table Talk,* Theodore Tappert, ed. and trans., Fortress Press, Philadelphia, 1967, 363.

14. Oberman, *Luther,* 288-89.

15. Stevenson, *Nuptial Blessing,* 130-31.

16. Roper, Lyndal, "'Going to Church and Street': Weddings in Reformation Augsburg," *Past & Present,* No. 106 (February 1985), 100.

17. Stevenson, and Searle, *Documents of the Marriage Liturgy,* Pueblo Publishing Company, New York, 1992, 213.

18. Calvin, *Institutes,* 2.8.41.

19. Ibid., 2.8.42-43.

20. Calvin, John, *Commentaries on the First Book of Moses called Genesis,* vol. 2, trans. John King, Calvin Translation Society, Edinburgh, 1850, 286-87.

21. Ibid., 210.

22. Calvin, John, *Harmony,* vol. 1, trans. William Pringle, Edinburgh, 1845, 293.

23. Richard, James W., "The Church and Divorce," in *The American Journal of Theology,* vol. X, no. 3, (July 1906), 458-64.

24. Ibid., 461.

25. Ibid., 468. The phrase comes from the 1552 report of an English commission which reflects the reformed view.

26. Ibid., 460.

27. Schillebeeckx, *Marriage,* 257.

28. Orsy, *Marriage in Canon Law,* 31-33.

Chapter Eight

1.   Gillis, John R., *For Better, For Worse: British Marriages, 1600 to the Present,* Oxford University Press, New York, 1985, 38.

2.   Ibid., 111. Lawrence Stone calls it "a society in which marriage was delayed longer than in any other known society." *The Family, Sex and Marriage in England 1500 to 1800,* Harper and Row, New York, 1977, 81.

3.   Roper, "Going to Church and Street," 82.

4.   Ibid., 82.

5.   Stone, Lawrence, *Uncertain Unions: Marriage in England 1660-1753,* Oxford University Press, Oxford, 1992, 11.

6.   Gillis, *For Better, For Worse,* 75-76.

7.   Stone, *Uncertain Unions,* 9.

8.   Flandrin, J.L., "Repression and Change in the Sexual Life of Young People in Medieval and Early Modern Times" in Wheaton, R. and Hareven, Tamara K., *Family and Sexuality in French History,* University of Pennsylvania Press, 1980, 31, 37.

9.   Gillis, *For Better, For Worse,* 47, 50, and Roper, "Going to Church and Street," 96.

10.   Ibid., 198.

11.   Stone, *Uncertain Unions,* 17.

12.   Stone, Lawrence, *Road to Divorce: England 1530-1987,* Oxford University Press, Oxford, 1990, 57.

13.   Ibid., 115.

14.   Ibid., 121.

15.   Gillis, *For Better, For Worse,* 140.

16.   Stone, *Road to Divorce,* 131.

17.   Stone, Lawrence, *Uncertain Unions,* 31.

18.   Gillis, *For Better, For Worse,* 99.

19.   Ibid., 198.

20.   Ibid., 211-17.

21.   Stone, *Road to Divorce,* 143-48.

22.   *Ibid.,* 166-67.

23.   Carlier, Auguste, *Marriage in the United States,* De Vries, Ibarra and Co., Boston, 1867, xiii.

24.   Carlier, *Marriage in the United States,* vii-viii.

25.   Ibid., 114-15.

26.   Ibid., xiii.

27.   Rendall, Jane, *The Origins of Modern Feminism,* Macmillan Publishers Ltd., London, 1985, 37.

28.   Carlier, *Marriage in the United States,* viii.

29.   Ibid., 105-06.

30.   Gillis, *For Better, For Worse,* 57, 81. See also the *Oxford English Dictionary.*

31.   The American Book of Common Prayer, for two centuries, had the priest say, "I now pronounce you man and wife," which, in effect, said nothing at all about a change of status for either. "Wif" was any woman in Anglo-Saxon and "wer" was any man, but the "wer" had passed out of use except in relation to werewolves, so "man and wife" meant only "man and woman." Cranmer had written (and most English-language Prayer Books continued to say) "man and wife together" which puts the emphasis on the unity of the two, not their change in status, and may be intended simply to recall the uniting of the first man and woman in Genesis.

32.   Roper, "Going to Church and Street," 86.

33.   Gies, Frances and Joseph, *Marriage and the Family in the Middle Ages,* Harper and Row, Publishers, New York, 1987, 4.

34.   Wheaton, R. "Affinity and Descent in Seventeenth-Century Bordeaux," in Wheaton, R. and Hareven, Tamara K., *Family and Sexuality in French History*, 115-16.

35.   Wheaton and Hareven, *Family and Sexuality in French History,* 6.

36.   Gillis, *For Better, For Worse,* 82.

37.   Rendall, *The Origins of Modern Feminism,* 27.

38.   *The Merchant of Venice,* Act 3, Scene 1.

39.   Stone, *The Family, Sex, and Marriage*, 5.

40.   Ibid., 192.

41.   Ibid., 70.

42.   Ibid., 7.

43.   Wheaton and Hareven, *Family and Sexuality in French History*, 17.

44.   Gies, *Marriage and Family in the Middle Ages*, 12-13.

45.   *The Lady's Magazine*, 1774, quoted in Stone, *The Family, Sex, and Marriage*, 75

46.   These were copied at random from tombstones in the churchyard of St. Deiniol's Church, Hawarden, Wales, but any old cemetery will provide further examples.

47.   Richard, "The Church and Divorce," 470.

48.   Calvin, *Institutes* Book II, Chapter 8, section 44.

49.   Roper, "Going to Church and Street," 101.

50.   These quotations are from Taylor's sermon "The Marriage Ring" which is included in *Famous Sermons*, ed. Macleane, Douglas Sir Isaac Pitman and Sons, Ltd., London, 1911.

51.   *The Works of John Milton*, Columbia University Press, New York, 1931, Vol. III, Part II, 381-82.

52.   Stone, *The Family, Sex, and Marriage*, 328.

53.   Ibid., 329.

54.   Gillis, *For Better, For Worse*, 251-52.

55.   Rendall, *The Origins of Modern Feminism*, 42.

56.   Wollstonecraft, Mary, *A Vindication of the Rights of Woman*, Third Edition, printed for J. Johnson, London, 1796, 340.

57.   Ibid., 444.

58.   Gillis, *For Better, For Worse*, 229.

59.   Ibid., 244.

60.   Ibid., 237.

61. Ibid., 285.

62. *The Lambeth Conference, 1958,* SPCK Press, London, and Seabury Press, New York, 1958, 2.150.

63. *The World Almanac and Book of Facts, 1993,* ed. Mark S. Hoffman, Pharos Books, New York, 1993.

64. Stone, *Road to Divorce,* 409.

65. Forster, Greg, *Marriage Before Marriage?: The Moral Validity of 'Common Law' Marriage,* Grove Ethical Studies No. 69, Grove Books Limited, Bramcote, Nottingham, 1988.

66. Article in *The Independent,* Thursday, September 23, 1993.

67. *Whitaker's Almanac, 1993,* J. Whitaker and Sons Ltd., London, 1993.

68. Stone, *The Family, Sex, and Marriage,* 34-35.

69. Gillis, *For Better, For Worse,* 282.

70. Alvarez, A., *Life After Marriage: Love in an Age of Divorce,* Simon and Schuster, New York, 1981, 21.

71. Stone, *The Family, Sex, and Marriage,* 55.

72. Ibid., 56.

73. cf. Ecclesiastes 1.9.

74. Stone, *Road to Divorce,* 411.

75. See above, 95.

76. Gillis, *For Better, For Worse,* 251.

77. Alvarez, *Life after Marriage,* 241.

78. Alvarez, *Life after Marriage,* 216, ("Thus Morton and Bernice Hunt in The Divorce Experience...").

79. Schillebeeckx, *Marriage,* vii.

Chapter Nine

1. Bolt Robert, *A Man for All Seasons,* Samuel French, Inc., New York, 1962, Act I, 669.

2.   Le Guin, Ursula, *Dancing at the Edge of the World,* Grove Press, New York, 1989, 19.

3.   Ibid., 150-51.

4.   Forster, *Marriage before Marriage?,* 9.

5.   Silbermann, Eileen Zieget, *The Savage Sacrament: A Theology of Marriage after American Feminism,* Twenty-Third Publications, Mystic, Connecticut, 1983, 50.

6.   Richard, "The Church and Divorce," 452.

7.   Oppenheimer, Helen, *The Marriage Bond,* The Faith Press, Leighton Buzzard, Beds, 1976, 80.

8.   Ibid.

9.   Stone, *Road to Divorce,* 5-6.

10.   Kemp, Eric Waldram, *An Introduction to Canon Law in the Church of England,* Hodder and Stoughton, London, 1957, 19-20.

11.   Orsy, Ladislas, *Theology and Canon Law,* The Liturgical Press, Collegeville, Minnesota, 1992, 53-56.

12.   Provost, James H.(ed.), *Code, Community, Ministry: Selected Studies for the Parish Minister Introducing the Revised Code of Canon Law,* Canon Law Society of America, Washington, D.C., 1982, 107.

13.   Kemp, *Introduction to Canon Law,* 75.

14.   Orsy, *Theology and Canon Law,* 44-45.

15.   Ibid., 76.

16.   Provost, *Code, Community, Ministry,* v.

17.   Kemp, *Introduction to Canon Law,* 56.

18.   Mark 1.27 and parallels.

19.   Berman, *Law and Revolution,* 78.

20.   Ibid., 79.

21.   Caffarra, Carlo, "Marriage as a Reality in the Order of Creation and Marriage as a Sacrament," in Malone, Richard and Connery, John R.,(eds.) *Contemporary Perspectives on Christian Marriage, Propositions and Papers from the International Theological Commission,* Loyola University Press, Chicago, Illinois, 1984, 147.

22.   Thompson, William, *Appeal to One-Half the Human Race, Women, Against the Pretension of the Other Half, Men,* quoted in Gillis, *For Better, For Worse,* 224

23.   *Victorian Women: A Documentary Account of Women's Lives in Nineteenth Century England, France, and the United States,* eds. Erna Olafson Hellerstein, Leslie Parker Hume, and Karen M. Offen, The Harvester Press, Brighton, England, 1981, 258.

24.   Silbermann, *The Savage Sacrament,* 44.

25.   Ibid., 49.

26.   *The Constitution of the Presbyterian Church (U.S.A.)* Part II Book of Order. Louisville, Kentucky: The Office of the General Assembly, 1991, W-4.9001.

27.   See, for example, Davidson, Robert, "Covenant ideology in ancient Israel," in *The World of Ancient Israel,* ed. R.E.Clements, Cambridge University Press, Cambridge, 1989, 22.

28.   Ehrlich, Rudolf J., "The Indissolubility of Marriage as a Theological Problem," *The Scottish Journal of Theology,* Vol. 23, No. 3, August 1970, 66.

29.   Nelson, James B., *Between Two Gardens: Reflections on Sexuality and Religious Experience,* The Pilgrim Press, New York, 1983, 88. For a Roman Catholic example, cf. Philippe Delhaye, "Nature and Grace in the Theology of Vatican II," in Malone, *Contemporary Perspectives,* 290. Delhaye uses contract and covenant as parallel terms: ". . . to the natural contract, to the purely human covenant. . . "

30.   Torrance, James B., "Covenant or Contract? A study of the theological background of worship in seventeenth-century Scotland," *The Scottish Journal of Theology,* Vol. 23, No. 1, February 1970, 56.

Chapter Ten

1.   *The Canons and Decrees of the Council of Trent,* trans. Buckley, Theodore George Routledge and Co., London, 1851, 52.

2.   *Semel autem initum connubium in civitate Dei nostri, ubi etiam ex prima duorum hominum copula quoddam sacramentum nuptiae gerunt, nullo modo potest nisi alicuius eorum morte dissolvi.*
"But a marriage once for all entered in the city of our God, where even from the first the marital joining of two humans carries a certain sacramentality, can no way be dissolved except by the death of one of them." (Augustine, *On the Good of Marriage,* 17.)

3.   Augustine, *Expositions on the Book of Psalms,* Psalm 74, v. 4.

4.   Rowe, Trevor, *St. Augustine, Pastoral Theologian,* Epworth Press, London, 1974, 61-62.

5.   Epistles 185.23; Rowe, *St. Augustine,* 64.

6.   Ibid., 71.

7.   Forsyth, P.T., *Marriage: its Ethic and Religion,* Hodder and Stoughton, London, 16-17. (Forsyth lived from 1849 to 1921.)

8.   Baillie, D.M., *The Theology of the Sacraments,* Charles Scribner's Sons, New York, 1957, 48.

9.   Gelpi, Donald L., *Committed Worship: A Sacramental Theology for Converting Christians,* (2 volumes), The Liturgical Press, Collegeville, Minnesota, 1993, xiv.

10.   Rowe, *St. Augustine,* 67.

11.   Martos, Joseph, *The Catholic Sacraments,* The Liturgical Press, Collegeville, Minnesota, 1983, 11.

12.   Nelson, *Between Two Gardens,* 85

13.   Rahner, Karl, "What is a Sacrament?," *Worship,* Volume 47, No. 5, May 1973, 275-76.

14.   Williams, Charles, *Outlines of Romantic Theology,* William B. Eerdmans Publishing Company, Grand Rapids, Michigan, 1990, 44.

15.   Rahner, Karl, *The Church and the Sacraments,* Burns and Oates, London, 1963, 19.

16.   Häring, Bernard, *The Sacraments in a Secular Age,* St. Paul Publications, Slough, England, 1976, 19.

17.   Gelpi, *Committed Worship,* iv.

18.   Oppenheimer, *The Marriage Bond,* 33.

19.   1 Corinthians 6.16.

20.   1 Corinthians 6.15.

21.   Gelpi, *Committed Worship,* Vol. 2, 64.

22.   Mackin, *The Marital Sacrament,* 611.

23.   Schillebeeckx, Edward, "Christian Marriage and the Human Reality of Complete Marital Disintegration," 52-53, cited in Mackin, *The Marital Sacrament,* 612.

24.   Williams, *Outlines of Romantic Theology,* 44.

25.   Mackin, *The Marital Sacrament,* 664.

26.   Oppenheimer, *The Marriage Bond,* 87.

27.   Mackin, *The Marital Sacrament,* 674-75.

28.   Meyendorff, John, *Marriage: An Orthodox Perspective,* St. Vladimir's Seminary Press, Crestwood, New York, 1984, 16-17.

29.   1 Corinthians 7.9.

30.   Lawler, Michael G., *Secular Marriage, Christian Sacrament,* Twenty-Third Publications, Mystic, Connecticut, 1985, 105-10.

31.   Mackin, *The Marital Sacrament,* 611.

32.   Ibid., 65.

33.   Mackin, *What is Marriage?,* 21.

34.   Gelpi, *Committed Worship,* Vol. II, 64.

35.   *The Lambeth Conference, 1958,* 2.150.

36.   Brooke, Christopher, *The Medieval Idea of Marriage,* 274-75.

Chapter Eleven

1.   1 Corinthians 7.26-27, 31-32.

2.   Augustine, *On the Good of Widowhood,* ch. 25.

3.   Augustine, *On Marriage and Concupiscence,* ch. 14.

4.   Ibid., ch. 19.

5.   Augustine, *On Remission of Sins,* ch. 57, (vol.5, 37).

6.   Canon 1055,1.

7.   Augustine, *On the Good of Marriage,* ch. 3.

8.   Silbermann, *The Savage Sacrament,* 64.

9.   Abbot, Walter M., *The Documents of Vatican II,* Guild Press, New York, 1966, 250.

10.   Mackin, *What is Marriage?,* 19.

11.   Lederer, William J. and Jackson, Don D., *The Mirages of Marriage,* W.W. Norton & Company, New York, 1968, 7.

12.   Augustine, *On Marriage and Concupiscence,* ch. 19.

13.   Mackin, *What is Marriage?,* 610.

14.   Lederer and Jackson, *The Mirages of Marriage,* 42.

15.   Ibid., 43.

16.   Ibid., 42.

17.   Ibid., 42.

18.   2 Corinthians 1.2.

19.   The Book of Common Prayer, 1979, 423.

20.   Lederer and Jackson, *The Mirages of Marriage,* 59.

21.   Genesis 29.20.

22.   Williams, *Outlines of Romantic Theology,* 73.

23.   Thomas, R.S., *Later Poems,* Macmillan Publishers Ltd., London, 1984, 76.

24.   Williams, *Outlines of Romantic Theology,* 46-47.

25.   Williams, Charles, "Sensuality and Substance," *Theology,* Vol. XXXVIII, No. 227, 353.

26.   Ibid., 357.

27.   Ibid., 360.

28.   Williams, *Outlines of Romantic Theology,* 81.

29.   Ramsey, Paul, *One Flesh: A Christian View of Sex Within, Outside, and Before Marriage,* Grove Books, Bramcote, Notts,1975, 16.

30.   Ibid., 6.

Chapter Twelve

1. Stevenson, *To Join Together,* 189.

2. Van Gennep, *The Rites of Passage,* 13.

3. Ibid., 3.

4. Ibid., 11.

5. "Marriage Preparation Policy, Diocese of Paterson, New Jersey," in *Perspectives on Marriage: A Reader,* eds. Kieran Scott and Michael Warren, Oxford University Press, New York, 1993, 427-29.

6. Gillis, *For Better, For Worse,* 307.

7. Amos 3.2.

8. *The New York Times,* June 9, 1989; A1, 28, cited in Stone, *Road to Divorce,* 411.

9. Stevenson and Searle, *Documents of the Marriage Liturgy,* 203-4.

10. Genesis 24.

11. Goody, *The oriental, the ancient, and the primitive,* 315.

12. 1 Peter 2.9.

13. Evdokimov, Paul, *The Sacrament of Love,* St. Vladimir's Seminary Press, Crestwood, New York, 1985, 68-69.

14. Oppenheimer, *The Marriage Bond,* 26-27.

15. Ramsey, Paul, *One Flesh: A Christian View of Sex Within, Outside, and Before Marriage,* Grove Books, Bramcote, Notts,1975, 20, paraphrased.

16. Ibid., 17. "The presumption was that their betrothal consent to be married in the future was changed in the 'internal forum' of their consciences into a present consent to marry before they engaged in sexual relations. The presumption was that they were fully, responsibly married without the ceremony and before their acts of sexual love, which were then an expression and the nurturing of the bond between them. This bond, their marriage, was present by their own making preceremonially; and of course by the very nature of marriage-responsibility, marriage had to be present (if it was present) before copulation, since no number of acts of copulation are able to make a marriage. The parties alone make marriage, and only they can say whether this was their meaning and their intention toward one another."

17.   Williams, Charles, *The Descent of the Dove,* The Religious Book Club, London, 1939, 14.

18.   Williams, *Outlines of Romantic Theology,* 34-35.

19.   Midgley, John M.V. and Midgley, Susan Vollmer, *A Decision to Love: A Marriage Preparation Program,* Twenty-Third Publications, Mystic, Connecticut, 1992. This is, on balance, a very useful guidebook.

20.   Job 41.1.

21.   Genesis 15.5.

22.   "Love," in *The New International Dictionary of New Testament Theology,* vol. 2, ed. Colin Brown, The Paternoster Press, Exeter, 1976, 539.

23.   Williams, *Outlines of Romantic Theology,* 39.

24.   Ibid., 94.

A Story

1.   Weil, Simone, *Waiting on God,* London, Fontana Books, 1959, 85.

Bibliography

PRIMARY SOURCES

Adams, Henry. *Mont-Saint-Michel and Chartres.* Doubleday Anchor Books, Garden City, New York: 1959.

The Ante-Nicene Fathers. American reprint of the Edinburgh Edition. Wm. B. Eerdmans Publishing Company, Grand Rapids, Michigan: 1979.

The Basic Writings of Thomas Aquinas. ed. Pegis, Anton C., Random House, New York: 1945.

Aristotle. "Politics." *Introduction to Aristotle,* ed. Richard McKeon. Random House, New York: 1947.

Augustine. *The City of God.* The Modern Library, New York: 1950.

Blackstone, William. *Commentaries on the Laws of England* (facsimile edition). University of Chicago Press, Chicago: 1979.

Calvin, John. *Commentaries on the First Book of Moses called Genesis,* Vol. 2, (trans. John King). Printed for the Calvin Translation Society, Edinburgh: 1850.

Calvin, John. *Harmony,* Vol. I (tr. William Pringle). Edinburgh: 1845.

Calvin, John. *Institutes of the Christian Religion,* The Library of Christian Classics. The Westminster Press, Philadelphia: 1960.

Carlier, Auguste. *Marriage in the United States.* De Vries, Ibarra and Co., Boston: 1867.

Chrysostom, St. John. *On Marriage and Family Life.* Translated by Catherine P. Roth and David Anderson, St. Vladimir's Seminary Press, Crestwood, N. Y.: 1986.

Luther, Martin. "On the Babylonian Captivity of the Church," in *Three Treatises.* Fortress Press, Philadelphia: 1970.

Luther's Works, Vol. 54; Table Talk. Edited and translated by Theodore Tappert. Fortress Press, Philadelphia: 1967.

The Nicene and Post-Nicene Fathers. American reprint of the Edinburgh Edition. Wm. B. Eerdmans Publishing Company, Grand Rapids, Michigan: 1979.

Thomas, R.S. *Later Poems*. Macmillan, London: 1984.

Wollstonecraft, Mary. *A Vindication of the Rights of Woman*. 3rd ed. Printed for J. Johnson, London: 1796.

The Works of John Milton. Vol. 3, Part 2. Columbia University Press, New York: 1931.

OTHER PRIMARY SOURCES INCLUDING STATISTICAL REPORTS AND STATEMENTS ISSUED BY CHURCHES AND COMMITTEES

Adult Conversion and Initiation. The Liturgical Press, Collegeville, Minnesota.

The Canons and Decrees of the Council of Trent. Translated by Buckley, Theodore. George Routledge and Co., London: 1851.

The Church and the Law of Nullity of Marriage. Report of a Commission appointed by the Archbishops of Canterbury and York in 1949. London, SPCK: 1955.

The Constitution of the Presbyterian Church (U.S.A.) Part II/Book of Order. The Office of the General Assembly, Louisville, Kentucky. 1991.

The Documents of Vatican II. ed. Abbot, Walter M., Guild Press, New York: 1966.

The Interpreter's Bible. Abingdon Press, New York: 1952.

The Lambeth Conference, 1958. SPCK, London; and Seabury Press, New York: 1958.

"Marriage Preparation Policy, Diocese of Paterson, New Jersey," *in Perspectives on Marriage: A Reader*. eds. Kieran Scott and Michael Warren. Oxford University Press, New York: 1993.

The New International Dictionary of New Testament Theology. Vol. 2. ed. Colin Brown. The Paternoster Press, Exeter: 1976.

Putting Asunder: A Divorce Law for Contemporary Society. Report of a group appointed by the Archbishop of Canterbury in January 1964. SPCK, London: 1964.

Whitaker's Almanac, 1993. J. Whitaker and Sons Ltd., London: 1993.

The World Almanac and Book of Facts, 1993. Mark S. Hoffman, editor. Pharos Books, New York: 1993.

SECONDARY SOURCES

Allen, Joseph. *Love and Conflict: A Covenantal Model of Christian Ethics.* Abingdon Press, Nashville: 1984.

Alvarez, A. *Life after Marriage: Love in an Age of Divorce.* Simon and Schuster, New York: 1981.

Andersen, F.I., and Freedman, D.N. *Hosea,* Anchor Bible, Volume 24. Doubleday, Garden City: 1980.

Bagot, Jean-Pierre. *How to Understand Marriage.* Crossroad Publishing Company, New York: 1987.

Baillie, D.M. *The Theology of the Sacraments.* Charles Scribner's Sons, New York: 1957.

Barth, Marcus. *Ephesians 4-6,* The Anchor Bible. Doubleday, New York: 1974.

Bassett, William and Huizing, Peter, eds. *The Future of Christian Marriage.* Herder and Herder, New York: 1973.

Berman, Harold J. *Law and Revolution, The Formation of the Western Legal Tradition.* Harvard University Press, Cambridge, Massachusetts: 1983.

Biddle, Perry. *Abingdon Marriage Manual.* Abingdon Press, Nashville, Tennessee: 1987.

Bockle, Franz, ed. *The Future of Marriage as an Institution.* Herder and Herder, New York: 1970.

Bolt Robert. *A Man for All Seasons.* Samuel French, Inc., New York: 1962.

Brooke, Christopher. *The Medieval Idea of Marriage.* Oxford University Press, New York: 1989.

Brown, Peter. *The Body in Society: Men, Women, and Sexual Renunciation in Early Christianity.* Columbia University Press, New York: 1988.

Caffarra, Carlo. "Marriage as a Reality in the Order of Creation and Marriage as a Sacrament," in Malone, Richard, and Connery, John R., eds., *Contemporary Perspectives on Christian Marriage, Propositions and Papers from the International Theological Commission.* Loyola University Press, Chicago, Illinois: 1984.

Childs, Brevard. *Old Testament Theology in a Canonical Context.* Fortress Press, Philadelphia: 1985.

Cooke, Bernard, ed. *Alternative Futures for Worship, Vol. 5; Christian Marriage.* The Liturgical Press, Collegeville, Minnesota: 1987.

Countryman, L.William. *Dirt, Greed, & Sex: Sexual Ethics in the New Testament and Their Implications for Today.* SCM Press Ltd., London: 1988.

Davidson, Robert. "Covenant Ideology in Ancient Israel," in *The World of Ancient Israel.* Edited by R.E. Clements, Cambridge University Press, Cambridge: 1989.

Delhaye, Philipe. "The Development of the Medieval Church's Teaching on Marriage," in *The Future of Marriage as an Institution.* Edited by Bockle, Franz, Herder and Herder, New York: 1970.

Dominian, Jack. *Marriage, Faith, and Love.* Fount Paperbacks, London: 1984.

Duby, Georges. *The Knight, the Lady, and the Priest, The Making of Modern Marriage in Medieval France.* Pantheon Books, NewYork: 1983.

Edwards, Robert R. and Spector, Stephen, eds. *The Olde Daunce: Love, Friendship, Sex, & Marriage in the Medieval World.* State University of New York Press, Albany: 1991.

Ehrlich, Rudolf J. "The Indissolubility of Marriage as a Theological Problem." *Scottish Journal of Theology.* 23, no. 3 (August 1970).

Evdokimov, Paul. *The Sacrament of Love.* St. Vladimir's Seminary Press, Crestwood, New York: 1985.

Flandrin, J.L. "Repression and Change in the Sexual Life of Young People in Medieval and Early Modern Times" in Wheaton, R. and Hareven, Tamara K., *Family and Sexuality in French History.* University of Pennsylvania Press, Philadelphia: 1980.

Forster, Greg. *Marriage Before Marriage?: The Moral Validity of 'Common Law' Marriage.* Grove Ethical Studies No. 69, Grove Books Limited, Bramcote, Nottingham: 1988.

Forsyth, P.T. *Marriage: Its Ethic and Religion.* Hodder and Stoughton, London: 1912.

Fox, Robin Lane. *Pagans and Christians.* Alfred A. Knopf, Inc., New York: 1987.

Gallagher, Charles A., Maloney, George A., Rousseau, Mary F., and Wlczak, Paul E. *Embodied in Love: Sacramental Spirituality and Sexual Intimacy.* Crossroad Publishing Company, New York: 1986.

Gelpi, Donald L. *Committed Worship: A Sacramental Theology for Converting Christians,* 2 volumes. The Liturgical Press, Collegeville, Minnesota: 1993.

Gies, Frances and Joseph Gies. *Marriage and the Family in the Middle Ages.* Harper and Row, Publishers, New York: 1987.

Gillis, John R. *For Better, For Worse: British Marriages, 1600 to the Present.* Oxford University Press, New York: 1985.

Gold, Michael. *Does God Belong in the Bedroom?* The Jewish Publication Society, Philadelphia: 1992.

Goody, Jack. *The development of the family and marriage in Europe.* Cambridge University Press, Cambridge: 1983.

Goody, Jack. *The oriental, the ancient, and the primitive: systems of marriage and the family in the pre-industrial societies of Eurasia.* Cambridge University Press, Cambridge: 1990.

Gramunt, Ignatius; Hervada, Javier; Wauck, LeRoy A. *Canons and Commentaries on Marriage.* The Liturgical Press, Collegeville, Minnesota: 1987.

Häring, Bernard. *The Sacraments in a Secular Age.* St. Paul Publications, Slough, England: 1976.

Hillman, Eugene. "The Development of Christian Marriage Structures," in *The Future of Marriage as Institution.* Bockle, Franz, ed. Herder and Herder, New York: 1970.

Hoffman, Paul. "Jesus' Saying about Divorce and its Interpretation in the New Testament Tradition" in *The Future of Marriage as Institution.* Bockle, Franz, ed. Herder and Herder, New York: 1970.

Hunt, Edmund. *St. Leo the Great: Letters.* Fathers of the Church, Inc., New York: 1957.

Hunter, David G. *Marriage in the Early Church.* Fortress Press, Minneapolis: 1992.

Kasper, Walter. *Theology of Christian Marriage.* Crossroad Publishing Company, New York: 1991.

Kemp, Eric Waldram. *An Introduction to Canon Law in the Church of England.* Hodder and Stoughton, London: 1957.

Kooper, Erik. "Loving the Unequal Equal: Medieval Theologians and Marital Affection," in *The Olde Daunce.* Edwards, Robert R. and Spector Stephen, eds. State University of New York Press, Albany: 1991.

Lacey, W.K. *The Family in Classical Greece.* Cornell University Press, Ithaca, New York: 1968.

Lawler, Michael G. *Ecumenical Marriage and Remarriage.* Twenty-Third Publications, Mystic, Connecticut: 1985.

Lawler, Michael G. *Secular Marriage, Christian Sacrament.* Twenty-Third Publications, Mystic, Connecticut: 1985.

Leclercq, Jean. *Monks on Marriage.* The Seabury Press, New York: 1982.

Lederer, William J. and Jackson, Don D. *The Mirages of Marriage.* W.W. Norton & Company, New York: 1968.

Leeming, Bernard. *Principles of Sacramental Theology.* Longmans, Green and Co. Ltd., London: 1956.

Le Guin, Ursula. *Dancing at the Edge of the World.* Grove Press, New York: 1989.

Lincoln, Andrew T. *Ephesians.* Word Books, Publisher, Dallas, Texas: 1990.

Mackin, Theodore. *The Marital Sacrament.* Paulist Press, New York: 1989.

Mackin, Theodore. *What is Marriage?* Paulist Press, New York: 1982.

Malone, Richard and John R. Connery, eds. *Contemporary Perspectives on Christian Marriage, Propositions and Papers from the International Theological Commission.* Loyola University Press, Chicago, Illinois: 1984.

Martos, Joseph. *The Catholic Sacraments.* The Liturgical Press, Collegeville, Minnesota: 1983.

Meek, Theophile. "The Song of Songs," Introduction in *The Interpreter's Bible,* vol. 5. Abingdon Press, New York: 1956.

Meyendorff, John. *Marriage: An Orthodox Perspective.* St. Vladimir's Seminary Press, Crestwood, New York: 1984.

Midgely, John M.V., and Susan Vollmer. *A Decision to Love.* Twenty-Third Publications, Mystic, Connecticut: 1992.

Miles, Margaret Ruth. *Augustine on the Body.* Scholars Press, Missoula, Montana: 1979.

Miles, Margaret Ruth. *Desire and Delight.* The Crossroad Publishing Company, New York: 1992.

Moore, George Foot. *Judaism in the First Centuries of the Christian Era: The Age of the Tannaim.* Harvard University Press, Cambridge, Massachusetts: 1927.

Nelson, James B. *Between Two Gardens: Reflections on Sexuality and Religious Experience.* The Pilgrim Press, New York: 1983.

Nelson, James B. *Embodiment: An Approach to Sexuality and Christian Theology.* Augsburg Press, Minneapolis: 1978.

Oberman, Heiko. *Luther: Man Between God and the Devil.* Yale University Press, New Haven: 1982.

O'Meara, John J. *Studies in Augustine and Eriugena.* The Catholic University of America Press, Washington, D.C.: 1992.

Oppenheimer, Helen. "The Churches and Marriage," in *The Future of Christian Marriage.* Bassett, William and Huizing, Peter, eds. Herder and Herder, New York: 1973.

Oppenheimer, Helen. *The Marriage Bond.* The Faith Press, Leighton Buzzard, Beds., England: 1976.

Orsy, Ladislas. *Marriage in Canon Law.* Michael Glazier, Wilmington, Delaware: 1986.

Orsy, Ladislas. *Theology and Canon Law.* The Liturgical Press, Collegeville, Minnesota: 1992.

Packard, Vance. *The Sexual Wilderness.* D. McKay Co., New York: 1968.

Provost, James H., ed. *Code, Community, Ministry: Selected Studies for the Parish Minister Introducing the Revised Code of Canon Law.* Canon Law Society of America, Washington, D.C.: 1982.

Rahner, Karl. *The Church and the Sacraments.* Burns & Oates, London: 1963.

Rahner, Karl. "What is a Sacrament?" *Worship, 47,* no. 5 (May 1973).

Ramsey, Paul. *One Flesh: A Christian View of Sex Within, Outside, and Before Marriage.* Grove Books, Bramcote, Notts. England: 1975.

Reilly, Christopher C. *Making Your Marriage Work.* Twenty-Third Publications, Mystic, Connecticut: 1992.

Rendall, Jane. *The Origins of Modern Feminism.* Macmillan Publishers Ltd., London: 1985.

Richard, James W. "The Church and Divorce." *The American Journal of Theology,* 10, no. 3 (July 1906).

Ritzer, Korbinian. "Secular Law and the Western Church's Concept of Marriage," in *The Future of Marriage as an Institution,* Bockle, Franz, ed. Herder and Herder, New York: 1970

Robinson, John A.T. *The Body.* SCM Press Ltd., London: 1952.

Roper, Lyndal. "'Going to Church and Street': Weddings in Reformation Augsburg." *Past & Present,* no. 106, (February 1985).

Rowe, Trevor. *St. Augustine, Pastoral Theologian.* Epworth Press, London: 1974.

Sampley, J.Paul. *'And The Two Shall Become One Flesh' A Study of Traditions in Ephesians 5:21-33.* Cambridge University Press, Cambridge: 1971.

Schillebeeckx, Edward. *Marriage: Human Reality and Saving Mystery.* Sheed and Ward, London: 1965.

Schmeiser, James A. "Marriage: New Alternatives." *Worship,* 55, no. 1 (January 1981).

Schulman, Grace. "The Song of Songs," in *Congregation.* David Rosenberg, ed. Harcourt Brace Jovanovich, New York: 1987.

Scott, Kieran and Warren, Michael. *Perspectives on Marriage.* Oxford University Press, Oxford: 1993.

Shideler, Mary McDermott. *The Theology of Romantic Love: A Study in the Writings of Charles Williams.* Harper and Brothers, New York: 1962.

Silbermann, Eileen Zieget. *The Savage Sacrament: A Theology of Marriage After American Feminism.* Twenty-Third Publications, Mystic, Connecticut: 1983.

Spencer, Bonnell. *Ye Are the Body.* Holy Cross Press, West Park, New York: 1950.

Stevenson, Kenneth W. *Nuptial Blessing: A Study of Christian Marriage Rites.* Oxford University Press, New York: 1983.

Stevenson, Kenneth W. *To Join Together. The Rite of Marriage.* Pueblo Publishing Company, New York: 1987.

Stevenson, Kenneth W. and Mark Searle. *Documents of the Marriage Liturgy.* Pueblo Publishing Company, New York: 1992.

Stone, Lawrence. *The Family, Sex and Marriage in England 1500 to 1800.* Harper and Row, New York: 1977.

Stone, Lawrence. *Road to Divorce: England 1530-1987.* Oxford University Press, Oxford: 1990.

Stone, Lawrence. *Uncertain Unions: Marriage in England 1660-1753.* Oxford University Press, Oxford: 1992.

Taylor, Jeremy. "The Marriage Ring" in *Famous Sermons.* Macleane, Douglas, ed. Sir Isaac Pitman and Sons, Ltd., London: 1911.

Temple, William. *Nature, Man and God.* Macmillan and Co. Limited, London: 1935.

Thomas, David M. *Christian Marriage: A Journey Together.* Michael Glazier, Wilmington, Delaware: 1983.

Torrance, James B. "Covenant or Contract? A study of the theological background of worship in seventeenth-century Scotland." *Scottish Journal of Theology,* 23, no. 1, (February 1970).

Trible, Phyllis. *God and the Rhetoric of Sexuality.* Fortress Press, Philadelphia: 1978.

Trigg, Joseph W. "What Do the Church Fathers Have to Tell Us About Sex?" *Anglican Theological Review,* 74, no. 1, (Winter 1992), 18-24.

Turner, Philip, ed. *Men and Women: Sexual Ethics in Turbulent Times.* Cowley Press, Cambridge, Massachusetts: 1989.

van der Toon, Karel. "Female Prostitution in Payment of Vows in Ancient Israel." *Journal of Biblical Literature,* 108 (1989).

van der Wald, Nicholas. "Secular Law and the Eastern Church's Concept of Marriage," in *The Future of Marriage as Institution.* Bockle, Franz, ed. Herder and Herder, New York: 1970.

van Gennep, Arnold. *The Rites of Passage.* Translated by Monika B. Vizedom and Gabrielle L. Caffee, Routledge and Kegan Paul, London: 1960. (Published as *Les rites de passage* in 1908.)

Victorian Women: A Documentary Account of Women's Lives in Nineteenth Century England, France, and the United States. Erna Olafson Hellerstein, Leslie Parker Hume, and Karen M. Offen, eds. The Harvester Press, Brighton, England: 1981.

von Rad, Gerhard. *Old Testament Theology.* (two volumes) Harper and Row, New York: 1962.

Wegner, Judith Romney. *Chattel or Person? The Status of Women in the Mishnah.* Oxford University Press, New York: 1988.

Weil, Simone. *Waiting on God.* Fontana Books, London: 1959.

Westermarck, Edward. *The Future of Marriage in Western Civilization.* Macmillan and Co. Ltd., London: 1936.

Wheaton, R. "Affinity and Descent in Seventeenth-Century Bordeaux," in Wheaton, R., and Tamara K. Hareven, *Family and Sexuality in French History.* University of Pennsylvania Press, Philadelphia: 1980.

Wheaton, R. and Tamara K. Hareven. *Family and Sexuality in French History.* University of Pennsylvania Press, Philadelphia: 1980.

Wieseltier, Leon. "Leviticus," in *Congregation.* David Rosenberg, ed. Harcourt Brace Jovanovich, New York: 1987.

Williams, Charles. *The Descent of the Dove.* The Religious Book Club, London: 1939.

Williams, Charles. *He Came Down From Heaven.* Faber and Faber, London: 1950.

Williams, Charles. *Outlines of Romantic Theology.* William B. Eerdmans Publishing Company, Grand Rapids, Michigan: 1990.

Williams, Charles. "Sensuality and Substance." *Theology,* 38, no. 227 (May 1938).

Index